HB
G.W.T

GUIDEPOSTS

STORIES I COULDN'T TELL WHILE I WAS A PASTOR

BRUCE McIVER

Guideposts®
CARMEL • NEW YORK 10512

This Guideposts edition is published by special arrangement with Word Publishing.

STORIES I COULDN'T TELL WHILE I WAS A PASTOR

Library of Congress Cataloging-in-Publication Data

McIver, Bruce.
Stories I couldn't tell while I was a pastor / Bruce McIver
p. cm.
ISBN 0–8499–3418–4
1. McIver, Bruce. I. Title.
BR1725.M3566A3 1991
286.1'092—dc20
91 13224
CIP

Printed in the United States of America.

To My Grandchildren

Emily Paige Allen

and

Alexandra (Ali) Shea McCarthy

"Don't let the fun stop"

CONTENTS

ACKNOWLEDGMENTS

These stories could have not been written without the help of a lot of people. Some deserve special mention:

Lawanna—wife, companion, and friend for thirty-one years—has been my chief critic and primary encourager. She has patiently read every line of this manuscript again and again. Her creative input and loving affirmation have been invaluable.

Our three daughters, Kathie McIver, Shannon Allen and Renie McCarthy, have chuckled and grinned with me as stories about them have been reviewed. They've even volunteered some things that I never knew, and a few things that I'd just as soon not write! Kathie, who now teaches English in college, has worked overtime giving me crash lessons in sentence structure, tense, and basic grammar.

Barbara Jenkins, who once walked across America and is now a best-selling author, believed in me and encouraged me to share these stories. This classy lady talked me through the "dry seasons" when the words did not flow, and affirmed me when the words and sentences blended to tell the stories. She's been a dear, tough, and helpful friend.

Barbara and Wayne Swearingen, Judy and Jim Roberts, and Emily and Richard Park marched into my study at home shortly after I retired as pastor of Wilshire, set up a personal computer, wished me a belated "Merry Christmas," and walked straight out the front door with the admonition, "Now start writing!" Their gracious gift has enhanced this entire writing project.

Robert Wolgemuth and Mike Hyatt of Wolgemuth & Hyatt, Publishers, Inc., my publishers and editors, have expressed to me confidence and encouragement from the beginning. They have been helpful, patient, and understanding. I'm grateful to them.

Bob Harty of J. C. Harty Publications, Inc., publisher of my first book, *Grinsights,* in 1977, graciously gave me the privilege of retelling a few of the stories that first appeared in that book. Thank you.

The Wilshire Baptist congregation asked me to become their pastor at a time when I had little pastoral experience and many personal needs. They welcomed me, affirmed me, celebrated with me through good experiences and hurt with me through painful times. They were patient, understanding and encouraging. And, through it all, we learned to laugh together. It's been a good journey—one that I wouldn't trade with anyone. I am a fortunate person.

Finally, I am indebted to the dozens of people who are a part of these stories. Without them, and their permission for me to write about them, this book could not have been published. In most cases the real names of the persons in the stories are used. In a few cases, the names have been changed to protect . . . *me!*

INTRODUCTION

Question:
How does a pastor remain in one church for thirty years?

Answer:
By threatening to write a book entitled,
Stories I Could Not Tell While I Was A Pastor.

That's the way this whole thing got started. In lighter moments I mentioned to my congregation the possibilities of writing such a book, often adding in jest, "And after all these years I've got something on somebody in every pew!" Great fun. They loved it.

When it became necessary for me to step aside as pastor after my second heart surgery, the questions came from all directions: "What about that book?" "Are you going to write about the time when . . . ?" "Are you going to tell *everything?"*

Heavens! I thought. *These people have taken me seriously. Now they're asking for it. Well, why not?*

So the stories began to flow—wild weddings, awkward hospital visits, pulpit bloopers of the worst kind, a funeral service where one disaster led to another, and the front page newspaper story about my dog getting drunk!

In the months that followed I discovered slowly, and sometimes painfully, that many of the stories came full circle and focused on my own pilgrimage—growing up in the hills of North Carolina, moving to Texas and working with college students, coping with my own grief, trying to be both father and mother to a four-year-old little girl, becoming the pastor of a fast-growing young church in the heart of Dallas while still struggling as a single parent, and celebrating the gift of new love, new life, and a growing family. I also discovered, delightfully, that the journey had been made easier because of grins . . . and chuckles . . . and laughter. My late friend, Grady Nutt, often said, "Laughter is the hand of God on the shoulder of a troubled world." It is, Grady; it really is.

Why did I wait until now to tell these stories?

While a few of them have been shared on special occasions, it's not easy to write down stories and experiences while preparing sermons, juggling schedules, attending committee meetings, marrying the living, and burying the dead. The beauty of hindsight is that it affords us the luxury of absorbing and appreciating what we missed the first time around.

There's another reason why these stories have not been shared until now. Humor should never embarrass anyone. Wisdom and discretion (and my safety!) have dictated that some things can best be told later—after people have laughed with you, or after they have moved on, or after time has changed the scenery.

Did I tell everything? Not on your life . . . or *mine!*

But I've already started another file of stories . . . just in case.

So, read on, enjoy and remember: "A cheerful heart is good medicine . . ." (Proverbs 17:22, NIV).

STORIES I COULDN'T TELL WHILE I WAS A PASTOR

1

BEFORE AND AFTER

"Daddy, will the store be opened this early in the morning? Can we have an ice cream soda? Mr. Brewer makes them real thick—'specially for me. Can I look at some new coloring books? He had some new dolls last week. Can I see them? Please?"

Four-year-old Kathie's barrage of questions continued through the door and down the first aisle of the store. She was an inquisitive, challenging little girl who could seldom be satisfied with simple answers, or a statement like "just because." She was always looking, always exploring, always thinking—sometimes, two or three steps ahead of me.

"No, Kathie, it's too early in the morning for an ice cream soda. Besides, Mr. Brewer isn't here yet. Now, stay close to me and try not to knock anything off the display racks. Okay?"

"Okay, Daddy, but could I . . ."

"Please, Kathie, we're in a hurry. We've got a lot to do this morning. Here, let me take you by the hand." I pulled her gently, but firmly, up the aisle while she tugged for the freedom to explore on her own.

"Daddy, do you need any shaving cream?"

"No, I have plenty at home."

"Any toothpaste? Toothbrushes?"

"No, Kathie, we're in good shape when it comes to toothpaste and toothbrushes."

I paused for a second, and she was gone.

"Daddy, Daddy," she called from two aisles away, "what does 'fem . . . i . . . nine hy . . . giene' mean?"

"Put that back this minute!" I ordered in a loud whisper. "And don't touch anything else on the shelves."

I glanced around and was glad that we were the only two customers in the store. My mission was awkward enough without having to stop and explain it to friends and neighbors. Besides, I wasn't sure what Kathie might pull off the shelves next.

"Sir, can I help you?"

A tall, stately woman came from behind the soda fountain and moved in our direction. The hint of a smile on her face told me that she knew I was fumbling around with little sense of direction.

"Thank you. I'd sure appreciate some help. I'm trying to find some Spoolies. They're little round pink things that look like miniature car wheels without tires on them. I've never seen any, but a friend told me about them yesterday. I was told you could roll hair on them."

"Oh, yes," she smiled warmly, "I think we have some on the next aisle. Let me see if I can find them for you."

"I really appreciate your help," I said. "You see, I'm facing this situation and . . ." My voice trailed off and the sentence was never completed. There was no need to try to explain this to a stranger, I reasoned. There were a lot of things I'd had to learn to keep to myself in recent days.

"By the way," I said to the nice clerk, "I also need a bottle of lanolin. I think it's a kind of oil or . . ."

"I know exactly what you mean," she replied graciously. "We have that in stock, also."

The Spoolies and lanolin were found and the sale was rung up on the old cash register that went "clang" as the drawer opened. I thanked the lady and we walked rapidly toward the door, pausing only for a second while Kathie looked at the dolls and coloring books once more.

As we backed away from the curb and headed toward home, Kathie asked, "Daddy, what are Spoolies?"

"Honey, Spoolies are little things that we're going to roll your hair on. We'll put some of this lanolin on each strand, roll it up,

"I'm trying to find some Spoolies. They're little round pink things that look like miniature car wheels without tires on them."

and then flip the sides of the Spoolies so each strand will be tightly in place. We'll let it stay that way for a few hours, unpop the Spoolie, and . . . presto! Fluffy hair!"

"How long will it take for my hair to get fluffy again, Daddy?"

"Not long. And it's real simple to do."

"Have you ever done it, Daddy?"

"No, but Mrs. Jackson, Melinda's mother, told me how to do it yesterday. She's a real nice person. And, she's very nice to help us, isn't she?"

"Yeah. Can we roll my hair on them as soon as we get home?"

"In ten minutes," I grinned.

What's the world coming to? I marveled, as we arrived back at our house. Right here in the middle of the '50s we have fin-tailed automobiles, air conditioning, color television, prepackaged fish sticks and beef pot pies, duck tails and hula-hoops, rock and roll and Elvis, Sputnik . . . and Spoolies. Unbelievable.

But I was relieved, for those newfangled Spoolies just might be the answer to one of my pressing problems at the moment.

Those little pink round things were something tangible that I could pick up, handle with my hands, and work with. I resolved to do just that, and I vowed that when I was through, my little girl's hair would be as fluffy and curly as it had ever been. I'd show everybody that a thirty-year-old single parent could be both father and mother to his four-year-old, hazel-eyed child. I'd need a lot of other answers in the days ahead, but right now I had to get to work with Spoolies.

"Hey, kid," I said teasingly, "climb up on the stool and let's get this show under way. You can pay me later."

Kathie giggled, threw her arms around my neck, and kissed me on the cheek. Her light brown hair brushed against my face, and her eyes danced with delight.

"We're going to have a good time together, aren't we, Daddy?"

I swallowed hard and longed for the innocence of childhood. *Yep,* I thought, *we're going to have a good time together, and we're going to make it—somehow.*

I looked down into her face, hugged her up close to me, and smiled.

I was surprised at myself, for it was the first time that I had smiled in many days. I had been busy walking through painful experiences that I had always assumed happened to other people. But this time they had happened to me, and my own emotions had been twisted and bent and stretched almost to the breaking point. Like a cork in troubled waters, I had bounced from one bobbing emotion of grief to another—shock, disbelief, paralysis, fear, hope, loneliness, struggling faith, and finally resignation. The winds of the storm that had thundered down into my life had now blown on through, but they left behind an eerie calm and a lot of debris. Like a confused and bewildered pilgrim, I stumbled around in the wreckage, wondering which piece to pick up in the rebuilding chore before me.

I picked up a Spoolie, fingered it, and began to roll Kathie's hair.

"You're going to be one of the prettiest little girls in church today," I announced with confidence. "Daddy's going to fix your hair, and we're going to make it look as pretty as ever."

Within an hour the entire head of hair had been thoroughly soaked in rich lanolin. My theory in applying the oil was simple: If a little is good, a lot must be better. The last strand had been carefully rolled, and the last Spoolie flipped into place. I then stepped back, admired my work, and said to Kathie, "See, honey, it wasn't hard at all. We make a great team."

"Yeah," she exclaimed excitedly. "We can roll my hair every day!"

"Kathie giggled, threw her arms around my neck, and kissed me on the cheek. . . . 'We're going to have a good time together, aren't we, Daddy?' . . . Yep, I thought, we're going to have a good time together, and we're going to make it—somehow."

I wasn't sure about her "every day" proposal, but there was a warm feeling in knowing that the two of us had made it through our first major project together. I was confident that we would make it through a lot of others down the road.

Two hours later it was time to begin dressing for the Sunday church service. Just the two of us in attendance was another "first" for us, and I was determined that we would look and act our best. This meant that together we had to select the right dress, petticoat and panties, and socks and shoes. All of this should have been simple enough, but between what I thought she should wear and what she wanted to wear we managed to waste a good thirty minutes. When all the clothing had been selected and laid out in perfect order, we turned our attention to curly and fluffy hair. I could hardly wait for the miracle that I knew was about to unfold before my very eyes.

Kathie climbed up on the stool in the tiny kitchen and giggled all over in anticipation. I reached out nervously and took the first

Spoolie in my hand, held my breath and "un-popped" it. I then slowly unwound it so that the strand of hair could fluff and bounce—just like it was supposed to do. But it didn't fluff and bounce; the entire strand was one soggy, oily ringlet from the top of Kathie's head to her shoulders. I couldn't believe what I saw. My poor child's hair was doomed! The other Spoolies produced the same results. Twelve wet, gooey strands of hair. Melinda's mother had failed to tell me that lanolin comes from the fatty coating of sheep's wool and that it is extremely greasy.

"Please, Daddy, can I see how pretty it is?" she asked as she jumped off the stool and moved quickly toward the mirror.

"Honey, wait a minute," I said as I took her arm. "Let's see if Daddy can't touch it up just a bit."

That satisfied her for the moment while I surveyed the disaster. After the first glance I knew that it would take a lot more than a mere touching up to save this situation.

"I've got a great idea," I said, smothering the panic that I felt within. "Why don't we find a pretty colored scarf or a kerchief and we'll tie your hair up in it? You'll be the only little girl at church wearing something as beautiful as that."

"Yeah! That's a real good idea," Kathie said with total trust as she ran to her room and began to search for the right scarf to wear.

I rolled my eyes, looked upwards and sighed with exasperation, "I'm trying, Jean. I'm trying."

The drive from our house to the church ordinarily took about ten minutes. On this day we drove slowly, very slowly. I figured that if we were fifteen minutes late even the last of the stragglers would be seated. My plan was for us to sneak into the back of the sanctuary and then head quickly for a remote part of the balcony, preferably the last row in the top section. I wanted to get as far away from anyone who might recognize us as possible. We made it from the parking lot to the front door without bumping into a single person. The two ushers just inside the doors greeted us warmly and kindly. When they gave Kathie special attention, she pointed with pride to her bright purple kerchief. She then volunteered cheerily, "It's my very favorite color." I ducked my head and tried to guide her on past them as quickly as possible.

I don't remember a thing the preacher, Ralph Langley, said that day.

He and I had been roommates in college, and I regarded him as one of my best friends. He had a sharp mind and a remarkable ability to communicate his thoughts through words. But nothing he said that day found any lodging in my preoccupied mind. In all fairness, it wasn't Ralph's fault; I was still thinking about lanolin and Spoolies. I just wanted to sink lower and lower in the pew and then get out the doors as soon as the service was over. Meanwhile, Kathie sat up straight and smiled proudly at everyone who

"Please, dear Lord, forgive me. But, Lord, have you ever tried to work with lanolin and Spoolies?"

glanced our way. She even waved at two ladies who smiled at her. I lowered my head, scratched my eyebrow, and pretended to be praying.

No four-year-old child has ever been as proud of a bright purple kerchief as she was; no thirty-year-old widower has ever wished more for the final "Amen" of a service than I did that day. When it finally was pronounced, I slipped out of our pew, took Kathie by the arm, and sped down the balcony steps three at a time. Poor little Kathie kept saying out loud, "Daddy, you're pulling on my arm!" and "Daddy, wait for me!" We darted out the door without a word to anyone, including the two friendly ushers who followed us out the door and to the edge of the parking lot just to make sure that everything was all right. I waved to them that everything was fine.

In three days most of the greasy lanolin had been washed out and the hair had finally dried. On the fourth day I plotted a new course.

"Honey," I said, "how would you like to have short hair?"

"How short, Daddy?"

"Well . . . er . . . real short. I think that's going to be the new style, and you know that I want you to have the latest style in haircuts."

(Please, dear Lord, forgive me. But, Lord, have you ever tried to work with lanolin and Spoolies?)

"That'll be great, Daddy! Let's get it cut off real short."

"Real short, honey; I promise."

The next day we went to the beauty salon. For the next four years Kathie wore cropped, straight hair—the shortest of any child in the neighborhood.

And I have "before and after" pictures to prove it.

"Before and after." One short phrase—not even enough to make a complete sentence, but when dropped unexpectedly upon life, it rewrites entire chapters.

AN ORANGE HOUSE AND A BRIGHT FUTURE

The "before" involved studies at Mars Hill College in North Carolina and later at Baylor University in Waco, Texas. It also included meeting Jean, an attractive and radiant junior class student from Goose Creek, Texas. Her positive attitude toward life, grounded in common sense, was contagious. Two years later we were married. Life was good, and a whole world of possibilities and adventures lay before us. The sky was the limit—if we didn't overshoot it!

"Before" also included graduate studies at Southwestern Baptist Theological Seminary in Fort Worth. On the very day of graduation, after three years of preparation for some kind of Christian ministry, I accepted a challenging opportunity to teach Bible courses and direct the Baptist Student Union work at Southwest Texas State University in San Marcos, Texas. The timing had been perfect, so Jean and I loaded the old '41 Chevy with our few worldly possessions and headed southwest toward the Texas hill country where the university was located. The five years spent on that scenic campus and in that community established roots and relationships that will remain throughout life. But even more importantly, that's where Kathie entered our lives—colic and all—and that very special event in 1952 still makes the place all the more meaningful.

"Before" also involved a similar kind of teaching and administrative responsibility at Texas Tech University, located in Lubbock. The hearts of the people out West are as big and wide as the plains themselves. Doors are opened immediately to new people, friendships form quickly, and strangers are made to feel at home. The two brief years there left indelible impressions on our lives.

> ***"Life was good, and a whole world of possibilities and adventures lay before us. The sky was the limit—if we didn't overshoot it!"***

Then a surprising call came from Dallas encouraging me to consider a new job responsibility ministering to college and university students on campuses throughout the state. While emotions cried, "No!"—reason, coupled with a broader perspective answered, "Yes." The job would put me in contact with students and student leaders on more than sixty campuses in Texas. The travel would be demanding, but the personal rewards would be most satisfying.

So, the car had been loaded again and the three-hundred-mile trek east toward "Big D" was begun. By now, however, we had accumulated enough secondhand furniture, baby toys, and books to fill the small moving van that followed us. Kathie was four, Jean and I were both thirty, and life was good.

"We're very fortunate people," I said to Jean as we drove through the vast open spaces of Texas on our way to Dallas. "I'm amazed how well things have worked out. This is the third time the doors have opened for us in seven years. And this new challenge looks like it will be the best ever."

There was no need for further comments. The only sound was the steady whistle of the wind as it flowed through the open windows of the second-hand DeSoto with a plush interior and a sorry engine. Kathie was sound asleep on the back seat. We were family . . . together . . . growing . . . speeding across the desolate plains . . . toward tomorrow. And even a "lemon" of an automobile couldn't dampen our spirits.

Yes, life was very good, and we were thankful.

Adequate housing in Dallas was difficult to find, but with the help of friends we were able to locate a small two-bedroom duplex in a nice residential neighborhood. The house was trimmed with wood that had been painted a hideous orange color. I nearly walked away from it because of the paint, but Kathie loved it and insisted, "But, Daddy, it's the brightest color of any house on the block! Can't we live here?"

"Let's take it," Jean added. "It's in a good area of the city. There's a park a block away and Kathie will enjoy playing there. Besides, we'll be thinking about buying our own house in a few months. Until then, this will be fine, even with orange trimming."

The lease was signed, and the next day crates and barrels, lamps and tables, cooking utensils and sealed boxes were stacked everywhere. Just walking from one room to another was like trying to move through an obstacle course. Strangely, the momentary clutter and inconvenience didn't seem to matter that much. Boxes and crates became a part of transition, a transition that would lead to new plateaus.

WHEN LIFE TUMBLES IN

But it was not to be. Before all the boxes could be opened and before the curtains could be hung, the wide open road toward the future had turned into a lonely path of uncertainty. We were thrust into another kind of transition—one that turned our world upside down and carried us, not to new plateaus, but through the depths of valleys.

The crisis came unannounced and without expectation, shortly after our ninth wedding anniversary: suddenly Jean was experiencing severe headaches . . . waves of nausea that refused to respond to medication . . . acute pain in the legs and arms and throughout the entire body . . . slurred speech . . . more headaches . . . and more nausea . . . a hurried trip to the hospital . . . and a restless night.

"Mr. McIver," the nurse said early the next morning, "why don't you step outside the room and let me give your wife her

"The wide open road toward the future had turned into a lonely path of uncertainty. We were thrust into another kind of transition—one that turned our world upside down and carried us, not to new plateaus, but through the depths of valleys."

bath? It'll only take about ten minutes, and you can walk down the hall and get a cup of coffee."

"But she's had a bad night," I protested, "and she's just closed her eyes. Can't you let her sleep for a few minutes and give her the bath later?"

"It would be better to do it now," she replied with hesitation. "I understand how you feel, but I'll be through shortly and I'll come and get you personally." Then she added with a smile, "I promise."

Sitting on a counter stool, I slowly stirred the cup of stale, tasteless coffee. The monotonous process of stirring gave me something to do as I pondered the last three or four days. Jean had seldom been sick, but the intensity of the headaches had incapacitated her. The pulsating pains had been accompanied by nausea and fever, and soon her entire body was thrashed by some kind of virus within her. While she had remained at home she had not responded to any of the medications, so the decision had been made to admit her to the hospital.

"It should take only a couple of days and she'll be on her way to recovery," the kindly doctor had told me. "We'll start some fluids and give her something to help her rest tonight. She should begin to feel better by tomorrow."

I continued to stir the cold coffee even though I used neither sugar nor cream and though I did not intend to drink it. This is tomorrow, I thought, and she's not better; she's worse. I just want the hurting to stop and I want her to begin to feel better, and . . .

"Mr. McIver! Mr. McIver! Come quickly! Please! Now!"

I dropped the spoon, raced down the hospital corridor behind the nurse who had been bathing Jean, threw open the door to her room, and found her bed encircled by a dozen doctors and nurses, all frantically working over her.

"What happened?"

No response.

"Somebody please tell me what happened! What are you doing? How's my wife?"

One of the doctors nodded to another and said softly, but firmly, "Please take him outside and talk with him."

"Mr. McIver," the doctor said when we were outside the room, "we don't know what happened. Your wife stopped breathing. All vital organs have shut down. We're trying to resuscitate her now. We're doing all we can, but we don't know if she will make it."

"Make it?" I asked in disbelief. "You mean, live? You don't know if she will live?"

"Crash cart! Code blue! Clear the halls! Please clear the halls!"

The doctor and I pressed against the wall as the lifesaving apparatus was pushed hurriedly past us and into Jean's room.

"I'm sorry, sir," the doctor continued. "I need to go back in your wife's room. It would be best for you to remain out here. We're doing all we can."

"Clear the halls! Clear the halls!"

I pressed against the wall again and watched another piece of bulky equipment being rolled into her room.

This went on for five hours. Five long, agonizing hours standing in a cold, sterile, institutional hall . . . alone. There were no relatives to stand with me since none of them knew of the sudden turn of events. I hesitated to leave my station outside the room to dial friends in Dallas because I might be needed for consultation with the doctors. These hours were the loneliest I've ever experienced in my life.

And so it went throughout most of the day.

One door, made and installed by man, separating me from the known and the unknown; one door, with a handle for everyone, except me.

I tried to understand this. I knew in my mind that it was best for me not to be in the room, but pain and frustration have difficulty listening to reason.

About two o'clock in the afternoon most of the nurses and doctors began filing out of the room, quietly and somberly. The older, white-haired physician in charge walked with me to the end of the hall. He then put his hand on my shoulder and broke the news.

"Your wife is alive," he said, "but only because of the machines."

I listened in stunned disbelief.

"All bodily functions have ceased," he added. "There are no reflexes, no responses. She is in a deep coma. It is urgent that we move her across the city to the isolation wing of Parkland Memorial Hospital. We're not sure what kind of virus she has, and since Parkland is the county hospital, they're better equipped over there to handle cases like this. I must tell you, however, that I'm not sure she will live through the transfer."

He then tightened the grip of his hand on my shoulder, looked me squarely in the eyes, and said with profound empathy, "I'm sorry."

In that moment I knew that he had done all he could behind that closed door. I thanked him, sighed, and leaned heavily against the wall.

Jean lived through the transfer to Parkland but remained in the coma for seven days.

And then she died.

The diagnosis: polio. The year: 1956—the year of the Salk vaccine, but because of the shortage, it was given only to preschool children and pregnant women. I remembered that Jean had made sure that Kathie had received her vaccine, and for that I was grateful.

So near—so far.

I gathered the fragments of hopes and prayers and dreams and plodded my way back to the newly rented orange duplex. Kathie was staying with some dear friends from college days, Mary Louise and Foy Valentine.

I unlocked the door, stepped into the living room, reached out, and touched . . . emptiness.

In that moment I knew that the "before" was over—just a memory. I was now living in the "after."

A few days later, my grief welled up inside as I crumpled in exhaustion in my favorite chair and shed some of my first tears since Jean's illness and death. I was a child again, trapped in the brokenness of life, needing comfort and reassurance. For a few brief moments I vented my feelings and expressed my emotions.

Then I looked at the clock on the wall, blew my nose, wiped my eyes, and rose from the chair. It was time to drive across the city to the Valentines' home and pick up Kathie. As I prepared to leave, I paused at the door and slowly scanned the room. The unopened boxes and the curtains and the drapes could wait.

But some things could not wait. Kathie would have a lot of questions, and simplistic answers and "just because" would not satisfy her inquiring mind. She would need love and a warm blanket of security—more than ever. And I'd have to figure out how to turn on the stove . . . and pick out dresses . . . and iron frilly things . . . and cook fish sticks and beef pot pies . . . and how to be a "single parent" (before the words were ever invented) . . .

***"And then she died.
The diagnosis: polio. . . .
So near—so far. . . .
I . . . plodded my way back to
the newly rented orange duplex. . . .
I unlocked the door, stepped into
the living room, reached out,
and touched . . . emptiness."***

And, goodness . . . somehow . . . something had to be done about Kathie's hair!

2

QUARANTINED!

I stepped off the plane at Love Field in Dallas, located my car in the crowded parking lot, paid the parking ticket, and drove east on Mockingbird Lane toward our rented duplex. Since my wife's death and memorial service ten days earlier, I was now returning from speaking at a national student gathering in New Mexico. I had planned to cancel the long-standing engagement for personal reasons, but Mother and some close friends insisted that I keep it. Mother, who had volunteered to stay several days with us after Jean's death, reassured me that she and four-year-old Kathie would be fine without me for a couple of days. Her maternal instincts must have told her that her son needed a change of scenery and time away from all the sadness that had engulfed us.

True, the brief trip had provided a respite, but the thirty-minute drive from the airport toward home brought me back to reality—harsh reality. I sensed all too painfully that I was returning home to face a lot of unanswered questions and painful decisions.

Where would I turn for help after Mother had gone back to her home in North Carolina? What about Jean's clothes and personal possessions? When could I possibly find time to write all those "thank you" notes? How would I answer Kathie's perceptive questions? What about other speaking engagements and commitments on my calendar? What in the world would I do with those unopened boxes stacked in every room? And, what do little girls wear?

In the midst of these uncertainties, I thought again of Mother waiting at the house for my return. Just knowing that she would be there gave me reassurance. So many times in my life her very presence seemed all the answer I needed. As I drove past Southern Methodist University and crossed crowded Central Expressway I realized that I was wearing three hats. I was a husband who had lost his wife; I was a father who had suddenly become a single parent; and I was also a little boy searching desperately for solid ground in the quagmire of life. Mother could help me, for her roots had always provided stability and meaning to life.

On my left—just across the railroad tracks—was the historic Dr. Pepper plant, one of Dallas's oldest and most familiar landmarks. I noticed that new complexes and high rise office buildings were taking shape all around the distinctive, yet simple, facility. The land on which the plant was located was some of the most valuable in the city; yet, for the time being, it was not for sale. Dr. Pepper seemed oblivious to the changing skyline and to the bumper-to-bumper traffic one block away on Central Expressway.

I smiled at the large "10-2-4" logo in front of the rambling building. The sign daily gave the exact time and also the temperature reading. Ironically, the building, the sign, and the clock reflected consistency . . . and courage.

Within blocks of my house my mind was still racing wildly—forward, toward a future filled with perplexities; and backward, searching for roots that could hold me steadily while everything around me crumbled.

GRANDPA MOODY—A LESSON IN COURAGE

Roots. Consistency. Courage. No person had ever needed these more than I felt I did as I drove home late that afternoon. As I turned right and headed south on Greenville Avenue I remembered a story Mother had told me years before. It unfolded in my mind like a gift.

Her father, Grandpa Moody, was a dirt-poor farmer who lived in the Rives Chapel area of Chatham County, North Carolina. He was a strong, silent person who did most of his speaking through hard work and integrity. He and Grandma made a great team. She did the talking and organizing; he did the thinking and plodding. Talking and organizing, thinking and plodding were all necessary in grubbing out enough food to support ten growing children.

Shortly after the turn of the century, when Mother was about ten years old, Grandpa saddled his favorite horse and headed toward the county seat ten miles away in Pittsboro, North Carolina. His journey took him along Tick Creek, across Rocky River, and through a densely wooded area at the foot of Hickory Mountain. In one side of his saddle bags he tucked a few ham biscuits that Grandma had prepared for a snack; in the other side he carried money that had been carefully saved from the recent cotton crop. It was exactly enough to make the last payment on the note he had borrowed to build the homeplace, a two-story farmhouse. Grandma and all the children celebrated the occasion while Grandpa rode steadfastly on his mission.

When he arrived in Pittsboro, he hitched his horse behind the courthouse and transacted his business. He lingered just long enough to feed and water the horse and to chat briefly with some of the farmers about the weather and the crops and world events. He glanced at the sun and reckoned it would be nearly sundown by the time he would arrive back home. A lot of chores still needed to be done before he could call it a day.

On the return journey Grandpa rode much lighter in the saddle for a tremendous weight was off his shoulders. The bank note was paid in full; the folded receipt in the saddle bag was proof of the transaction. It was a great new day for the entire Moody family. As Grandpa topped the last hill before arriving home he reined in his horse, paused, and surveyed the 250 acres before him with a sense of genuine gratitude. This land was his, and on this land he would grow cotton and wheat and tobacco and corn. On this land he would raise pigs and hatch a brood of chickens and graze cattle. And, near his now-paid-for-house, he would plant a garden of beans and peas and okra and onions and potatoes and squash and . . .

Grandpa squinted, for out of the clump of trees where his house had been built there rose a white spiral of smoke. He continued to stare in confusion and bewilderment, as Mr. Bill Dowd galloped up on his own horse to meet him. Mr. Dowd, a good neighbor and friend, had been watching for Grandpa's return from the day's trip to the county seat.

"I'm sorry, Jasper," Mr. Dowd said with compassion. "Your house has just burned to the ground."

Grandpa made no response, but looked straight ahead in an empty, dead silence.

After a couple of minutes the silence was broken and Grandpa turned to his neighbor and asked in a slow, monotone voice, "Was anyone hurt?"

"No," said Mr. Dowd.

Grandpa watched the last wisps of smoke fade and blend into the twilight that settled over the valley. He then replied softly, but with determination, "We'll build it back."

And he did.

During my boyhood days, nothing delighted me more than running through and around and under that house that Grandpa built back. It was never painted and some of the boards were weathered and warped, but to me, as a child, it looked more beautiful than Tara in *Gone With The Wind*.

Grandpa died when I was nine years old. I remember his long mustache, his broad-brim hat, his overalls, and his scuffed brogans with twine for laces. As a growing boy I sat with him on the porch and was fascinated at the way he stoked his old pipe endlessly, using the stiff end of a broom straw or the head of a nail to tamp the tobacco. Then, after a good smoke, he'd reach in the pocket of his overalls and fill the pipe again with crumpled leaves of tobacco that he had grown on his own farm and cured in the tiny loft upstairs. One of my boyhood thrills was to climb the narrow, winding steps to the loft over the kitchen, smell the tobacco that was hanging from the ceiling, and sample the peanuts, or groundpeas (or goobers), that were spread out for drying on the floor. I'm convinced that most of the world is poorer for

" 'I'm sorry, Jasper,' Mr. Dowd said with compassion. 'Your house has just burned to the ground. . . .' Grandpa watched the last wisps of smoke fade and blend into the twilight that settled over the valley. He then replied softly, but with determination, 'We'll build it back.' "

having missed the unique aroma that comes from peanuts and tobacco being shut up together for weeks in the same room.

The night Grandpa died Mr. Bill Dowd sat by his bed all night. He never left the side of his neighbor and friend. I tried to rest on a sofa in the front parlor where the old pump organ sat in the corner. The smell of coffee in the kitchen, the hushed voices of people coming and going throughout the night, and just knowing that Grandpa was hurting kept me awake.

Grandpa died just before daybreak. I cried.

His funeral was the first I had ever attended. They sang "What a Friend We Have in Jesus," and "Jesus Is All the World to Me." When the church service was over, we walked behind the building and buried Grandpa in the church cemetery. Neighbors, including Mr. Dowd, had dug the grave, and everyone—neighbors, children, and grandchildren—took turns with shovels as the grave was covered with dirt. I remember the sounds of the clods as they hit the wooden box that covered the casket. It was an act of love and a final tribute to Jasper Moody, my grandpa.

I remember all this.

I wish I could recall his voice. I've tried again and again, but even the tone inflection escapes me.

Maybe he said it all—through courage and steadfastness and integrity.

Maybe paying off a debt, and then vowing to "build it back" was all this strong, silent man needed to say.

Now, two blocks from my own duplex, I spoke aloud through tears, "Thanks, Grandpa. I don't know how, but we'll also build it back."

My car was in the driveway before I saw the huge black and white sign that covered the front door. I stared at it in absolute disbelief. The bold letters read "QUARANTINED"! What in the world had happened?

I jumped out, ran to the door, hugged little Kathie, and whispered in an aside to Mother, "Who in the world did this? What does it mean?"

"I don't know, Son," she answered sadly. "The County Health Department people came this morning and nailed it up. They said there was a question about the nature of Jean's illness and how contagious the virus was."

I listened in disbelief as Mother continued, "They then told me that the house was quarantined and that Kathie could not leave until the sign came down. They also said that none of her friends could come over and play with her until further notice."

My emotions bounced from anger to frustration to futility. But these had to be bottled up inside for the sake of Mother and my four-year-old little girl who couldn't possibly comprehend what was happening.

Later that evening, after dinner, I walked out into the backyard. I stood alone for a few minutes, and then looked up and spoke softly.

"Grandpa, I'm trying 'to build it back,' but it's 'quarantined.'"

Three days later, after endless telephone calls and confused memos between departments in the public health system, I was told that the sign could come down. They said the whole thing had all been a mistake. Again, I tried to understand that bureaucratic mistakes happen, but the shock of the sign lingered for days. The good news, however, was that Kathie was now free to play with her friends. This more than made up for any frustration that I felt. Like a freed prisoner, I ripped the sign off the door, tore it into pieces, and threw it in the trash can.

"Now, two blocks from my own duplex, I spoke aloud through tears, 'Thanks, Grandpa. I don't know how, but we'll also build it back.' "

A couple of days later I drove Mother to the airport, thanked her, kissed her good-by, and saw her off for home in North Carolina. The drive back across Dallas was a lonely, pensive one. The reality of the new responsibilities before me began to settle in. As I pondered this, I was quite sure that no person anywhere was less prepared for the challenge of trying to be both mother and father to a little girl than I was.

A CONVERSATION WITH A FOUR YEAR OLD

"Honey, this is a chicken potpie, and this is a beef potpie. Which do you want? They're really delicious."

"Now, let's see, we just turn this knob on the stove, strike a match and . . . oops! A little too much gas."

"No, I don't know where your favorite coloring book is. Have you looked in your closet and under your bed?"

"Yes, God is everywhere. . . . Yes, He's right here in our house. . . . No, we can't see Him. . . . Well, just because . . ."

"Kathie, I know the top doesn't match the shorts, but couldn't you wear this just for today? Please? You couldn't? Well, you'll just have to!"

"I'm sorry your hair isn't curly and fluffy, but it still looks pretty."

"No, your mother isn't sick anymore, and she's very happy in heaven."

"Well, heaven is . . . up . . . heaven is . . . a long way off . . . er. . . . Why don't I read you one of your favorite stories?"

"I'd love to take you to the park today, but Daddy has to go to work."

"Yes, I really do love you."

"No, I don't think we can get a dog. No, we can't get a cat. Maybe later."

"We'll fly to see Mommie Mac and Daddy Mac next summer, and we'll drive to Baytown soon to see Grandmother Withers and Pops."

"Honey, nice little girls don't use words like that. Where did you hear that word? . . . Sunday School? Well, we can't use it around here."

"Kathie, please don't tell people that I'm going to get married so you'll have a new mother. And, for heaven's sakes, don't tell anybody else that I'm going to marry that nice lady I was talking to on the church parking lot. She's already married!"

"Okay, we've had our bath, and I've read you a story. It's past your bedtime."

"Yes, I'll be here when you wake up in the morning. Now, good-night."

Another day. Another evening. Another night settles in.

Tomorrow will come.

CHASING SNAKES!

I collapsed across my bed, bone-tired and heartsick. I was aroused from a deep sleep by a tug on my pajama sleeve and by the words, "Daddy, I don't feel good."

I awakened enough to mumble the question, "Where do you hurt, honey?"

"All over," Kathie replied.

Suddenly, an emotional wave of panic overwhelmed me! For a brief moment there was an instant replay of Jean's illness and the trauma of the last few weeks. My mind reeled in anxiety and my spirits sank in despair.

Oh, God, could it be?

Please, Lord, it just can't be! Not again!

As Kathie continued to cry and to tug on my sleeve, I reached out to hug her. Somewhere in that simple movement, that reach-

"Honey, nice little girls don't use words like that. Where did you hear that word? . . . Sunday School? Well, we can't use it around here."

ing out, I discovered that my own emotions and fears and fatigue could wait: my child needed me. There was nothing dramatic or heroic in what I did; it's just a part of being a parent. There are times when you do what you have to do. The past is gone and the future isn't reality; you just do it now—present tense!

"Okay, honey," I said as I took my daughter by the arm, "Why don't you get in the bed with me for a few minutes until you feel better."

That was the very invitation Kathie had expected, and she quickly snuggled in next to me. "It's just a touch of insecurity," I rationalized, for in that moment I was an authority on that subject. "She'll drop off to sleep in no time and will be fine."

I closed my heavy eyes and was nearly asleep myself when I was jolted by a shrill, piercing cry.

"Daddy! Daddy! They're crawling all over you! Run! Run fast!"

"What's all over me?" I asked as I threw the covers back and sat upright in bed.

"Snakes!" Kathie cried. "There are snakes everywhere!"

I got out of bed quickly, turned on the light, and tried to reassure my child that there were no snakes on me or anywhere else. Even with the light on, she "saw" them clearly and distinctly.

"Daddy, they're crawling all over your pajamas!" Kathie screamed in terror. "Don't get close to me!"

For the next several hours we wrestled with those snakes. Nothing I could do, lights on or lights off, could convince Kathie that they weren't real. My body ached with fatigue, my mind blurred in confusion, and my fears mounted.

Is my child losing her mind? Am I losing my mind? Has the stress of the last few weeks been too much for her? For me? Those were questions without answers.

Sometime about dawn, as the gray morning light crept through the Venetian blinds, I knew I could handle the situation no longer. I got out of bed, stumbled to the phone, and called two dear friends, Myrtice and Woody Brownlee, and explained to them the situation. "Bring her right over to our house," Myrtice insisted. "I'll take care of her."

With a silent prayer of gratitude for such friends, I threw a blanket around Kathie and in less than five minutes we were at their house. Myrtice, a mother of four, took her temperature immediately and saw that it was elevated. This was the first clue to the problem.

"What kind of pajamas were you wearing?" Myrtice wisely asked me as I stood helplessly in her den.

"Just ordinary ones with a narrow red border," I replied.

"The fever must have made her hallucinate," she added. "And the red border of your pajamas must have been those 'snakes' she kept seeing."

The next day little red spots appeared all over Kathie's body.

Measles!

We were "quarantined" again.

The childhood diseases began to come one after another. It was as though gremlins were lining up in rows and sending out the orders: "Attack the McIver house. 6005 Marquita. Everybody move." And did they ever move in on us! Red measles, German measles, chicken pox, whooping cough, scarlatina, mastoid ear infection, and tonsillitis.

Next to the Bible, I read "Dr. Spock" most. And, if you won't tell anyone, there were some days when I read "Dr. Spock" more than the Bible! I became a walking encyclopedia of every childhood illness, but I whimpered through every one of them.

MOTHERS—AND ONE FATHER—IN WAITING

The surgical waiting room at Gaston Hospital was tiny and cramped—definitely too small for nine mothers and one father. We huddled in the crowded, institutional-like room because we shared one thing in common: each was the parent of a child scheduled for a tonsillectomy. Our children had already been taken, most of them tearfully, to another area where they were being "prepped" for the surgery. The mothers, some of them tearful, had been ushered into the waiting room. I became a part of the "mothers-in-waiting."

There is no chatter anywhere worse than nervous chatter. While we waited, I learned more about people and problems and illnesses and things than I cared to know. I also heard, in more subdued tones, a great deal about husbands.

While the mothers discussed needlepoint, recipes, fashions, Bluebirds and Brownies, in-laws, and the latest operations, I tried to play it cool. Giving every impression of confidence (some would call it macho) and relaxation, I casually browsed *Woman's Day* and *Reader's Digest*, the only two magazines I could find in the waiting room. (There was a copy of *Cosmopolitan*, but someone grabbed it immediately.) As we sat there, I had the strange feeling that I was being watched out of the corners of eyes and that wheels were turning in the minds of others seated around me.

"Who is he? . . . What's he doing here by himself? . . . Poor thing."

Of course, most of this was over-reaction and hypersensitivity on my own part. But I did feel just a little out of place, like a fifth wheel.

A gracious, middle-aged lady seated next to me reached out to include me in the fraternal . . . er . . . maternal spirit of the gathering. She asked with concern a few lead questions that gave me an opportunity to interpret my situation as a single parent, or widower. I sensed immediate rapport with her, and soon this rapport rippled across the room because most every word spoken by anyone was heard by everyone. From that moment on they included me in the circle.

I talked with the women about the latest styles in little girls' dresses; the best beauty salons for short, straight haircuts; measles, and other childhood illnesses. I even contributed to the discussion on cooking as I marveled about the convenience of fish sticks and beef potpies! To their everlasting credit, my companions listened without snickering.

Soon we became a bonded group, united in conversation and mutual concern.

Periodically, the nurse supervisor of the operating room would enter our room and announce to various ones, "Your child has entered surgery," or "Your child is just out of surgery," or "Your child is in recovery and is doing fine." This eased tensions and worked beautifully until . . . until Kathie's surgery lasted a little longer than expected.

I glanced at the large clock in the room and knew that too many minutes had ticked away without some word from the nurse. I tried to stay calm and collected because I knew that little things in a surgical area could delay the process. But I kept watching the clock—minute by dragging minute.

Others were keeping up with the time, also. Soon the room became quieter and quieter, and an eerie hush settled over it.

The stillness was broken when one mother asked me, "How long has your little girl been in there?"

"Oh, about an hour," I answered coolly.

"My son was out in forty-five minutes," she volunteered with a hint of compassion.

Another observed that her neighbor's child had hemorrhaged during this kind of surgery. She then added, "Anything can happen, you know."

I gulped and muttered weakly, "I know."

Ten . . . fifteen more minutes passed . . . ever so slowly. Nothing else could be heard but the ticking of the clock and an occasional sigh. The sigh was usually accompanied by a sympathetic glance in my direction. I imagined the silent thoughts of my new "friends."

"Poor little girl. . . . Poor, pathetic father. . . . They're probably in serious trouble back there in surgery. . . . How will they break the news to him?"

Once again, my imaginations were swirling out of control. It was time to find out what was going on. Time to crash through those "No Admittance" doors that led to the forbidden area of surgery. Time to yank masks off doctors and nurses and get some answers.

Time to act. Now!

But reason held me back for a moment. A fleeting note of sanity told me that if I bolted for surgery, my nine new friends

"Once again, my imaginations were swirling out of control. It was time to find out what was going on. Time to crash through those 'No Admittance' doors that led to the forbidden area of surgery. Time to yank masks off doctors and nurses and get some answers."

would crash the doors with me, or ahead of me. I wasn't sure the surgical suite could survive that kind of frenzied onslaught. Neither could I.

So I waited . . . and waited . . . with my eyes glued on the doors leading into the surgical suite. My heart quickened at the sound of footsteps from behind the doors. I braced myself for the worst as a familiar nurse in a white uniform came through the doors and walked straight toward me. Her smile was all the reassurance I needed as I breathed a sigh of relief.

"Mr. McIver, your little girl is out of surgery and is now in recovery. She's doing fine. No problems at all."

The tension in the room lifted immediately, and from every corner my new friends chimed in: "I knew she was okay. . . . These delays sometimes happen. . . . I wasn't worried at all."

But I was too emotionally drained to respond.

Three hours later I checked Kathie out, cradled her in my arms, and took her back to our orange duplex. We were met at the front door by our friend, Myrtice, who asked, "How was it?"

I smiled with confidence and answered like an old pro, "Great. Nothing to it. Nothing at all."

I then opened the door, carried my sleeping little girl inside, placed her on the bed, bowed my head, and said wearily, "Thank you, Lord."

I walked out of the room, paused, and said with a grin, "And please, dear Lord, forgive me for lying."

On June 19, ten months after Jean died, Kathie's pediatrician dismissed her as a patient and released her except for routine check-ups. The doctor's medical books indicated that there were no more childhood diseases available for my daughter to catch!

3

AFTERSHOCKS

Sir, I understand your position," I said to the young airline agent who stood at the door leading to the plane that was now late for departure. He looked nervously at his watch, tightened his lips, and listened to my pleas for the third time.

"I realize that you gave the final boarding call five minutes ago," I continued, "but I'm begging you to give me three more minutes—just three. Please. I have a real crisis on my hands, and with any luck at all, I think I can solve it by then."

Without waiting for his response, I dashed off down the wide corridor of the Atlanta airport, glancing in all directions. I was hoping and praying that I would see some matronly or grandmotherly looking woman who might understand. There was no time to waste. That frustrated agent wasn't going to hold the plane much longer.

About thirty yards from the boarding gate I saw an older woman coming down the walkway who looked like a good prospect to assist me. She was tiny in size, slightly stooped, and walked with a cane. A big straw bonnet covered a part of her face, but I had a feeling there might be help under that bonnet. She was alone.

"'Scuse me, Lady. Please excuse me, but I wonder if I might ask you to help me?"

The older lady just stopped and looked at me without a word. I was grateful that she at least stopped and looked. It gave me a chance to continue without catching my breath.

"Thank you," I sighed, "I'm from . . . we're from Dallas. That is, my four-year-old daughter and I are from Dallas. We're on our way to her grandparents in North Carolina, and she's in the ladies' restroom and refuses to come out. She's been in there twenty minutes, and they've announced the final boarding twice. I've got the agent holding the plane, but they're ready for take-off, and his patience is about exhausted. He says they have a schedule to meet."

At this point I was practically begging.

"Please, Ma'am, I sure do need help. I can't go into the ladies' restroom and . . ."

She straightened up slightly—as much as she could—and tilted back her head, looked me squarely in the face, and chuckled. Then the lady planted her cane solidly on the floor with one hand, reached out and took my elbow with the other, and said reassuringly, "Now, now, young man, don't you fret another minute. I'll find your little girl for you. I've raised six myself," she added with a twinkle in her eyes, "and I have eleven grandchildren. Now, what's her name?"

"Her name is Kathie," I answered with a sigh of relief. "I don't think there's anything wrong with her. She's probably playing a game with me and just won't come out, and . . ."

"We'll be back in no time," the woman said as she picked up her cane and limped off in a hurry straight toward the restroom. "Don't you go away," she exclaimed as she looked back over her shoulder.

As she hastened through the door, I began pacing around in small nervous circles in the corridor, wondering how long the agent would keep holding the plane.

In no time the tiny, stooped lady came back out the door, walking hand-in-hand with Kathie. Both of them were grinning.

There was not time for a formal introduction or even for an appropriate "thank you." I grabbed Kathie by the hand, waved at the lady, raced by a not-so-happy airline agent, and stumbled into our seats. I hunkered down in my seat, for I could feel 168 people looking at us in disapproval. And that number didn't include the captain and the crew up front.

Neither of us said anything as the plane taxied out, nor was there any talk during the take off. Kathie was too excited, and I was too exasperated.

When we reached the cruising altitude I turned to her and asked, "Honey, what in the world were you doing back there?"

"Playing a game," she smiled. "And guess what, Daddy?"

"What?" I sighed.

"We're on our way to her grandparents in North Carolina, and she's in the ladies' restroom and refuses to come out. She's been in there twenty minutes, and they've announced the final boarding twice."

"I won!" she exclaimed proudly.

We were nearly to North Carolina when Kathie looked up from her coloring book and said, "That sure was a nice lady back at the airport."

I nodded a weary assent.

"Daddy, do you think she would marry us?"

A BLUE CHRISTMAS TREE

Kathie wiggled next to me while I read the newspaper in my favorite chair. It was nice to have her sit with me, but I knew her well enough to know that her closeness was usually followed by some special request. I was not wrong, for she soon leaned over and whispered into my ear the kind of Christmas tree she wanted.

"You want what color Christmas tree?" I asked quietly, hoping the expression in my voice would hide my bewilderment.

"A *blue* one," Kathie responded emphatically as she stuck out her lower lip.

I braced myself for another logical, sensible discussion with my little daughter. Phrases were already zinging through my mind, ready to be spoken: "Whoever heard of a *blue* Christmas tree? . . . *Blue* will clash with the furniture in the living room. . . . Nobody else has a *blue* tree."

"The neighbors will stare at that *blue* tree through the windows."

There was no doubt about it; this had to be dealt with from a rational and grown-up perspective. I resolved that a hideous, spray-painted *blue* Christmas tree would not be found in our *orange* duplex this year.

So, there. My mind was made up.

Until . . . I felt two tiny arms around my neck . . . and looked into two twinkling eyes that asked more than any words could ever ask.

In that moment I remembered another day and another tree from long ago.

I was a boy back in the rolling hills of North Carolina. It was summer and time for playing baseball, swimming in the muddy creek (after we had frightened the snakes away), and skipping flat stones across ponds.

It was also time to begin scouting the woods for the perfect Christmas tree. After all, Christmas was only six months away.

Across the field from our small white bungalow was a thick wooded area that belonged to our friendly neighbor, Mr. Dark. Beyond the clump of trees there was an old, dilapidated house that sat overlooking a steep hill. Behind the vacant house was the very tree that I had picked out. I stumbled on it one day while on my way to my favorite fishing hole at the foot of the hill.

The tree was cedar, not pine, and had some gaps between branches. It was bent over and crooked, as though it had been designed to blend with the rolling landscape. But if you walked around to the other side, you couldn't see the gaps and the crooks.

I kept my eye on that tree and checked on it throughout the rest of the summer and during the fall. I usually went alone when I visited the tree for I didn't want anyone else to know the treasure I had found. That tree had my name on it!

In the second week of December, just after the first snow, I pulled on my boots, crawled into my leather jacket, and snapped my aviator's cap (equipped with goggles!) under my chin. As I stepped out into the cold, I put on my gloves that were lined with soft rabbit fur. Then, with hatchet in hand, I waded happily in snow across the field and through the woods until I came to the old house.

My tree was waiting for me. An hour later I returned home, dragging my prized possession behind me.

A crude base was hammered together to hold the tree. Old green and red decorative ropes, found in the attic, were wrapped around the cedar arms and branches. Strings and strings of popcorn helped cover the gaps. A small packet of tinsel purchased at Rose's Five-and-Ten-Cents Store added the final touch.

There was only one place in our house worthy of my tree—the front room.

"There was no doubt about it; this had to be dealt with from a rational and grown-up perspective. I resolved that a hideous, spray-painted **blue** ***Christmas tree would not be found in our*** **orange** ***duplex this year."***

This was the room that was opened and heated only when special guests—like the pastor, or the visiting preacher, or some out-of-town relative—came for a visit. The room contained a maroon mohair sofa that scratched your legs if you wore short britches. There were also two large stuffed chairs, a secondhand piano, two tables that Dad made in his workshop, a framed picture of a farm from a calendar, and a statue of Rebekah at the Well that Mother purchased with her egg money.

The special room now had the special Christmas tree. The little tree wobbled in its crudely constructed base, leaned in the wrong direction, and had glaring gaps in the branches that were obvious to everyone—except to an eight-year-old boy.

To me, it was the perfect Christmas tree.

I remembered that special tree as Kathie continued to snuggle next to me. I thought about it until logic no longer seemed important.

And who cared about being rational? Especially at Christmas.

"A blue tree?" I pondered half aloud. "Why not a blue tree?"

I reached around and touched Kathie's smiling cheek and gave her a big hug.

"Let's go, honey," I said. "Let's buy the *bluest* tree in town."

Kathie and I put on our coats and headed for the car without another word. We drove quickly to the grocery store in the Skillman Shopping Center and purchased on the spot the last gaudy blue tree available!

It wasn't the prettiest tree ever grown; it had some sagging branches with gaps between them; it never did stand up straight, regardless of how many times we adjusted the metal stand; and, I'm sure the neighbors must have stared many times at that lighted, spray-painted *blue* tree through the window.

But to a four-year-old child, it was perfect.

And, to a father who remembered, it looked mighty good, also.

BONITA'S IN TOWN

It was Friday afternoon, and I had just gotten home from the office. The lady that had been keeping Kathie had gone for the day, and I welcomed a few hours of quiet and solitude. Kathie and I would read and talk during the evening and then get a good night's rest. Tomorrow we would run some errands and do some grocery shopping. It was nice to be home.

The telephone rang ten minutes later.

"Hi!" a chirpy voice said on the other end of the telephone, "I'm here!"

"Well . . . er . . . that's nice," I replied in confusion. "But who are you and where are you?"

"Oh, this is Bonita," she answered with a giggle.

The momentary silence on my end of the line must have been a dead giveaway. I was scratching my head as I thought, *Bonita? Bonita who?*

"You remember," she continued teasingly. "You spoke to the youth group in our church several weeks ago. I drove you to the airport, and you said just before you left, "If you're ever in Dallas, give me a ring and we'll have a cup of coffee together."

I remembered. It had just been a simple gesture of goodwill, sort of like saying "Thanks" to one of the fellows. The problem was that Bonita was no fellow, and she was on a mission to prove it.

"Well, Bonita, that's nice," I lied. "How long do you plan to be in the city?"

"All weekend," she giggled again. "And I don't have any plans—none at all."

While I stalled and racked my brains for some appropriate answer, she continued, "I'm staying with a friend of mine. I'm on my way to her house now."

That's good, I thought. *Maybe her friend will keep her occupied.*

Then she added, "But I'm free tonight and tomorrow night and . . ."

I was trapped; boy, was I ever trapped!

"Well, Bonita," I said as politely as possible, while trying to cover my frustrations, "let me do some checking on my schedule and see if I can make some arrangements for Kathie. I'll call you later at your friend's house."

I hung up the phone, shook my head and muttered, "I'm in a mess!"

Two of my former Texas Tech students, Wanda and Andy Edmondson, had moved recently to Dallas. They were not only former students; they had also become friends, and nobody needed a friend more than I did in this situation. I dialed their number.

"Wanda, I need you and Andy badly," I pleaded. "And I need you tonight."

"Is something wrong with Kathie?" Wanda asked with concern.

"No," I said, "There's something wrong with me. And you have to help me out . . . please!"

Briefly, I tried to explain my recent telephone conversation, but Wanda kept laughing so hard she missed most of what I was saying.

"Please, Wanda," I begged. "It's not funny. Stop laughing and listen!"

"You know," I reasoned with my friend who had been my former student, "that I've dated several girls in recent months. "It's helped me to heal, but I've got to have the freedom to choose my own dates. Bonita just plopped in."

Wanda cackled over the phone. I ignored her and continued the mostly one-way conversation.

"I'm sure Bonita is a nice girl. She seems to be efficient in her work, but she's just not my type. She talks too much and she laughs too loudly. And, I don't know just how to say this, but she's a little on the hefty side. No, she's more than hefty; she's large!"

Wanda was laughing so hard she was nearly out of control, but that didn't slow me up one bit.

"And another thing. She uses some kind of gosh-awful perfume that reeks. Believe me, it's really strong stuff, and it smells sweet and sickening. I know what I'm talking about 'cause I rode with her in her car all the way to the airport. I can't stand it."

That was too much for Wanda. She lost it completely, and the more she laughed, the more impatient and irritable I became. I had a feeling that she actually enjoyed seeing her old college teacher in this kind of pickle.

"And another thing," I shouted in the phone, "if you were in my class today I'd flunk you!"

"Okay, okay," Wanda choked, "I get the message. Now, what do you want Andy and me to do?"

"Just don't leave me alone with that girl," I pleaded.

"Look," I said, "Find out what's playing at the summer musicals tonight—either in Dallas or Fort Worth. Anywhere. Buy four tickets and I'll pay for them. Just make sure you don't leave us alone."

"And another thing. She uses some kind of gosh-awful perfume that reeks. Believe me, it's really strong stuff, and it smells sweet and sickening."

She was kind enough to get the tickets, and we all went to the musical together. After one whiff of Bonita's sweet-smelling lilac perfume, I considered sitting between Wanda and Andy, but common sense—what was left of it—told me that this wouldn't be the wisest thing to do. So I just sat it out for three long, miserable hours in the seat assigned to me.

Wanda and Andy snickered and nudged each other all the way through the performance. This confused Bonita since the show wasn't that funny. I started once to comment that she must have missed a punch line, but the perfume got in the way and I gave up. Thankfully, the curtain finally came down.

Later, I drove Bonita back to her friend's apartment. She seemed oblivious to my uneasiness during the evening and began to talk about plans for us the next day. I listened in disbelief and mumbled something about "a busy day," or "Kathie's schedule," or a "headache."

I told her good-night and good-by. I never saw Bonita again.

Wanda and Andy are still laughing.

Every now and then, on crowded elevators or in small restaurants, I catch a whiff of sweet lilac perfume and wonder if Bonita is back in town.

OUT OF ASHES

The three-day professional seminar was a requirement for me since I worked with college students and taught accredited Bible courses. The lectures were often long and tedious, the bunk beds sagged in the wrong places, and the showers were cold—always cold. More than anything else, however, I didn't like being out of town for three days and nights in a row. So, when the final session of the seminar came to a close, I breathed a sigh of relief and headed home.

Home had become very special to me. It was a sanctuary, a haven, where I could drop appearances and pretenses and just be myself. Home was a place of acceptance and love and peace . . .

. . . and loneliness.

The loneliness really didn't hit me until I parked the car in the driveway, moved up the steps, and unlocked the door. As I crossed the threshold, words of greetings had already formed on my lips.

"Hi! I'm back! Everything okay? Oh, it was a good seminar, but I got tired of all the lectures. For the life of me, I can't figure out why intelligent people plan programs with one speaker following another and another. It's a known fact that one end of the body can absorb only what the other end can endure. And that 'other end' of my body is tired—worn out from all that sitting. But, it's great to be home. Say, let me tell you one of the funniest things that happened. You won't believe this. Tom was trying to climb into the upper bunk, and . . ."

Then, like cold water in my face, it hit me.

My house was empty.

I stood there paralyzed, overwhelmed by the lonely void. I gulped, and swallowed the greetings that I yearned to say—but there was no one to hear.

The chill of the cold winter wind prompted me to close the door. Wearily, I dropped my luggage—a suitcase and a new leather briefcase—to the floor, turned up the thermostat, walked across the room and collapsed into a lounge chair. I had an hour before I was to pick up Kathie from the house of friends who had kept her while I was away. Just enough time for a quick nap.

Sometime later, I was awakened from a deep sleep by a burning odor. Slowly opening my eyes I saw nothing except a blur. The pictures on the wall and the furniture around the room were hidden by a thick cloud of smoke. My eyes began to water and I started coughing. Jumping quickly from the chair, I began to grope around the room trying to find what was causing the smoke.

Then I remembered. The floor furnace was located at the entrance of the room, immediately inside the front door. The thermostat was on the wall to the right as you stepped across the threshold. That's where I had dropped my luggage, and that's where I had turned on the heat!

I fumbled around until I found the handles of the suitcase and the new briefcase. They were blistering hot. As fast as I could, I opened the door and pitched both of them out onto the front lawn. The oxygen in the fresh air provided the combination needed for combustion and the luggage burst into flames while in mid-flight.

There was nothing left to do but stand and watch helplessly as fire devoured both pieces of luggage. Suits, shirts, sweaters, ties, underwear, books, correspondence, mementos, and even notes from a dull seminar were charred beyond use.

I stood motionless on the lawn until the flames had done their work. The flickering embers seemed to keep guard to make sure that nothing worthwhile could be salvaged.

The cold wind no longer bothered me.

I moved slowly up the steps and across the threshold for the second time. The house seemed more empty than ever.

I realized that I could do one of two things. I chose the second.

I laughed.

If the phoenix can rise from ashes, I thought, as I shut the front door and moved toward the phone, *maybe my insurance will at least buy me one set of new underwear.*

NOW I LAY ME DOWN TO SLEEP

"Okay, honey," I coaxed, "you've had your supper, taken your bath, and we've just finished reading fourteen of your favorite stories. It's time for bed. You're tired, and Daddy's tired."

"Just one more story," she pleaded with a whine in her voice. "This is really my favoritest of all."

I was beginning to learn in the dual role of both father and mother that any story that delays bedtime becomes the "favoritest," or "most favoritest."

We finished the last story and, amazingly, Kathie climbed down from my lap and moved immediately into her room. I thought the delaying tactics were over, but I soon learned better.

Like a little angel, she knelt beside her bed for prayers. I knelt beside her.

"Dear Lord," she began, "please bless Clara and Tommy, and Bobby and Bo, and Nancy, and Uncle Roger and Aunt Martha, and Grandmother and Pops, and Mommie Mac and Daddy Mac, and Annie Kay, and Daddy, and Mother up in heaven, and Uncle Bill and Aunt Ella, and the Millers, and Mary and GiGi, and . . . ."

I wasn't sure where she was headed or how long it might take us to get there, but my knees began to hurt. With an unuttered sigh, I shifted my weight from one knee to the other, opened the right eye to look at Kathie, and caught her looking back at me through her left eye. There we were eyeball-to-eyeball, four inches apart.

We both grinned, and she continued, "And, dear Lord, thank you for fish sticks and beef potpies and ice cream and bacon and eggs and candy and. . . ."

"Lord," I thought, *"How many different things has she eaten this week?"*

Finally, and thankfully, she wore herself out praying. She had just about run out of people and things and her voice grew softer and fainter.

"We're almost there," I hoped.

At this moment she became rejuvenated and revived, long enough for one last request.

"And please, God," she asked in a tone louder than usual, "send me a little brother or little sister."

"Amen."

"If the phoenix can rise from ashes, I thought, as I shut the front door and moved toward the phone, maybe my insurance will at least buy me one set of new underwear."

I tucked her in, kissed her good-night, told her that I loved her, and moved down the hall to my own room.

I turned out the light and fell into the bed, utterly exhausted. My arm flopped out and I felt the empty space beside me.

For a long time I stared at the ceiling. Then I smiled and added my own prayer.

"Lord, if You can pull this one off . . . we've got a real miracle."

God must have smiled also, for I was asleep before I could finish the sentence.

4

GETTING MY FEET WET

I was returning to Dallas late one night from speaking to a group of college students in another city. As often happened when it was necessary for me to be away, friends volunteered to let Kathie spend the night with them. The support that several families and individuals continued to give us warmed my heart. *I just couldn't make it,* I thought, *without their friendship.* The lights of Dallas loomed on the horizon in the distance. Although I had lived in the city only a few months, it was beginning to feel more and more like home—even with some of the moving boxes still unopened.

When I arrived home thirty minutes later, I found a note taped to my front door. I opened it and read: "Important called meeting of the pulpit committee. Come to Billie Newsom's home as soon as possible. We will wait for you."

I glanced at my watch. It was after ten o'clock. Strange. A meeting of the committee at this hour of the night?

"Heaven help us," I groaned. "I'm in no mood for another tedious committee meeting. I'm worn out. It's late and I have to be at the office early in the morning. Besides, I'm having a hard time understanding that committee."

Indeed, I was.

It had been nine months since our pastor, Ralph Langley, had resigned to assume new responsibilities in Houston. In some church denominations there are bishops to lead in the selection of new leadership for local congregations. In others, presbyteries and synods assist. Every Baptist church, however, is responsible for seeking out and "calling" its own pastor. The individual church elects from its own membership a pastor search, or a pulpit committee. I was one of the nine elected by Wilshire to serve in this capacity.

Getting the names of candidates was no problem. Our church had an excellent reputation as a strong, growing congregation north of downtown Dallas, two miles east of Southern Methodist University and just west of White Rock Lake. This was a choice area of the city. Also, Wilshire was young enough not to be bound by traditions, but stable enough to provide a solid ministry to persons of all ages. In short, it was a desirable pulpit for any candidate.

The names of prospective pastors poured in—more than ninety in all. And, several of the candidates recommended themselves! Those particular résumés were usually accompanied with statements like "I feel that my work is about over where I am," or "I feel that the Lord is leading me to your church," or "I've always thought I could minister effectively in the Dallas area." On closer examination, however, our committee often discovered that the church members where those pastors were serving had declared their work was "over." Furthermore, the congregation was helping them get "led" somewhere else. Anywhere else.

But among the ninety-plus names before us were many good persons who were more than qualified to lead our church. Several of these were researched and interviewed. I was excited about our opportunities for securing excellent leadership.

Then, a puzzling thing happened. After six months of positive, concerted effort, the work of the committee seemed to slow down. Traveling to hear prospective pastors preach was reduced dramatically, and the meetings became more and more routine as we shuffled papers and reviewed the obvious. This apparent change in attitude baffled me.

In fact, I became so discouraged that I was ready to resign, but I don't like quitters. That's why I walked wearily back to the car and drove to the Newsom home late that night.

"Settle down, Bruce," I told myself as I made the short drive. "You've just had a long day, and you're frustrated about a lot of things. Try to have an open mind. There must be some sensible explanation for this meeting."

I rang the doorbell and was greeted by Billie, the charming wife of Dr. Newsom, Sr., or "Big Doc," as he was affectionately

" 'We want to recommend you to the church as our pastor. . . .' 'But you folks don't understand,' I pleaded. 'I'm a member of the church, and I'm a member of this pulpit committee.' "

called by many. Both of them were special friends to me, and her warm smile was reassuring as she ushered me into the spacious living room.

One glance told me that every member of the committee was present—J. E. Smith, Johnnye Fildes, Vondyl Willis, Fred Herold, Jim Self, Jean Chastain, Bob Young, and Billie. This was unusual, especially at this late hour of the night. And, except for Billie's smile, they looked so somber.

As soon as I had seated myself on the sofa, J. E., the chairman, cleared his throat and said with a shaky voice, "Bruce, we haven't been fair with you. For several weeks we've been having brief meetings and dismissing them without much action. What you don't know is that we reconvened somewhere else as soon as you were gone. In short, we've been meeting behind your back."

So that explained it. I hadn't just imagined what had happened. But why?

"For a long time," he continued, "we've thought about this and prayed about it, and we've reached a unanimous conclusion: We want to recommend you to the church as our pastor."

I was stunned.

Time stood still while I tried to sort out my emotions. If ever a shot came out of left field or off the wall or. . . .

A second glance around the room told me that, right or wrong, these people really meant it. That scared me.

"But you folks don't understand," I pleaded. "I'm a member of the church, and I'm a member of this pulpit committee; I'm even vice chairman of this group. You elected me to that position. Remember? Besides, I know the members of the congregation too well to ever be their pastor. They're some of my closest friends. And another thing, friends in the ministry elsewhere have asked me to submit their names as prospective pastors for our church, and I've turned those names in to you and—"

"We know all that," the chairman responded firmly.

"But I'm a widower," I continued. "I'm trying to be both father and mother to my little girl, and the load gets heavy as it is. I don't know how in the world I could attend all the committee meetings that go on in a church, and I sure don't know what I could do about crisis calls at all hours of the day and night. I just couldn't leave Kathie at two o'clock in the morning to go to the emergency room of the hospital . . . and . . ."

"We've thought about that. We'll help you."

I was desperate. "But you don't understand. I've had very little experience pastoring a church. Most of my work has been on college campuses and in the classroom. I did pastor a small church on weekends while I was a student in the seminary, but the responsibilities there were nothing like those at Wilshire."

"We understand all that," J. E. replied patiently. "We've weighed these matters, and we are still convinced." He gave no ground.

"But, I've begun dating again," I continued. "I want my privacy. I must have it. The thought of living my personal life in a church goldfish bowl for everyone to see frightens me."

They all smiled understandingly, realizing that my own emotions were blocking out any rational answers that they might give me. What was happening was deeper than words could possibly convey. They recognized that I needed time to absorb the shock of their announcement and time to arrive at my own decision.

They quietly prayed for me. Then they asked me to go home, take all the time I needed, and pray about the situation.

"But some of my friends are still saying, 'If you want to pastor a good church, you must first get on the pulpit committee!' "

I did—if prayer includes arguing with God, fussing with God, stalking the floors, banging on the walls, and (forgive me) telling God that He needed to send clearer signals to the others on the pulpit committee.

My problem wasn't with the church or even with pastoring the church. My problem was the thought of trying to do this . . . and, at the same time, trying to provide for the needs of my daughter—alone.

One month later, after the committee had gone through the appropriate process and after I had gone through my own personal torture, the church "called" me as pastor.

It became a beautiful, growing, fulfilling relationship that lasted thirty years.

But some of my friends are still saying, "If you want to pastor a good church, you must first get on the pulpit committee!"

WORKING ON THE BAPTISMAL SPLASH METER

"Just a few more times, Bob," I insisted. "There's still room for improvement."

"But this is not in my job description," Bob retorted. "And besides, these ear plugs are beginning to hurt and the water is getting cold."

"Okay, okay," I said to my associate pastor and friend, Bob Feather. "I realize it's not in your job description, and I'm sorry about the plugs and cold water, but I've got to get this right."

"What if somebody comes through the door and sees us?"

"No way," I responded. "It's Saturday afternoon and all doors leading into the building are locked. I've checked them myself."

"Look," I added, "I haven't always been a pastor, and I've been sitting in the pews for several years watching baptismal services. I've seen people dipped, dunked, and dropped. I've seen the back row of the choir splashed as some hesitant person was thrown under the water by an overly-enthusiastic preacher. I've watched people slip and slide as they were put under the water. They'd often end up with their feet kicking wildly out of the water while the rest of their body was goodness-knows-where.

"Now, it seems to me," I continued, "since we Baptists baptize by immersion, we ought to do it with some dignity. There's nothing in the Bible that says we are to half-drown the candidate or drench the choir. And there's sure nothing that says I need to become a martyr and get kicked in the head by some upside-down baptismal candidate."

Bob agreed, but he wasn't happy about it. I put him under again and again as I practiced the method—fifty-three times in all!

It's been a secret until now, but Dr. Robert Feather, current vice president of Baylor University, holds an all-time record for being "baptized" more than any other person in the whole world.

"RESCUE THE PERISHING"

Because of that Saturday afternoon workout, things went smoothly in baptismal services at Wilshire . . . until . . . until I baptized Cecil.

Cecil was a seventy-seven-year-old church attender who decided that it was time for him to get some spiritual matters in his life settled. He decided to become a member of the church, and he asked me to baptize him. Everyone was thrilled over his decision, and numerous friends indicated that they would certainly be present when he was baptized.

The baptistry was filled with water on a Sunday afternoon. Cecil and I met in a small dressing room for what I called a "dry run."

"Don't worry about a thing," I assured him. "There's a metal bar similar to a towel bar, on the bottom of the baptistry. When you're in the water I'll guide you until your feet are under the bar. That will keep them from slipping." I was proud of that simple device that I had designed myself and had installed. It was bound to do wonders for baptismal services at Wilshire.

> ***"I was no longer concerned about a smooth, dignified baptism and not making a ripple. I knew I had to get Cecil off that bottom and back to the surface. We thrashed around like two alligators before I managed to pull him up."***

"Now, Cecil, when you're in the water, cross your hands high on your chest—just under your chin." Cecil nodded, and I continued. "I'll put my hand on top of your hands high on your chest—just under your chin." As I explained this to Cecil I went through the motions of placing my hand in the exact place indicated. "Then," I added, "I'll put my other hand firmly at the back of your neck. Okay?"

"Okay," Cecil answered. He was getting the hang of it.

"When I lean you back, don't resist. Just bend your knees slightly and let me lay you down on the water. Your feet are anchored under the bar and there's a buoyancy that will keep your body afloat. I'll simply put you under the water—only about two inches—and I'll guarantee that you couldn't swallow two teaspoons full of water if you tried."

Cecil smiled with confidence and we did our "dry run." No problem—none at all. I was pleased with the preparation for the baptism, and I was proud of myself for making it look so simple for my elderly friend. This is the way it ought to be done, I thought.

The worship service began, and I moved down the steps into the water. Cecil followed me and was obviously nervous as he waded out to the center of the baptismal pool. I kept whispering into his ear, "Everything's fine. Everything's fine."

Cecil cut his eye toward me and began to mutter, "eh? . . . eh? . . . eh?" He was on the third "eh?" before I realized that he had removed his hearing aids and couldn't understand a word I said.

"Dear friends," I intoned loudly, "This is Cecil. He made a beautiful decision recently in our worship service and requested baptism."

The lights were dimmed for effect, but I knew that people all over the congregation were nodding their heads in affirmation, thrilled to be a part of this happy occasion.

"Because of your faith and because of your open commitment, I now baptize you, my friend, in the name of the Father and the Son . . . and . . ."

At that very moment Cecil jumped the gun. He bent his knees, angled slightly to the right, rolled over, and sank.

I managed to go under with him far enough to keep my hands in place, one on the back of his neck and the other on the front of his neck. But this only added to the problem because my firm and determined hold, carefully designed to guide him, was now choking him. His own two hands were flailing around wildly on the bottom of the baptistry. I was no longer concerned about a smooth, dignified baptism and not making a ripple. I knew I had to get Cecil off that bottom and back to the surface. We thrashed around like two alligators before I managed to pull him up.

As he surfaced he spat out a mouthful of water, coughed, swayed back and forth, and held to me tightly. For a moment I was afraid we might go under a second time. But then he smiled weakly at me and whispered loudly in my right ear, "Thank you."

Cecil died several years ago. I've always wondered—did he thank me for baptizing him or for saving his life?

A BAPTISMAL CERTIFICATE WITH A BLUE RIBBON

Glynis was a vivacious, delightful elementary-school student. She had talked with me a couple of times about being baptized. We read the Bible together and discussed her commitment. The more we talked, the more enthusiastic Glynis became. She could hardly wait until it was scheduled.

"That girl is something else!" I marveled to members of the church staff. "I don't think I've ever seen anyone more excited about being baptized."

The moment finally arrived and I moved into the baptistry and made a brief, introductory statement. I then nodded to Glynis who moved down the steps into the water from the ladies' dressing room. She was grinning from ear to ear. I grinned back and thought, "It's wonderful to see a young person so thrilled. Maybe some of the youth are listening to my sermons after all."

The baptism went without a flaw. Without a ripple, also. I couldn't help but feel grateful for such a meaningful moment.

Glynis then turned around to wade back toward the steps leading to the dressing room. She paused, gave me an angelic smile, put her face back under the water, and swam across the entire baptistry, using some of the most beautiful free-style strokes and smoothest kicks ever seen in a Baptist church.

The next day I learned that she was the star pupil on her special synchronized swimming team.

ON ENVYING THE METHODISTS

"Pastor, it's about time for the service to begin," one of the associate ministers said through the closed door of the baptismal dressing room.

"Almost ready," I replied as I hurriedly pulled on the rubber waders that most Baptist preachers use. I reached for a spotless white robe neatly hanging on the rack, put it on, and zipped it up, breathing a sigh of relief that the zipper didn't catch in the fabric. This was one baptism that should be smooth and perfect.

I remembered with gratitude the events that had led to this very moment.

Carol Brady, an attractive young adult, had indicated a strong desire to join our church. Her husband and other members of the family were already members and vitally involved in the programs and ministries of Wilshire. Carol liked everything she knew about the church and was quick to pass this along to others—everything, that is, except baptism.

This was her "big-time hang-up" as she put it. The thought of putting on a robe, stepping into a big "tub" (again, her word) and being immersed before the entire congregation was too much for her.

The more I tried to reassure her, the more nervous she seemed to become. I tried gentle persuasion, understanding, and a touch of firmness, but it got us nowhere.

"Okay, Carol," I said one day, "We've about talked this subject to death. I'll leave the matter with you. If and when you are ready to be baptized, just let me know. Meanwhile, we'll let it rest here for a while."

"Agreed," she responded.

Several weeks went by and the subject was not mentioned by either of us. I determined to give her all the freedom she needed to reach her own decision.

One Friday morning my telephone rang. Carol had only one crisp statement: "Fill the baptistry!"

"When?"

"This Sunday night!"

"It's done."

"And, Bruce," she added, "do it right. A lot of my family and friends will be there."

Now, Sunday night had come and the moment had arrived. The last preparations had taken place. I glanced down again at the waders, smoothed the wrinkles out of the white robe, and waited impatiently for the conclusion of the first congregational hymn. I knew that Carol was waiting in the ladies' dressing room on the other side, preparing to descend the steps into the water to finalize her long and difficult decision.

"It will all be over in five minutes," I thought. "Carol will be glad; her friends and family will be happy for her; and I'll be relieved."

The last note of the hymn had been sung. This was my cue. I opened the door, entered a small hallway, made a right turn, and started down the stairs into the water.

One . . . two . . . three . . . steps.

I froze.

No water. Absolutely bone dry, like a desert.

Carol was halfway down the steps on the opposite side, facing me and giving me this "what-do-I-do-now?" look.

Good question, I thought. *What do we do now?*

Slowly I walked to the center of the empty baptistry and made some weak, lame apology about "breakdown in communications." With a painfully forced smile, I then added some inane comment like, "These things just happen in the best of situations."

Out of sight of the congregation, Carol covered her face, snickered, and headed quickly for the ladies' dressing room.

As the next hymn was announced, I slowly ascended the dry steps on my side of the baptistry.

I paused at the top, also out of view of the congregation, looked down at the large, empty tank, and mumbled a prayer:

"Lord, if it's all the same to you, just now I think I'd rather be a Methodist!"

5

BY-THE-STILL-WATERS

Scene One: A small restaurant in Dallas. A conversation between two friends is taking place over a cup of coffee.

One speaks hesitantly as he stirs his coffee. "Bruce, have you ever considered dating a seminary girl . . . I mean . . . a girl who is a student at the seminary?"

"Heavens, no, Bill. That's the last place I care to look for dates!"

"Why?"

"Well, to begin with, I'm a frequent visitor on the campus and I'm a friend of most of the faculty and administration. Also, I taught and worked with some of the seminary students while they were still in college. I may be overly sensitive, but I'd just as soon keep my personal life personal."

My friend listens silently while I continue. "And another thing, when I was a student at the seminary, there just weren't that many good-looking girls on the campus."

He smiles while I ramble on. "Don't get me wrong; I've met some sharp, attractive girls who have been students there, but . . . well. . . . No, I don't think that's the place for me to look for dates."

"Besides," I add with a boast, "my social calendar's pretty well booked-up as it is."

Bill O'Brien, minister of music at Wilshire and student at Southwestern Baptist Theological Seminary in Fort Worth, gives me a knowing look and finishes his coffee. He knows better than to take seriously my empty boast. He and his wife, Dellanna, are special people in my life. They realize that nearly four years of living without a wife has been a lonely, difficult journey for me. They know me well enough to know that I will not marry just to find someone who will be a mother for Kathie. They know, also, that I will not marry just to marry. Life is too short to settle for that.

That's the joy and pain of friendship. Friends know, really know, what's deep down inside a person. And they care.

The coffee session is over. Bill slips out of the booth while I linger for a last look at the dregs in my empty cup.

"Lord, can my cup ever be filled again?"

❧ ❧ ❧

Scene Two: A small restaurant in Fort Worth. A conversation between two friends is taking place over a quick cup of coffee between classes.

"Lawanna, have you ever considered dating someone older than you?"

"How much older? I dated a boy in high school who was a year older than me."

"Ten years."

"Ten years? You've lost your mind! I wouldn't think of it. Not in a thousand years!"

"Have you ever dated a guy who's been married?"

"Are you kidding? I've never had any reason or occasion to. Besides, what on earth would we have in common to talk about?"

"Have you ever considered dating someone who has a child?"

"Come on, Bill O'Brien! You're wasting your time, and you're wasting mine! I thought you were my friend. Look, I've got to go," she said as she grabbed her purse and stood to leave.

"Hold it, Lawanna. Sit back down for a minute. One last question. Have you ever considered dating a preacher, a pastor?"

"Heavens no! I could never see myself as a pastor's wife. I'm just not the type. Besides, I've been around some of the ministerial students here long enough to make me want to look elsewhere! No preachers, thank you. The answer is "no" to every question. See you back in class."

❧ ❧ ❧

Scene Three: An orange duplex in Dallas. It's a cold November morning and the rains are pelting the windows of the house. The phone rings.

"Heavens no! I could never see myself as a pastor's wife. I'm just not the type. Besides, I've been around some of the ministerial students here long enough to make me want to look elsewhere! No preachers, thank you."

"Say, Bruce, I hate to bother you on your day off, but I want to ask a favor of you. Would you mind driving me to Fort Worth? I have to deliver an important paper to one of my professors at the seminary, and it has to be turned in today or it will be late. I know you're probably reading or resting on your day off, but I could surely use your help."

Use my help? Why does Bill need my help? He has his own car and he's perfectly capable of driving to Fort Worth. He makes the round trip drive almost daily to attend classes. But he is a friend, and friends don't have to ask a lot of questions, so . . .

"Okay, Bill. I'll do it if you really need me."

Those three scenes blended to change my life . . . and my future.

A DETERMINED MATCHMAKER

An hour later we parked the car on the seminary campus, walked in the rain to the main building, and stood briefly in the rotunda trying to get warm and comfortable. I noticed that Bill kept looking around the large spacious area.

"Why, hello, Lawanna! It's great to see you! Have you two ever met? Bruce, this is my special friend, Lawanna House. Lawanna, this is my pastor, Bruce McIver."

We exchanged greetings, and then Bill exclaimed, "I've got a great idea. Let me turn in this paper, and we'll go to the Mexican restaurant on Bluebonnet Circle for lunch. Lawanna, can you join us? Bruce, can you spare the time?"

Lawanna and I both nodded that we could.

About halfway through the luncheon specials we had ordered, Bill suddenly looked at his watch, jumped up, and excused himself with the words, "Oh, my goodness! I almost forgot. I've got an important appointment that I'm late for. Bruce, you and Lawanna go ahead and finish your lunch. Don't worry about me. Why don't you meet me in a couple of hours on the steps of Cowden Hall back on the campus?"

With those words he grabbed his coat and dashed out the door.

I looked at Lawanna; she looked at me.

Click! It all came together. If our mutual friend, Bill O'Brien, were playing the role of the Matchmaker in *Fiddler on the Roof* it couldn't have been more obvious. There was nothing left to do but laugh together. And try to get even.

"What are your plans for the afternoon, Lawanna?"

"Nothing, except to study."

"Okay, let's show him. Let's make him sweat."

We'd show him; we'd really make him pay for playing games. He had said for me to meet him in a couple of hours. Two additional hours tacked on might be good for him! So Lawanna and I drove and drove—all over Fort Worth, getting even with Bill . . . and getting to know each other. To my delightful surprise

I found her to be clever, creative, sharp, and attractive. The four hours sped by quickly, too quickly, and we made our way back to the campus for the belated rendezvous with Bill.

He was standing on the steps of Cowden Hall, getting drenched in the rain . . . and grinning.

JOY TO THE WORLD?

It was the Christmas season and everyone seemed to be in a festive mood. Families decorated their houses, and shoppers strolled through the malls looking for the perfect gifts for special people. Carols were played and sung everywhere—in churches, in department stores, and on street corners. Business associates, Sunday school classes, and youth groups planned dinners and parties. Relatives finalized plans to travel and gather with loved ones around the Christmas tree. "Joy to the World," and I dreaded the days immediately before me. This would be my third Christmas alone with Kathie. The "Silent Nights," followed by "silent days" haunted me. Of course, I knew the deeper meaning—the true meaning—of this season. I preached about it, and I preached about it with sincerity. But few things are lonelier than trying to celebrate . . . anything . . . with a part of your heart missing. I longed for January 2, when life would resume a normal routine.

The telephone rang. I was invited to a Christmas party at the home of Dot and Asa Newsom, Jr. Six or eight couples, including Bill and Dellanna O'Brien, were getting together to celebrate the special time of the year. As always, my invitation was conditional. "You can attend," the close-knit group said, "but you have to bring a date." My friends loved checking out and testing my dates. The men were all either deacons or church staff members at Wilshire, but that didn't make me any less nervous when I showed up with a new girl. And their wives didn't help one bit! I learned later that the group always "graded" my date after she and I left.

But this time I had no date. I was a victim of "busy schedules," "out of town visits," and "last minute shopping."

It had been more than three weeks since Lawanna and I had spent the afternoon together driving around Fort Worth. We had not seen each other or talked again during those weeks. We were both busy. She was completing her seminary work in anticipation of graduation, and I was involved in the numerous church activities surrounding Christmas.

"Why not?" I thought. I called her and was pleased to discover that she was still in Fort Worth and was free for the party on the evening of December 19. She indicated that she would be "delighted" to go with me. Deep down, I found myself being "delighted," also. And a little nervous, especially since I knew my friends would soon get the word that my date was a seminary student. I didn't have the heart to try to prepare Lawanna for what might be before us.

After dinner that evening, we played games. Asa, a physician who specializes in obstetrics and gynecology, was in charge. One of his games was for everyone to identify the contents of ten sterilized (so he said!) urine specimen bottles from his office. We were told to do this by smelling the ingredients. He assured us that they were commonly used in all households. The person who correctly guessed the most items was the winner.

Asa was true to his word—up to a point. In the bottles were ordinary household items such as toothpaste, cocoa, iodine, and laundry detergent. But it doesn't take a lot of imagination to figure out what an ob-gyn would put in some of those other bottles, especially knowing that his pastor's date was a seminary student! When I discovered what some of the other items were, I protested, insisting that all those contents were not ordinary in the household of a widower! Admittedly, it was a feeble effort to protect my date, but all my protests were drowned out by the riotous laughter.

But that wasn't the worst. The party was just getting warmed up. Asa's next game was charades, and the category drawn was children's songs. The idea was to pantomime the animals in "Old MacDonald's Farm." Bob Feather, my associate, whom I had baptized fifty-three times, attempted to imitate a mooing cow. When he had finished, I wished that I had baptized him fifty-four times—and had left him under the last time! Hugh Williams, chairman of the church's personnel committee, tried to sound like a "honking goose." I'm convinced I could have gotten a larger raise the next year if I had only recorded Hugh's act. James Baldwin, a dentist, became a "neighing horse" and loped all over the room.

Silly? You bet. I looked around the room and thought, *These are my deacons, my staff, my faithful members. If the congregation could only see us now, we'd all probably get kicked out of the church! What's happening to my world? And to my ministry? And what is my date going to think about this Christmas party?*

Someone interrupted my worrying and told me that it was my turn to act out a nursery rhyme—any nursery rhyme. Without

"I looked around the room and thought, These are my deacons, my staff, my faithful members. If the congregation could only see us now, we'd all probably get kicked out of the church!"

much forethought, I chose "This Little Piggie Went to Market." Big mistake! I got down on all fours, as dignified as possible, and began to "oink . . . oink . . . oink . . ." across the room. It sounded like a pretty good "oink" and everybody guessed the right answer immediately.

"Well," I thought, "at least, that's over."

But not until James Baldwin hollered loudly over the laughter, "Pastor, I'm really relieved. I was afraid you were going to "wee . . . wee . . . wee . . . all the way home!"

That did it.

Jeannette, Hugh's wife and my secretary, laughed so hard she fell off the ottoman; Carolyn and Bob Feather were gasping for breath; Myrtice and Woody Brownlee, the couple that had helped so much with Kathie, had tears streaming down their cheeks; Asa and Dot Newsom were doubled over in hysterics; and Bill and Dellanna O'Brien were contorted and holding their sides. Hugh tried to pick Jeannette up but only added to the problem because he was groaning and laughing as hard as she was.

I was embarrassed for my seminary date . . . until I saw her on the other side of the room, crumpled across a chair, banging the top of a table with her hand and guffawing out of control. She kept muttering something about this being the "wildest" and "best" party she had ever attended.

Finally, Lawanna and I told the others good-night, and we headed back to Forth Worth. We were so "laughed out" that we only had energy left for an occasional chuckle—one about every five miles.

Between those chuckles I began to realize that I had experienced more fun and laughed harder than I had in nearly four years. I realized, also, that the Christmas holidays were immediately before us and Lawanna would be leaving to be with her family in Alabama. We had found common ground in laughter and fun, but there was so much more I wanted to know about this remarkable, attractive girl.

"'Lawanna' is an unusual name," I said. "What does it mean?"

"It's an Indian princess name," she said. "It means 'By-the-Still-Waters.'"

While we continued to drive west toward the seminary campus, the others at the party were grading her.

"By-the-Still-Waters" made a hundred!

"HELLO, POLICE DEPARTMENT?"

Four days later, December 23.

"Meridian Police Department," a man with a heavy southern accent answered.

"Sir, my name is McIver, Bruce McIver. I live in Dallas, Texas, and I'm trying to locate a young lady who is supposed to be passing through your city. She's driving . . . "

"Is this an emergency?"

"Well, Sir, you might call it that. You see, I'm a pastor and . . ."

"Glad to help you, Reverend. When was this young lady last seen?"

"I happened to see her on Monday night. We had a cup of coffee together."

"Did she seem to be in good spirits? Were there any problems?"

"No, as a matter of fact, she seemed to be unusually cheerful. She's passing through Meridian on her way home to Alabama and may be spending the night there."

"How's she traveling, Reverend?"

"She's driving a white '59 Ford Fairlane, trimmed with red stripes. It could be that she is staying with some people who are members of First Baptist Church since she has served there recently as minister of youth, but I don't know their names, and—"

"Know a lot of them First Baptist folks. Good people, they are. Now, don't you worry, Reverend, we'll get right on it. And we'll call you if we get any leads."

I thanked him and hung up the phone. *Bruce, what in the world have you done?* I thought. *You've only been with her three times. The first time you spent four hours trying to get even with your minister of music. The second time—the only real date you've had with her—you spent the evening trying to identify the contents of weird little bottles, and the third time, just two nights ago, the two of you went out for a cup of coffee. What's happened to you?*

"And what's more," I rambled on, "it's midnight."

"And one other thing—for the record, you hate to be called, 'Reverend.'"

I didn't know what had happened to me, but I was thrilled when the phone rang an hour later. The police in Meridian, Mississippi are efficient. "By-the-Still-Waters" was on the phone.

We talked . . . and talked . . . and talked . . . through much of the night . . . through the brief Christmas holidays while she was home in Alabama . . . through the movie, *Ben Hur,* on New Year's Eve back in Dallas . . . through the Cotton Bowl football game the next day (don't ask who played or what the score was!) . . . and during the drive back to Fort Worth after the game. We talked and listened, oblivious to chariot races and touchdowns . . . and telephone bills.

I told Lawanna good-bye on the Barnard Hall dormitory steps at the Seminary, and headed back to Dallas.

But I wasn't through talking. I parked the car, walked straight into the house, dialed her on the telephone . . . and asked her to marry me.

She said, "Yes!"

A NEW YEAR—AND A NEW LIFE!

The calendar said that tomorrow was "January 2," the day that I had longed for so I could return to a "normal routine." I was to learn soon, however, that with Lawanna, there is no such thing as a "normal routine."

I quickly dialed my parents in North Carolina.

"Dad, I'm getting married!"

"That's great, son. When?"

"February 13. Six weeks from now."

"Son, why in the world are you waiting so long?"

A few days later Mother wrote me: "Son, we are thrilled that you are getting married. We've worried so much about you and Kathie. You need a wife and she needs a mother. We're very, very happy about this."

Then, Mother added a P.S. to her letter: "What is her name? The relatives and neighbors are asking."

We were married at Wilshire six weeks later. Bill O'Brien sang, and beamed with pride. Bob Feather assisted with the ceremony. Scores of friends pitched in to help wherever they were needed. (Goodness, we really should have invited the Meridian

Police Department.) The deacons were affirming; the pulpit committee, including me, was happy and relieved. The pastor had found a wife.

"The calendar said that tomorrow was 'January 2,' the day that I had longed for so I could return to a 'normal routine.' I was to learn soon, however, that with Lawanna, there is no such thing as a 'normal routine.' "

We paid for all that long distance talking . . . and talking . . . after the honeymoon.

That was more than thirty-one years ago, and we're still talking . . . and talking . . . and laughing.

And, miracle of miracles, He still "leadeth me 'By-the-Still-Waters.'"

6

SEEING DOUBLE

Kathie's prayers for a baby brother or a baby sister were answered—not once, but twice!

Shannon was born ten months and twelve days after we were married. Those months and days may not seem important, but they are if you are the pastor of a church and some sweet little ladies, and a few deacons, have begun to count on their fingers the exact number of months—and days—since their pastor married! Maureen, or "Renie," was born fifteen months after Shannon. Lawanna's poor mother thought that we were starting up some kind of baby factory.

I was jolted into the reality of this when I came home late one afternoon and found two baby beds in one room. That was a shocker for a thirty-six-year-old former widower who had grown to appreciate moments of quietness and solitude. It was also a jolt to a former seminary student who relished the fun and freedom of life. "By-the-Still-Waters" was caught in the rapids of life—without a paddle.

Two baby beds in one room. It couldn't be. But it was.

OUT OF THE MOUTHS OF BABES

It had been a difficult week for Lawanna. I had been out of town speaking at a youth camp, and she was left home to mother three girls, two of them still in diapers. Her week had gone from crisis to crisis. When I arrived back in town on Friday afternoon she was waiting for me at the door. There was an ashen look on her face and dark circles under her eyes. There was no "Darling, it's so good to have you home," or "Tell me all about your week," or "Come on in; I've planned a special meal in honor of your homecoming." None of that.

Instead, there was a low, guttural cry that rose in pitch to a near wail: "Get me out of here!"

I looked at her in disbelief, wondering what in the world had happened to my bride. As I stood there with my mouth open in amazement, the slow, agonizing cry started again.

"Anywhere—I don't care where—just get me out of this house for a few hours. I can't take it any more."

Then, in a staccato kind of monotone she continued, "Shannon and Renie ruined the bathroom by emptying an entire bottle of Ajax cleanser into the tub while they were taking their baths . . . and they washed the car with the windows down and soaked the upholstery . . . and they colored on the den wall with crayolas—'drawing pretty pictures for Daddy'. . . and a drunk man has been making obscene telephone calls . . . and the dog got sick . . . and I've had a headache . . . and the tire on Kathie's bicycle is flat . . . and Bobbie Bedford called to tell me that she was thinking about divorcing Kenneth . . . and Mrs. Grayson thought the organ was too loud last Sunday . . . and . . ."

"Okay. Okay," I interrupted, "I'll call Mrs. Heed and see if she can babysit tonight. We'll take in a movie, or do something special. I promise."

"Anything," Lawanna repeated. "Just get me out of here—for the sake of my sanity."

And for the sake of my marriage, I thought.

Mrs. Heed was a lovable, grandmother-type person. She had a sensitive concern for lonely and sick people and often delivered a vase of cut flowers to them from her garden. She was also concerned about Lawanna and me and our family. She often dropped by the house with a "mess" of turnip greens or some ripe tomatoes or some fresh corn. She also made a standing offer to babysit for the children anytime we needed her. Lawanna was always grateful for the turnip greens and other things from Mrs.

Heed's garden, but the offer to babysit was about the finest gift anyone could make to her.

The children liked it when "Mama Heed," as they affectionately called her, showed up for an evening. She would pamper them, read to them, play games with them, and, as she put it, "chew on" them. That was one of her favorite expressions: "When can I come over and 'chew on' my babies?"

Something told me that this night was the perfect night for her to do some "chewing." I called Mama Heed even before I brought my luggage in from the car, and she was on the doorstep in thirty minutes.

"Lawanna has had a hard week and we'll probably take in a movie," I told her as she walked through the door, smiling and waving at Shannon and Renie. Kathie was in her own room doing her homework for school.

"Just fine, just fine. You folks get on out of here and leave me with my babies. Now scat!"

"Anywhere—I don't care where—just get me out of this house for a few hours. I can't take it any more."

But before we could leave there was one unfinished project. The family dog, Chrissy, had to take a pill. Or, more correctly, I had to give Chrissy a pill, which had been prescribed by our veterinarian.

Dr. John Melton was a tall, soft-spoken veterinarian who was a member of our church. His reassuring manner and grandfatherly attention to the animals, as well as the "parents" of the animals, had made him a favorite of pet owners all over north Dallas for years.

"How do I do it, Lawanna?"

"Dr. Melton said it was simple. Just take Chrissy firmly by the throat and force her mouth open. When this happens, put the pill way back on her tongue, and clamp her mouth shut. She'll have to swallow and the pill will go down. No problem."

No problem? I was a novice at this. Besides, I wasn't all that burdened about a long-haired, mix-breed dog. My bride was about to have her own "breakdown" and I had to get her away from the house—fast!

The children, especially Shannon and Renie, were fascinated that "Daddy was going to give Chrissy her medicine." They gathered in the den to watch me. Mrs. Heed sat on the couch.

Shannon, less than three years old, was on her knees beside me. Renie, nineteen months old, squatted on the other side of me. Shannon was ordering the dog to be still and telling me how she thought Dr. Melton would do it. I thanked her and ignored her.

Renie said nothing. This was not unusual, for Renie had never put together a complete sentence in her young life. She could say words like "Daddy," and "Mamma," and "hot," and "no." At times she could put two or three words together, like "go bye-bye," and "no, no, no!" But for some reason there had never been either the occasion or the desire for a whole sentence—nouns, verbs, and all the other parts of correct grammar that help make up wonderful, creative thoughts.

This concerned me. "The child's not talking," I said to Lawanna. "When do babies begin to talk? Didn't Shannon start making sentences before she was nineteen months old? Is there something we should do? Maybe see a speech therapist?"

"No, she's fine," Lawanna reassured me. "She'll put a sentence together when she feels there's something important enough to say."

So, we left it there, waiting for that special moment when a complete thought would be expressed and the exact words of her first sentence could be recorded in her little pink baby book. It would be the kind of treasure that someday she could pass on to her own children and to their children.

Chrissy spat the first pill out. I retrieved it, gripped her throat, shoved it back in and clamped the jaws—just like Dr. Melton had instructed. She spat it out the second time. The pill clattered to the floor and rolled under the sofa where dear Mama Heed was sitting.

"I'll get it, Daddy!" Shannon said as she crawled under the sofa.

"Isn't she sweet?" Mrs. Heed observed. Then, looking back at Renie she said to no one in particular, "Precious babies!"

On the third attempt Chrissy not only spat the pill out, but she snarled and snapped at me.

It was at this very moment that Renie chose to put together her first sentence. Still squatting, with wet diapers sagging to the floor, she pointed her finger at Chrissy and spoke the clearest words ever uttered in the English language: *"Take the pill, you damn dog!"*

Shannon looked at me. I looked at the ceiling. Lawanna dashed out of the bedroom, still brushing her hair for our night out, and looked at everyone. Mama Heed looked at a blank spot on the wall . . . and giggled.

OUR EVENING OUT

Neither Lawanna nor I knew what movie was playing at the Village Theater in the Highland Park area of Dallas. It really didn't matter. We just wanted to get away from the telephone, from snarling dogs posing as house pets, and from a nineteen-month-old "precious baby" who had just discovered something important enough to express in a complete sentence.

Whatever was playing at the movie must have been terrible, for, counting us, there weren't more than twenty people in the entire place. That suited us fine, and we stumbled around in the dark until we were ten rows from the nearest person, the kind of isolation we both craved. We collapsed in the seats—too tired even to hold hands!

As the movie droned on we became aware that the lone usher was moving up and down the aisles carrying a small, dim flashlight. He seemed to be leaning over and asking each person a question. We watched him as he slowly, deliberately moved toward us.

"Are you the McIvers?" he whispered.

"Yes, as a matter of fact we are. Why?"

"I hate to disturb you, but there's an emergency message from your baby sitter. Please call home immediately. You may use the phone in the manager's office."

Lawanna shot out of her seat and ran up the aisle. I followed as quickly as possible. The usher followed me. When we reached the office someone else was using the phone. The waiting only added to the anxiety as question after question swirled in our minds: Has there been another obscene phone call? Has something happened to one of the girls? To the baby sitter? To the dog? Has Renie put together another sentence?

Finally, Lawanna could stand the tension no longer. She turned to the usher and asked, "What was the message? Tell me the exact words. I must know."

"Well, lady, the person who called said she hoped she wouldn't alarm you, and I sure don't want to alarm you, but . . ."

"Tell me now!"

"She said to tell you that it looked like your little girls had eaten the dog's medicine and you might want to come home."

We raced to the car, burned rubber and left tire marks on the parking lot, ignored the speed limit, and squealed into our driveway. A quick check indicated that everyone, including Mama Heed, seemed okay. I then ran to the phone and called Dr. Melton.

"Dr. Melton, do you remember what was in that medicine you prescribed for Chrissy?" He remembered.

"Would it hurt a child?" No, he didn't think it would.

"How many pills were in the bottle?" Twenty-four.

For the next hour Lawanna and I, Shannon, Renie, and Kathie, Mama Heed, and Chrissy were on the floor, under the sofa, behind the chairs, under the tables, behind the bookcases—everywhere—finding pills that Shannon and Renie had been playing with . . . and dropped. When the last one was accounted for we breathed a sigh of relief. It was too late to return to the movie so we gave up on the "evening out."

Dear Mama Heed kissed the girls good-night, smiled weakly and moved toward her car. I moved back toward the den for a father-daughter talk with Shannon and Renie. Mrs. Heed might like to "chew on" them; I was more in the mood to "chew them out."

"I hate to disturb you, but there's an emergency message from your baby sitter. Please call home immediately. You may use the phone in the manager's office."

As I began to raise my voice, Shannon teared up and said, "But, Daddy, we were just playing a game with the pills."

Renie looked at Shannon for a long time. And then she looked at me. She didn't say a word. Silence.

Her one sentence had been enough for the evening.

LAW . . . AND LITTLE ORDER!

Kathie was quiet and studious. When not helping with her little sisters, which she enjoyed, she loved to go to her room and read a book or prepare homework for school. She also loved to write, and she was good at it.

Shannon and Renie also loved to go to their room . . . and leave! They were downright slippery. Before you could turn around twice they would be halfway down the street on their way to explore the neighborhood or play with friends. This went on day after day. Both Lawanna and I sat down and talked with them, loved them, and threatened them. Nothing helped. They would be here this minute and gone the next. We had just about run out of answers . . . and patience. Even "Dr. Spock" was silent on the subject.

One afternoon, the girls lay down in their matching baby beds for an afternoon nap. Lawanna read their favorite stories to them, and they hugged her lovingly in appreciation. She quietly closed the door, slipped down the hall to our room, and fell across the bed for a brief respite. These opportunities were few and far between so she cherished every reprieve that came her way. Ten minutes later she was asleep. Blessed sleep.

The ringing of the doorbell startled her from her peaceful nap. Wearily, she rose from the bed and trudged toward the front door.

"It's probably some of the neighborhood gang," she thought. With twenty-five kids under the age of six living on one block, it was impossible to synchronize afternoon naps, or anything else.

She opened the door to face a Dallas police officer.

"Lady, I'm Officer Boswick. Do the McIvers live here?"

"Yes," Lawanna replied with a puzzled look.

"Do you have two little girls about the ages of two and four."

"Yes," Lawanna answered hesitantly.

"Do you know where they are?"

"I surely do. I put them down for their afternoon nap a little while ago. They're in their rooms, safely tucked in their beds."

"Well, Lady, I don't want to alarm you, but I have two little girls out front of your house in my patrol car. They're about the ages of your children and one of the neighbors suggested they might live here. I found them a few minutes ago as they were walking down the middle of Trammel Drive, and you know how busy the traffic is on that street, so . . . ."

"They can't be mine, but I'll try to help you identify them," Lawanna said as the two of them hurried toward the car.

"Hi, Mommy. We've been riding in the police car. He's a nice policeman." Two little girls, side by side, with noses pressed flat against the window, waved from the back seat of the patrol car. Then they gave Mommy the most angelic look possible.

"What in the world? . . . How on earth? . . . When did they get out of the house? . . . Why didn't I hear them? But . . . but . . . the door was locked!"

The girls were right. He was a nice policeman. He smiled reassuringly at the sputtering mother standing with him by his car.

When she gathered her composure, Lawanna asked a logical question. "How did you know they were our children?"

The policeman hesitated and then replied. "When I saw them in the street I had a feeling that they lived somewhere in the neighborhood. I knocked on a door and asked a lady if she knew

" 'Hi, Mommy. We've been riding in the police car. He's a nice policeman.' Two little girls, side by side, with noses pressed flat against the window, waved from the back seat of the patrol car. Then they gave Mommy the most angelic look possible."

of any children who might have wandered off from their homes. The lady then asked, 'Do they have any diapers on?' I told her, 'As a matter of fact, they don't.' The lady then said, 'They must be the McIver girls, for they're always shedding their diapers when they get wet.'"

A logical answer to a logical question.

A FENCE AND A FLAG OF FREEDOM

"We'll have to fence them in," I told Lawanna sternly. "I don't like fences," I added, "but it's for their own protection."

"And for my sanity." Lawanna added.

Wayne Miles, a good friend and a deacon in the church, was a building contractor. I shared with him our dilemma, and he was helpful and encouraging.

"That can be done without any difficulty," he said. "I'll have a crew over at your house tomorrow and we'll begin to put a cyclone fence around the entire backyard." That was about the best news Lawanna had heard in a long time.

The work was begun on schedule, and a couple of days later she called me at the church office. "Come on home now," she said excitedly. "It's finished. The fence is up and Wayne is waiting for you to see it."

When I drove into the driveway of our house I had all kinds of good feelings down inside: gratitude for friends like Wayne, relief that Lawanna could now relax, and a warm sense of security for the girls.

"It's great, Wayne. Thanks so much for your help. This will solve a lot of our problems."

"Ole" Wayne, as we called him, turned to Lawanna and said, "Well, it oughta be worth at least a hug."

Lawanna threw her arms around him and they embraced, but only for a split second. Then, she gasped in disbelief and shock. From where she stood in the driveway—even while hugging "Ole" Wayne—she had a clear view of the back section of the yard. While the three of us stood in the driveway, celebrating the completion of the project that would solve our problems, Shannon and Renie had climbed over the fence in the back of the yard and were marching down the alley—off to explore more of the wonders of the neighborhood.

Renie was walking faster than usual, for she was not weighed down by soggy diapers. Hers had snagged on the top of the cyclone fence, and, somehow she had managed to slip out of them.

Her wet diaper hung there . . . like a banner of freedom.

Lawanna looked at Wayne . . . the fence . . . the diaper . . . and the girls as they skipped happily down the alley . . . and cried.

7

THE HEAD IS AT THE OTHER END

It was one of the coldest days on record in Dallas. An angry norther had swept down through the Rockies, blown with fury across the plains of west Texas, and plunged temperatures to single digit figures in our city. The rain that turned to sleet made the situation even more miserable. It was the perfect day to stay home, basking in the warmth of a glowing fire.

But no such luxury. I had been asked to conduct a funeral service for a man I had visited a couple of times in the hospital. He had no close ties with Wilshire, but he was a friend of one of our members. I was glad to call on him and found him to be warm, gracious, and receptive. Our friendship grew quickly, and when he died, the family asked me to lead the memorial service.

A dull, chronic pain in my back intensified as I tried to dress for the service. Every bone seemed to cry out for relief.

"My back is killing me!" I said to Lawanna. "I'm not sure I can make it through the service. And this weather is horrible."

"Why not call one of the deacons—perhaps one who's retired—and see if he will drive you to the funeral home?" she suggested. "I'd do it myself, but I can't leave the children."

"I wouldn't ask anyone to get out on a day like this," I replied. "The sleet is coming down, and the roads will be iced over in a couple of hours. Don't worry, I'll make it somehow."

While Lawanna and I were talking, the telephone rang. Kermit Whiteaker, my associate, was calling to check on me.

"Now, Pastor, don't you even think about driving to the funeral on a day like this. Be ready in thirty minutes and I'll pick you up at your house and drive you myself. You can relax on the way to the service and think about your message."

"That's just like Kermit," I said to a relieved Lawanna. "He's always thinking about little things he can do to help. Except in this case, what he's going to do is not little. I can really use his help."

Kermit was one of the most sensitive, caring persons I had ever met. He could size up a need and be on his way to solving it before most people recognized there was a need. There was added strength in knowing that he would be with me.

I fortified myself with a pain pill, groaned (that always seemed to help!), and waited. Kermit honked for me promptly on time. I uttered a silent prayer as I began the treacherous walk across the frozen lawn, crunching step by step toward his car.

We drove slowly on icy streets to the outskirts of Dallas and entered the gates to a large cemetery. We continued down narrow roads and lanes until we reached a small chapel nestled among some magnificent old trees. The stone building with arched windows is a favorite of mine. In a city of modern and contemporary structures, it is a quiet reminder of the blending of the centuries. We need something to keep that in focus, even if it has to be in the heart of a cemetery.

Kermit was kind enough to drive me to the back door of the chapel. The rain, mingled with sleet, pelted my face as I hobbled up the steps and through the door into a tiny room reserved for the minister. The privacy of this room provided an opportunity for the minister, the soloist, and the organist to compare notes and make any necessary last minute adjustments. Normally much of this was done in advance with input from everyone involved, including the family members. But the weather conditions made it impossible for us to meet until just before the time of the service.

In this brief session I learned that a special request had been made by some family member for a taped song to be played. One of the lines of the song was, "We'll say good night here, but good morning up there." I used to hear the song sung when I was a boy living in the hills of North Carolina. It would bring a tear to my eye and put a lump in my throat—even when no one had died! That was especially true if the words were sung in quivering tones and with a twang, "It will be goood night heeree . . . but goood mawnin' up therre." That's the way it was sung on the tape.

As the last note wafted throughout the exposed rafters of the small chapel, I summoned all the strength possible, rose from my chair, walked through the arched opening and faced a "standing room only" crowd of people. This surprised me, especially since the weather was so miserable. I was glad that so many had braved the elements to attend the service. As I scanned the audience, I saw row after row of men. Strange, I thought. Then I remembered that my friend who had died had been a used car salesman. It looked as though every used car salesman in Dallas had shown up to pay last respects! It was obvious that the taped song had pulled their emotions apart, but they masked it well, sitting like statues as they crowded shoulder-to-shoulder against each other.

The family of the deceased was in a small alcove to my left; the casket was on the floor level just beneath the pulpit; and flowers were everywhere—wall to wall.

HEART ATTACK IN THE FIRST ROW

Opening my Bible I read the first two lines of Psalm 103: "Bless the Lord, O my soul, and all that is within me, bless His holy name. Bless the Lord, O my soul, and forget not . . ."

"'Scuse me, Sir."

My first impression was to ignore the words. Maybe I hadn't heard them at all. It was probably my imagination.

Then, a second time, "Sir, 'scuse me, please!"

The voice came from an elderly, slightly-built woman who could have passed for anybody's grandmother. She had been sitting on the front row immediately in front of the pulpit. But now she was standing and speaking to me. Out loud.

"Sir," she continued, "I sure hate to interrupt this service, but my husband is having a heart attack!"

I looked down and saw a man had slumped into the lap of the person beside him on the pew. The man's mouth was open, his eyes were rolled back into his head and his glasses were dangling from one ear. His face was drained of all color.

The woman continued her one-way conversation with me.

"You see, sir, this here's his cousin," she said pointing to the casket. "They were very close as little boys. They used to play together, and they were in the same classes in school. My husband thought a lot of him, and he insisted on coming to this service today."

I watched in amazement as the focal point of the service moved from the pulpit to the front row. Without trying to do so, the anxious wife had taken complete charge of the service. I listened as she continued to talk without a pause.

"My husband hasn't been well and the doctor didn't want him to come over here today since we live in Fort Worth and since the roads are so bad because of the weather but he was determined to come and see his cousin so we got up early and drove over slowly and we've already been here for more than an hour . . ."

The crumpled figure beside her moaned and stirred slightly. She looked down, patted him reassuringly on the shoulder, and continued. "He has some nitroglycerin pills in his pocket, but I can't get them out 'cause I can't get my hand in his pockets . . ."

With that, she turned around and faced all those used car salesmen. By now they were nearly as ashen as her husband on the front row. They remained rigid, erect, stunned. It was obvious they hadn't bargained for this when they showed up to pay their respects to a friend and fellow-worker. None of us had.

With extended hand the wife continued,"If any of you men have any nitroglycerin pills in your pocket I would sure appreciate your passing them this way."

Pills came from everywhere—around pews, under pews, and over shoulders of people. From the looks of things, everybody present must have had some kind of heart problem.

" 'Sir,' she continued, 'I sure hate to interrupt this service, but my husband is having a heart attack!' "

Then I spotted Wally.

Wally was the funeral director assigned to this particular service. He was a short man with dark hair neatly parted on the left side. His horn rimmed glasses, blue serge suit, and conservative tie gave him the appearance of an executive. Wally was prompt, efficient, and caring. He was the kind of director I liked to work with, for I knew that any service he directed would be smooth and orderly.

There he was, standing in the back of the chapel, staring in astonishment at what was happening. Wally looked like he needed some kind of pill himself, since his funeral service was now completely out of hand.

I sized up the situation, and decided that it was time for me to leave the pulpit and try to help the man having the heart attack. Or, it was time to help his wife who was still talking and gathering nitroglycerin tablets. I took a few steps to the left and mumbled to myself, "How on earth do I get through that solid bank of flowers?"

Should I move the carnation spray or the floral wreath next to it? Would it be easier to rearrange two or three potted plants? The fragile wire stands that supported all these flowers caused me more problems. They weren't designed to be jostled or moved around or assaulted from the rear by a frustrated minister.

The answer was not simple, but the course had been dictated for me. I began to move back and forth behind all those flowers, trying desperately to find some opening. Incidentally, they don't look half as good on "this" side as they do on "that" side. Somehow, feeling a little like Moses trying to make it out of the bulrushes, I worked my way through the arrangements of "glads," carnations, and all kinds of greenery.

Meanwhile, Wally, the efficient funeral director, had moved as inconspicuously as possible from the back of the chapel to the front. He met me with the whispered words, "We'll terminate the service."

"No, Wally, we're not going to terminate the service," I replied. At the moment, it didn't make sense to me to weave my way through a floral obstacle course just to terminate a service.

"We came out in this weather to bury this man, and we're going to do it," I continued. Just how that was to be accomplished was still a mystery, but I was determined that we would finish what we had set out to do.

While this hushed conversation was taking place in front of a wreath of glads interlaced with sprigs of greenery, the poor man on the front row was gasping for breath.

"Wally," I asked, "Do you have an ambulance out here in this cemetery?"

"No."

"Do you have any oxygen?"

"No," he answered for a second time.

At that point I noticed Kermit, my associate, holding his position at the back of the chapel and motioned for him to come forward. When he reached the front I spoke to him in a quiet, but trembling, voice.

"Kermit, we've got problems—big problems. We've got one man in the casket whom we're trying to bury, and we've got another on the front row who may need to be buried if we don't do something fast. We've got an anxious wife who hasn't stopped talking for the last ten minutes, and we've got a chapel packed with used car salesmen who wish they were standing in the sleet on some corner lot trying to sell a jalopy!

"So, please, Kermit," I urged, "find a telephone, call the fire department, and get some oxygen and an ambulance out here."

Kermit nodded without a word and slipped quickly to the nearest exit.

" 'We came out in this weather to bury this man, and we're going to do it,' I continued. Just how that was to be accomplished was still a mystery, but I was determined that we would finish what we had set out to do."

For the next fifteen minutes not a person moved, except the two or three persons who were trying to make the man on the front row more comfortable. Not a word was spoken. Silence. The fifteen minutes felt like half a century.

Suddenly the doors at the back of the chapel banged open. Six helmeted firemen wearing hip boots and yellow slickers, moved in unison down the aisle, dragging a clattering tank of oxygen behind them. Clomp . . . clomp . . . clomp. They methodically cleared a path and began to work on the poor man gasping on the front row.

Seconds later the doors banged open again, and two ambulance attendants rushed down the aisle pulling a stretcher behind them. The wheels weren't lined up together, so the stretcher kept zigzagging, squeaking noisily, and bumping into the ends of the pews. The car salesmen sitting in the pews watched, moving their eyes, but not their bodies. They sat immobile—like zombies—hypnotized, wide-eyed, and spellbound. It was the kind of moment when someone could have given most any order or command and they would have responded like robots. No questions asked!

Within minutes, the man with the heart condition was stabilized, loaded on the stretcher and removed from the chapel. From the floor level (I wasn't about to try to make it through the floral arrangements to the pulpit again), I said a few words about the traumas of life and the uncertainties we all experience. We then had a prayer for the man on his way to the hospital, and I added a few concluding remarks about his "cousin" in the casket who had almost been forgotten in the excitement.

The benediction was pronounced, and we walked out of the chapel—into more rain and sleet—for the burial service.

FIRE AND ICE AT THE GRAVE SITE

The gravesite was only a few yards from the chapel so everyone walked to the spot. But in order to get there, we had to make our way up an incline and over a grassy knoll. The ground was completely covered with ice, and beneath the ice was mud—plain old slick mud. A couple of the pallbearers slipped as they moved up the incline, and I whispered my worst fear to Kermit, "They're going to drop the casket." I held my breath until they made it over the top of the knoll and then uttered a silent prayer of relief when they had reached the burial plot.

Surely nothing else can happen at this funeral, I thought hopefully.

Now, a couple of things will usually take place when the family of the deceased are seated at the grave site. The public is not aware of these since they are very subtle. A minister learns about them, not in the seminary classroom, but from observation and experience.

First, the funeral director will walk slowly with the minister to the casket and whisper to him, "The head is at the other end." It's amazing how he does this without ever moving his lips, but he does. In fact, I've heard this whisper from some who could have worked a second job as ventriloquists. They're good at this. Now, if I've had a bad day, I'll occasionally nod back at the director and then move deliberately in the opposite direction! It drives him up the wall, especially if he is a stickler for everything being proper.

The director also carefully studies the arrival of the people at the grave site. He scans in all directions to make sure the service does not begin until everyone is present. When he is satisfied that all stragglers have arrived, his eyes will lock in on the minister's eyes, and he'll give an ever-so-subtle nod, accompanied at times with a faint smile of approval. No words this time; just a nod and a hint of a smile. This is the signal from the director to the minister that the burial service can begin.

Well, on this particular day, with everybody freezing and slipping and sliding in mud, Wally had his hands full. Armed with one umbrella he moved quickly from person to person, offering whatever momentary relief he could. But he didn't have to worry about stragglers. Nearly seventy-five people crowded quickly under the tent. We were once again body-to-body.

Fortunately, because of the cold weather, the funeral home had arranged for a portable heater to be installed on a temporary shelf a few feet above the casket. As people moved under the tent there were audible sighs of relief as they felt the warm air blowing from the heater. Wally's eyes met mine, there was a slight nod, and I opened my Bible.

After a word or two of introduction, I began to read from the eighth chapter of Romans, verses thirty-eight and thirty-nine: "For I am persuaded that neither death nor life, nor angels nor principalities nor powers, nor things present nor things to come, nor height . . ."

Sputter . . . crackle . . . pop . . . hiss . . . bang!

The over-worked and over-wet electric heater exploded, and blue flames shot out across the heads of people. Some ducked as low as they could while others dashed for shelter—in the sleet!

Wally jumped past me and lunged over the foot of the casket in an attempt to unplug the heater. As he did so, he took the family floral blanket of flowers on the casket with him. All that could be seen of the efficient director was his muddy shoes, kicking wildly in the air over the end of the casket. Of course, I had already closed my Bible and stepped aside. Once again, the service was totally out of my hands.

The people under the tent waited for Wally to disentangle himself from the flowers and rise again from the other side of the casket.

But there was only silence. Eerie silence. Spooky silence.

Not a sound except the patter of sleet on the tent and the flap of the canvas in the wind.

After what seemed like an hour, Wally crawled up from behind the casket, brushed the floral petals off his coat, and straightened his tie. There was a stony look on his face, but his muddy feet and dazed eyes betrayed him. The dignity of this service was slipping fast.

Wally paused to get his composure, cleared his throat nervously, and stepped quickly to the edge of the tent where the pallbearers were standing. Then, taking a deep breath, he looked at me, smiled weakly, and nodded. Barely . . . but a nod anyway.

Mustering all the ministerial image possible, I took my place a second time by the casket. By now neither the "head" nor the "foot" mattered to me, and it didn't seem to make a lot of difference to Wally either. Both of us just wanted to get this thing finished. Fast! So, I opened my Bible to the eighth chapter of Romans.

"For I am persuaded that neither death nor life, nor angels nor principalities nor . . ." I began reading.

As I continued to read the passage I glanced toward Wally and noted that he seemed to be recovering slowly, if painfully, from his ordeal. His stony face had softened slightly, and some color had returned to his cheeks. His shoulders had straightened, and he began to look once more like the director in charge.

But then . . .

"Dear Lord," I gasped silently, "don't let Wally do what I think he's going to do."

The rain and sleet had been coming down with such force that the canvas tent was becoming water-logged. Wally saw this, and felt that the whole side might collapse if some of the water was not drained off. So, ever so gingerly, he took his closed umbrella and raised it like a prodding stick toward the tarpaulin over his head. In the process his already muddied feet slipped and he lost his balance. What was supposed to be a gentle nudge became a wild thrust. His umbrella jabbed into the canvas and a sheet of icy water splashed down the backs of the six pallbearers!

There were whoops and ouches and yipes!

I closed my Bible and stepped aside while Wally apologized helplessly to the shivering pallbearers and tried to brush the icy water off their necks and shoulders. This delay lasted for two or three minutes, giving Wally enough time to slip out from under

"The over-worked and over-wet electric heater exploded, and blue flames shot out across the heads of people. Some ducked as low as they could while others dashed for shelter—in the sleet!"

the tent and stand silently in the sleet. He looked so lonely. Maybe he thought nothing else would happen while he stood in the rain. As his glasses slowly frosted over with sleet and rain, he seemed perfectly content to keep his distance.

I took one look at him, and envied him out there—removed from the scene of action. I found myself longing to get out from under the tent and go stand with him!

But the perfectionist in Wally would not let him stand aside for long.

Maybe—just maybe—something in this service could yet be salvaged. So, from that distance, his eyes found mine, in spite of his icy, glazed-over glasses. I think I saw him nod, but any hint of a smile was gone. Instead, there was a pitiful plea for me to do something . . . anything . . . to finalize the service.

"For I am persuaded that neither death nor life, nor angels . . ."

I swallowed hard and began silently talking to myself.

". . . nor principalities nor powers . . ."

(*Steady . . . hold on . . .*)

"... nor things present ..."
(*This is a funeral.*)
"... nor things to come ..."
(*Uh-oh! I'm about to lose it.*)
"... nor height nor depth, nor any other created thing ..."
(*You don't laugh at funerals.*)
"... shall be able to separate us ..."
(*Swallow hard. Clear your throat.*)
"... from the love of God ..."
(*Almost there!*)
" ... which ... is ... in ..."
(*Go for it!*)
"... Christ Jesus our Lord!"

Then, without a pause or even taking a breath, I added, "Mr. Whiteaker will lead us in prayer."

Kermit had not been a part of the service. He didn't know the deceased or the family. He was just trying to be helpful to me on a bad day by driving me to the funeral service. He didn't have the foggiest idea that I would call on him for prayer. And, the truth is, he was gulping and strangling along with me as I tried to read the paragraph from Romans.

So, my request for him to lead in prayer was met with silence . . . and more silence. Then, from among the shivering mourners, I heard Kermit's hesitant voice thank God for something and ask God to do something ... for somebody. For once, I had the strange feeling that what he prayed really didn't matter. The Lord knew the mess we were all in, and He was probably chuckling Himself. Anyway, Kermit's prayer was about the shortest on record, and his "Amen" was one of the most comforting words I've ever heard.

With the closing prayer behind us I performed my last ministerial responsibility. Wearing a solemn face, I moved from person to person sitting in the chairs reserved for family members. I shook hands with each one, but I did not trust myself to look anybody in the eye. What I had mumbled to myself while reading the Scriptures was still true, "You don't laugh at funerals; if you laugh, you're finished!"

I nodded in the general direction of the wet pallbearers, and glanced with compassion at Wally, who was standing alone in the sleet with his closed umbrella in hand. The white sleet had already salt-and-peppered his hair and had gathered in clusters on his shoulders. Wally was oblivious, looking as frozen as the landscape. It had not been his day.

"For once, I had the strange feeling that what he prayed really didn't matter. The Lord knew the mess we were all in, and He was probably chuckling Himself."

Kermit and I then moved quickly to his car. He graciously opened the door for me without a word. He then walked around to the driver's side, opened his own door, slid in, and started the engine. With heads high, looking as pious as possible, we drove away.

Kermit drove down the narrow lanes of the cemetery, winding first to the right and then to the left. His direction, or lack of it, didn't bother me one bit. I was just glad to be on the move. I did know enough about the place, however, to realize that he wasn't even trying to find his way out. Instead, he was searching for a remote lane and a large tree.

He made a left turn, found the right spot, and pulled up behind a huge cedar tree. He then glanced over his shoulders to make sure that we were well out of sight, turned off the ignition . . . and . . . collapsed across the steering wheel while pounding the dash! If the windows had been down, I'm confident his guffaws could have been heard for half a mile. We both laughed until we cried and then laughed some more.

Finally Kermit wiped the tears from his eyes and started the motor. We pulled away slowly, almost reverently, and drove through the cemetery without another word. Seldom have two pastors looked more pious.

I went home and stayed in bed two days. Wally called later that afternoon just to check on how I was doing after the events of the morning. The widow wrote to thank me for "carrying on under such adverse circumstances."

The cousin who had the heart attack made it to the hospital and lived.

But the last I heard he and his wife had stopped attending funerals!

8

I DO— WITH LETTUCE, ONIONS, AND MUSTARD!

Hey, Preacher, there's somebody out here on the sidewalk that wants to talk with you."

What followed was like a scene from an old western movie. Everything in Echols' Cafe came to a halt. Coffee cups were suspended in mid-air; Mrs. Echols, who was presiding over the cash register, rang up a bill and then forgot to take the money; and Johnny, the cook, stopped frying eggs and bacon and peeped through the small opening where prepared dishes were placed. All eyes focused for a moment on me and the table where I was having a second cup of coffee with some ranchers. Then as if in slow motion, the heads turned and the eyes focused through the windows on the strangers outside.

I took a last sip of coffee, pushed my chair back, 'scused myself, and walked like a man toward whatever awaited me on Main Street, Walnut Springs, Texas—population 752 people and several thousand head of cattle. Most of my buddies set their cups down, picked up their hats, and followed me out the door. I knew, for I heard the shuffle of their chairs and the clomp of their boots.

Must be serious, I said to myself as I walked toward the strangers—a man and a woman. Anything's serious in Walnut Springs if it breaks up a good coffee-drinking session at Echols' Cafe on Saturday morning.

"Hi," I greeted them, "I'm the preacher." I never did like to be called *preacher*, but if they gave you a handle in this town, you lived with it.

The man said nothing; he just grinned at me. He was tall and lanky, and his hair was combed straight back and plastered down with some kind of heavy oil or cream. He was eating a hamburger. It was loaded with "the works"—meat, lettuce, onions, pickles, tomatoes, and mustard. Especially mustard. Between bites he would glance down proudly at the woman beside him.

She was much shorter than he in stature, had faded brown hair that was held down by bobby pins and clips, and wore a simple, drab print dress that came nearly to her ankles. Her hands were weathered from work, the kind of work done on a farm or ranch. Lines had begun to form on her face, but behind the lines was a hint of a nervous smile. It was obvious that she was shy and embarrassed.

"What can I do for you?" I asked as people gathered around us.

The man took another bite of his burger, chewed and savored it slowly, and said, "We want to get married, and we want to know if you'll do it."

With these words I gulped and looked down at the sidewalk. I couldn't afford to let this stranger see the fear in my eyes.

This was serious. He was asking me to marry them, and at this point as a seminary student I'd never performed a wedding ceremony. I'd only attended four weddings in my entire life. One of those was when I was four years old. Dad and I rode in his Model T Ford from Siler City, North Carolina, to Broadway where Aunt Beulah was getting married. I remember standing up and peeping over the dashboard most of the forty-mile journey, but I don't recall anything at all about the ceremony. Another wedding was my own, and I was too nervous to remember what the preacher said. I'd been to a couple of weddings of friends, but, frankly, I was more interested in decorating their cars than I was in observing the details of the service. I was a second-year seminary student, but marriage ceremonies had never been discussed in my classes.

"This was serious. He was asking me to marry them, and at this point as a seminary student I'd never performed a wedding ceremony."

I was in a mess—right here in the middle of Walnut Springs.

"Well," I replied with hesitation, "when would you like to get married?"

"Right now."

"Where?" I asked weakly.

"Right here's okay with us."

He grinned, took another bite of hamburger while she fidgeted awkwardly. The ranchers chuckled. They were really enjoying this.

I had to stall for time.

"I'll . . . I'll . . . marry you," I said with as much confidence as I could muster, "but it will take a little while for me to get ready. And I don't think right here on the street is the best place. Why don't we meet at the Baptist church around the corner in forty-five minutes."

She blushed shyly and said she liked the idea for it would give her a chance to go across the street to the variety store and purchase a new dress. He nodded his assent and I moved toward my old '41 Chevy that was parked at an angle in front of the cafe. Pausing before I opened the door, I swallowed hard, looked back at them and waved, hoping and praying that no one would guess the uncertainties churning inside me. She didn't see my wave for she was still looking shyly at the sidewalk.

But he looked me straight in the eyes and grinned broadly. I couldn't miss the grin for his mouth was outlined perfectly with mustard!

An older friend, Cecil Macbeth, was a seasoned pastor in Meridian, twelve miles east of Walnut Springs. When I reached the house I dialed him immediately and breathed a sigh of relief when he answered the phone.

"Cecil, I need help. Quick!"

"What's wrong, Bruce?"

"There's a couple over here in Walnut Springs that wants me to marry them."

"Well, go ahead and do it."

"I can't. I don't know how."

Cecil, a soft-spoken man, calmed me down and then asked if I had a copy of the *Pastor's Manual.*

"I think so," I replied hesitantly.

"Go find it and turn to the section on weddings. You'll find a sample of a ceremony on those pages. Just read that printed ceremony at the wedding and insert the names of the persons you're marrying."

"But I don't know their names," I protested.

"Well, my friend," he chuckled, "it's time you find out. And don't forget to sign the marriage license. Good luck."

Cecil also told me that we didn't need witnesses for weddings in Texas, so just the three of us showed up at the white frame church. I was relieved for I sure didn't want any of my coffee-drinking friends watching me stumble through this situation.

She was now wearing her new dress—a light blue clinging crepe one that came to her knees. It looked exactly like something that you would buy . . . well, it looked like something you would buy at a five-and-ten-cent store.

He was still wearing . . . mustard, clearly outlining his broad grin.

I closed the church doors, hoping and praying that no one would wander in.

They stood before me at the front of the little church and I read the introduction like an old pro. I had penciled their names in the black manual and breezed on through the "I do's." They did—without any hesitation.

"When they turned to thank me, I also smiled . . . for the first time . . . for both their mouths were now clearly outlined with mustard."

We made it through the ring ceremony, after he had dug through his pockets, searching for her wedding band. I led in a prayer and then pronounced them "husband and wife."

She smiled shyly. He grinned again, leaned over, and kissed her.

When they turned to thank me, I also smiled . . . for the first time . . . for both their mouths were now clearly outlined with mustard.

I headed toward home, thankful for Cecil and the *Pastor's Manual.*

As I drove slowly down Main Street, Walnut Springs, I prayed out loud, "Please, dear God, I hope she likes . . . mustard."

A GREAT HONEYMOON TRIP—ALONE!

My telephone rang at ten o'clock on Saturday morning. I looked up from my Sunday sermon notes and said, "Hello."

"Pastor McIver," a young man began, "I'm not a member of your church and you don't know me, but I've visited Wilshire several times and I sure do need to talk with you this morning. Could we visit over the phone?"

"How can I help?" I asked.

"Pastor, I'm scheduled to be married soon, and I'm not sure the girl I'm engaged to is the one I really want to marry."

"I understand," I replied, trying to play the role of a helpful counselor. "That's a heavy decision; you should spend plenty of time thinking through this matter before the wedding. Now, what's the date of your wedding?"

"This afternoon—at two o'clock."

"You mean today? This afternoon?" I asked in bewilderment.

"That's right, Pastor. And I'm in big trouble. We're having a formal wedding at the church where she's a member. All the bridesmaids and the groomsmen are here, and her parents arrived yesterday from Tennessee. She has a large family and they have all driven in for the occasion. We had the rehearsal and the rehearsal dinner last evening, and everybody seemed happy except me. Sir, I'm scared."

Then, he added, "We're scheduled to leave late this evening for a two-week honeymoon in Florida. All reservations and arrangements were made a month ago. I doubt we could get the deposits back."

Deposits are the least of your worries, I thought.

For fifty-five minutes I listened as he rambled through pros and cons, discussed his feelings and lack of feelings, confessed that he thought that he once loved her, but now he wasn't sure, and speculated on how he could get out of the fix he was in without hurting her.

The more I listened the more I knew that this prospective marriage wasn't going to get off the ground. But it's difficult to put it that bluntly to someone, especially three hours before the wedding ceremony. I wanted him to think it through and come to his own conclusion, but he rambled on and on as the clock ticked away.

Finally, I interrupted him. "Look," I finally said impatiently, "You're talking to the wrong person. Your fiancee is now—at this very moment—dressing for what she thinks is going to be her wedding. You need to be talking with her, not me. You owe it to her to let her hear some of your hesitations about this marriage. And she needs to hear them now."

"You're right, sir," he whimpered. "I'll call her right now. But, sir, please pray for me."

Boy, does he ever need it! I thought.

"Before you hang up," I added, "do me a favor. You've talked to me for nearly an hour this morning. I'm not asking anything out of our conversation except a word from you about how things go. Just call me and tell me the outcome."

He promised to do that.

Two weeks passed. In the rush of other responsibilities I had almost forgotten our conversation. My phone rang late one afternoon.

"Hi, Pastor McIver. I'm the fellow you talked to a couple of weeks ago who was having second thoughts about getting married. Remember? I'm back in town," he said excitedly.

"How did it go?" I asked. "What happened?"

"Oh, I phoned her immediately after talking with you and called the wedding off."

Admittedly, I felt a twinge of sadness for her and for him.

But I learned as he continued the conversation that any sympathy expended on him was totally unnecessary.

"I went on to Florida alone," he exclaimed, "and I had a whale of a time by myself!"

THE MISSING CANDELABRA

It was one of the largest weddings ever held at Wilshire. Fifteen minutes before the service was scheduled to begin, the church parking lots were overflowing with cars and scores of people were crowding into the foyer, waiting to be properly seated. It was the kind of occasion that warms the heart of a pastor.

But that was fifteen minutes before the service.

At exactly seven o'clock the mothers were seated, and the organist sounded the triumphant notes of the processional. That was my cue to enter the sanctuary through the side door at the front and begin presiding over the happy occasion. As I reached for the door a voice called from down the hall, "Not yet, Pastor. Don't open the door. I've got a message for you."

I turned and through the subdued lighting I saw the assistant florist hurrying as fast as she could toward me. Her speed didn't set any records for she was about eight months pregnant and waddled down the hall with obvious difficulty. She was nearly out of breath when she reached me. "Pastor," she panted, "we can't find the candelabra that you are supposed to use at the close of the ceremony. We've looked everywhere, and it just can't be found. What on earth can we do?"

I sensed immediately that we had a big problem on our hands. The couple to be married had specifically requested that the unity candle be a part of the wedding service. We had gone over it carefully at the rehearsal—step by step. The candelabra, designed to hold three candles, was to be placed near the altar. The mothers of the bride and groom would be ushered down the aisle, each carrying a lighted candle. Upon reaching the front of the sanctuary, they were to move to the candelabra and place their candles in the appropriate receptacles. Throughout the ceremony the mothers' candles were to burn slowly while the larger middle one remained unlighted. After the vows had been spoken, the bride and groom would light the center candle. This was designed to symbolize family unity as well as the light of God's love in the new relationship.

I felt good about all this at the rehearsal. I had a special verse of Scripture that I planned to read as the couple lighted the middle candle. We had it down to perfection.

We thought.

The notes from the organ pealed louder and louder as I was stalled in the hallway. I knew that the organist by now was glancing over her left shoulder wondering where in the world the minister was.

"Okay," I said to the perplexed florist, "we'll just have to 'wing it.' I'll cut that part out of my ceremony and improvise at the close."

With those words I opened the door and entered the sanctuary, muttering behind my frozen smile, "What on earth are we going to do?"

The groom and his attendants followed me in. The bride and her attendants came down the left aisle of the sanctuary. When the first bridesmaid arrived at the front, she whispered something in my direction.

The puzzled look on my face was a signal to her that I did not understand.

She whispered the message again, opening her mouth wider and emphasizing every syllable. By straining to hear above the organ and through lip-reading I made out what she was saying: "Go ahead with the unity candle part of the ceremony."

"But . . . how?" I whispered through my teeth with a plastic smile.

"Just go ahead," she signaled back.

We made it through the first part of the ceremony without any difficulty.

Everyone was beaming in delight because of the happy occasion—everyone except the first bridesmaid who had brought me

" 'That's the funniest thing I've ever seen,' the bride interrupted with a loud whisper."

the message. When I looked in her direction for some additional word about the candelabra, she had a stoic look on her face and her mouth was tightly clamped shut. Obviously, she was out of messages for me.

We continued with the ceremony. I read a passage from 1 Corinthians 13 and emphasized the importance of love and patience in building a marriage relationship. I asked the bride and groom to join hands, and I began to talk about the vows they would make. There wasn't a hitch. I was beginning to feel better, but I still had to figure out some way to conclude the service. Just now, however, we needed to get through the vows and rings.

"John, in taking the woman whom you hold by your hand to be your wife, do you promise to love her? . . ."

"That's the funniest thing I've ever seen," the bride interrupted with a loud whisper. I turned from the bewildered groom to look at her and noticed that she was staring toward her right, to the organ side of the front of the sanctuary. Not only was she looking in that direction; so were all the attendants, and so was the audience! One thousand eyes focused on a moving target to my left. I knew it was moving, for heads and eyes followed it, turning ever so slightly in slow motion style.

The moving target was none other than the assistant florist. She had slipped through the door by the organ and was moving on hands and knees behind the choir rail toward the center of the platform where I stood. The dear lady, "great with child," thought she was out of sight, beneath the rail. But in fact, her posterior bobbled in plain view, six inches above the choir rail. As she crawled along she carried in each hand a burning candle. To make matters worse, she didn't realize that she was silhouetted—a large, moving, "pregnant" shadow—on the wall behind the choir loft.

The wedding party experienced the agony of smothered, stifled laughter. Their only release was the flow of hysterical tears while they fought to keep their composure. Two or three of the bride's attendants shook so hard that petals of the flowers in their bouquets fell to the floor.

It was a welcomed moment for me when the vows were completed and I could say with what little piety remained, "Now, let us bow our heads and close our eyes for a special prayer." This was a signal for the soloist to sing "The Lord's Prayer." It also gave me a chance to peep during the singing and to figure out what in the world was happening.

"Pssst! Pssst!"

I did a half turn, looked down, and saw a lighted candle being pushed through the greenery behind me.

"Take this candle," the persistent florist said.

The soloist continued to sing, "Give us this day our daily bread . . ."

"Pssst. Now take this one," the voice behind me said as a second candle was poked through the greenery.

" . . . as we forgive those who trespass against us . . ."

I was beginning to catch on. So I was to be the human candelabra. Here I stood, with a candle in each hand and my Bible and notes tucked under my arm.

"Where's the third candle?" I whispered above the sounds of" . . . but deliver us from evil . . ."

"Between my knees," the florist answered. "Just a minute and I'll pass it through to you."

That's when the bride lost it. So did several of the attendants. The last notes of "The Lord's Prayer" were drowned out by the snickers all around me.

I couldn't afford such luxury. Somebody had to carry this thing on to conclusion and try to rescue something from it, can-

---

" 'Where's the third candle?' I whispered . . . 'Between my knees,' the florist answered. . . . That's when the bride lost it."

---

delabra or no candelabra. I determined to do just that as I now tried to juggle three candles, a Bible, and wedding notes. My problem was complicated by the fact that two of the candles were burning, and the third one soon would be.

It was a challenging dilemma, one that called for creative action—in a hurry. And there was nothing in the *Pastor's Manual* that addressed this predicament. Nor had it ever been mentioned in a seminary class on pastoral responsibilities. I was on my own.

I handed one candle to the nearly hysterical bride who was laughing so hard that tears were trickling down her cheeks. I handed the other to the groom who was beginning to question all the reassurances I had passed out freely at the rehearsal. My statements about "no problems," and, "we'll breeze through the service without a hitch," and, "just relax and trust me," were beginning to sound hollow.

I held the last candle in my hands. They were to light it together from the ones they were each holding. Miraculously, we made it through that part in spite of jerking hands and tears of smothered laughter. Now we had three burning candles.

In a very soft, reassuring voice, I whispered, "That's fine. Now each of you blow out your candle."

Golly, I said to myself, we're going to get through this thing yet.

That thought skipped through my mind just before the bride, still out of control, pulled her candle toward her mouth to blow it out, forgetting that she was wearing a nylon veil over her face.

"Poooff!"

The veil went up in smoke and disintegrated.

Fortunately, except for singed eyebrows, the bride was not injured.

Through the hole in the charred remains of her veil she gave me a bewildering look. I had no more reassurances for her, the groom, or anybody. Enough was enough.

Disregarding any other notes concerning the conclusion of the ceremony, I took all the candles and blew them out myself. Then, peering through the smoke of three extinguished candles, I signaled the organist to begin the recessional . . . now! Just get us out of here. Quickly!

Everything else is a blur.

But I still turn pale when prospective brides tell me about "this wonderful idea of using a unity candle" in their ceremony.

9

PULPIT BLOOPERS

It was a beautiful Sunday morning in Dallas. Winter was over and the signs of spring were all around. There were new buds on the trees and new blossoms on the shrubs. Tiny blades of green grass began to peek through dry stubble on the lawns. A new season was upon us and it was exciting.

As I drove into the church parking lot I was pleased to see that scores of people were already present. I knew in my heart that this was going to be a great day at the Wilshire Baptist Church, especially because it was Palm Sunday.

Palm Sunday, the Sunday before Easter, commemorates the triumphal journey that Jesus made through Jerusalem less than one week before His crucifixion. As He traveled through the narrow streets, the people waved palm branches—symbols of victory—and shouted *Hosannas*—exclamations of praise. All of this was to be the theme of the worship service that I would soon lead, and my sermon, carefully prepared, was to be an interpretation of the Biblical account of that last journey.

The brick chapel, where the congregation met before the larger sanctuary was built, was packed to and beyond capacity. Chairs were placed down the aisles and throughout the balcony. This added to the excitement as ushers scurried to accommodate the people. My heart was filled with gratitude and warmth when I saw so many faithful members who had gathered for worship.

The Patton family—mother, father, and four boys under twelve years of age—were in their usual place on the second row. Walter, the father, was a busy physician, but regular church attendance was a priority with the family. Wilma, the mother, had a touch of class seen in few women. She was poised and proper, but there were times when her one vote in the family circle outweighed those cast by the four boys and "Doc."

Just looking down at the boys lined up beside each other on the pew made me chuckle. They were tough little characters and usually looked like they had just posed for a Norman Rockwell painting. For instance, one Sunday I noticed that one of the boys had a broken arm, another had a bandaged scalp, and still another had a black eye. It was evident that a lot of activity had taken place around the Patton household that week.

On another Sunday I was impressed that each of the four boys held a hymnal in his hands and was singing with gusto. After the service was over I told the youngest that I was impressed by the way they all sang with such enthusiasm.

"Yeah, we had to," he replied in candor. "Dad told us that if we didn't sing, he'd make us join the Junior Choir."

Albert and Madge sat four rows behind the Pattons. They were both slightly beyond middle age and were regarded by most everyone as the "salt of the earth" kind of people. Their pattern of life was simple—without pretension and affectation. The reversals that life had dealt them worked positively, producing a genuine concern for others. This concern was frequently expressed to others through the sharing of what they gathered from their garden and from their fruit trees. They asked nothing in return for their kindnesses, and any attempt to return favors would have embarrassed them.

When I preached, Albert and Madge gave me continuous eye contact, often nodding their heads in unison to show their approval. They didn't realize it, but they made it a little easier to pastor a church.

The Stinson family sat in the center section of the chapel, just under the edge of the balcony. They were prompt, correct, and extremely conservative—in politics and in theology. The husband, a quiet man, was an executive with a major Dallas corporation. The wife, a petite woman, was anxiously and aggressively involved in one cause after another, trying to save the nation, the schools, and the church—from something. I found it difficult to figure out just who all our enemies were, but according to her

"One Sunday I noticed that one of the boys had a broken arm, another had a bandaged scalp, and still another had a black eye."

and to the literature she left constantly on my desk, they were lurking everywhere—even in pulpits and on the front pews of churches.

Mrs. Stinson monitored every activity provided through the church youth ministries to be certain that her children were not exposed to something "liberal" or "subversive."

The Stinson children were prim and proper. They smiled when the occasion called for it, but I never heard them laugh. I could never completely relax in the presence of the Stinsons, not even at church fellowships or at other happy gatherings. Their rigidity had a way of squelching joy and putting the lid on fun.

To my left was Flossie Fogleman. Flossie was eighty-plus years of age, drove a black vintage sedan, and wore a navy blue crepe dress. The dress became her uniform, and I began to wonder if she needed money for a new one. I soon learned that money was no problem; she just liked the dress she wore. Flossie used a lot of facial powder, which had a way of falling off her face and neck and getting on the front of her dress. It would also get on you if you stood too near her when you talked with her.

The church was just about the most important thing in Flossie's life. She would arrive early and park her car wherever she desired on the parking lot. Yellow stripes meant nothing to Flossie. In one maneuver of the steering wheel she could get that old vehicle across four of those stripes. People gave Flossie a lot of room when they spotted her car.

Flossie could be encouraging to a pastor, but it took energy just to listen to her.

"Pastor," she would say, "I just love my church and all my friends here and I think you are the most wonderful preacher in the whole world and my Sunday school teacher sure was good this morning and how are your wife and your darling children?"

When she paused for a split second I would inject, "Thank you, Flossie; they're fine, that's good, and everybody's well."

Flossie meant well in spite of the way she parked her car and in spite of the white powder that landed on my dark suit when I got close to her. I was glad to see her on this special Palm Sunday morning.

The diverse and faithful members were there in their places, and so were scores of others. There were college students who were home for spring break, friends from the neighborhood, guests of active members of the church, and several newcomers to the city who were looking for a new church home. It was just one of those days when everybody decided to show up.

I DIDN'T SAY THAT (OR DID I?)

At the appointed hour, the organist played a resounding fanfare and choir members began processing down the crowded aisles, led by little children waving palm branches. As they came forward, stepping around the added chairs for the occasion, they began to sing an uplifting, festive hymn. On the last stanza the entire congregation stood and joined in the singing. It was an inspiring experience, a signal of what was to follow.

Or, so I thought.

After the singing of the hymns, the receiving of the offering, a time of prayer, and some special music, I stood to read the Scripture. My text for the sermon was taken from Matthew's gospel, chapter twenty-two. I read from the King James translation the familiar account of Jesus riding through the streets of Jerusalem on an ass. The lowly beast of burden was in marked contrast to the white stallions usually ridden by victorious Roman generals. This was one of the truths I planned to underscore in my message.

My introduction to the sermon was drawn from a current news story about a man who made a last trip back to his hometown. He knew that he didn't have long to live, and he wanted to

"Yellow stripes meant nothing to Flossie. In one maneuver of the steering wheel she could get that old vehicle across four of those stripes. People gave Flossie a lot of room when they spotted her car."

take care of some unfinished business with his family and friends. Everyone in the audience, including the Patton boys, could relate to the story.

I made it through the opening remarks smoothly and moved quickly into the Biblical background of the story of the triumphal journey through the Old City. Relying on memories from my own recent visit there I described in detail the narrow gates and cobbled streets. I drew word pictures of the blind, the lame, and the poor that I had personally encountered while walking those streets. The people listened with rapt attention. Little children put down their pencils and paper and gave me undivided attention. The Patton boys leaned forward in the pew, hanging on to every word; Albert and Madge nodded affirmations; Flossie had an angelic look on her face and moved her lips in what I assumed to be a prayer; even the Stinsons seemed to relax and become a part of the procession through the streets.

This was a preacher's paradise. Words flowed quickly and freely. Spontaneous phrases found nowhere in my sermon notes were delivered in the inspiration of the moment and embellished every step of the journey. I described the cheering crowd, the waving of the palm branches, and the jubilant celebration of the disciples. I was on a roll, caught up in the excitement of the moment.

At the peak of this part of the message, I even had Jesus stopping the procession, getting off the ass, and ministering to people in the streets!

Then it happened.

With either a burst of some kind of inspiration or with unbridled imagination, I exhorted, "And, ladies and gentlemen, if we're going to do anything for God in this city, we're going to have to get off our *ass* and minister to people in the streets!"

There was a pause, but this time it was not for effect. It was a paralyzing pause. I was frozen by what I had said. So were others.

The Patton boys stared at me with their mouths open. Albert and Madge stopped nodding affirmations in "midstream." The entire Stinson family sat as rigid as fence posts. Flossie, who seemed to turn pale in spite of the powder, bowed her head and moved her lips. I wasn't sure if she was praying or what.

There are some guidelines that need to be followed by any speaker when this kind of catastrophe occurs. These have evolved in my mind as the "McIver Rules for Those Who Bloop."

First, keep talking. After the initial pause, move on. In a hurry. There's a kind of jet lag that most people in any audience experience. There is a lapse between the time a word is spoken and the time it is heard and internalized. If the speaker can recover, keep his composure, move forward quickly and smoothly, then some in the audience will miss the blooper.

Second, never apologize. If you've dug a hole and fallen in, apologies and explanations usually serve only to dig a deeper hole.

Third, never look at anyone. This is most important. No eye contact at all.

You have two alternatives here. You can look down at the floor, but this communicates the attitude of humiliation, and you certainly don't want to add humiliation to your *faux pas*.

On the other hand, you can look over the heads of the people. Find some object somewhere in the room and get a fix on it. Don't let your eyes move from it. Not even for a blink.

That is exactly what I did. The interior of our chapel is made of brick. I found one red brick just beneath the last chandelier and focused entirely on it. Meanwhile, I struggled verbally to complete the triumphal journey through Jerusalem, but my descriptions were sounding less and less triumphal.

> ***"There was a pause, but this time it was not for effect. It was a paralyzing pause. I was frozen by what I had said. So were others."***

Then a strange thing happened. With my eyes fixed on that single brick, with my face flushed in embarrassment and humiliation, and with the sound of my voice reduced to a monotone, I began a conversation with myself in my head.

"Bruce, did you hear what you just said?"

"I didn't say that," I protested. "It sounded like that, but I didn't say it."

"Yes, you did."

"I wouldn't say that. Not from the pulpit. I'm not that dumb."

"But you did. And you are. Besides, why didn't you use another translation of the Bible—one that reads 'donkey,' or 'colt' or 'beast of burden?'"

"But I was reading from the King James translation," I cried within. "If the King James translation was good enough for . . . ."

"No, Bruce, give it up; that won't work here."

While this drama was going on inside me another was taking place behind me on the platform.

Dan Pratt was our capable minister of music at the time. He had a great baritone voice and often sang the lead roles in operas performed in our part of the country. Dan's sense of humor was nearly as big as his body, which draped over the sides of the small, armless pulpit chair where he sat while I preached. For three or four minutes he swallowed hard and put on his best stone face. His opera training served him well at this particular moment.

But not for long.

As others in the congregation later described it to me, Dan sat rigid, staring straight ahead. Soon, however, his body began to bobble and his jolly jowls bounced up and down. The stone face of the opera actor caved in and tears came to his eyes. His groans of smothered laughter could be heard by those nearby, especially those seated immediately behind him on the front row of the choir. There was no doubt about it; Dan was losing control.

What the people in the congregation could not see, they soon sensed and heard. As the tension continued to mount, rustling sounds came from all directions. People leaned over, bowed their heads and scratched their eyebrows. From those head-in-hands positions they started peeking at the persons on either side of them. Then shoulders began to shake. Squelched snickers and muffled laughter began to rise to a rumble all over the chapel. By now Dan had virtually lost it; so had the choir.

When I recovered enough to assess the damage, I decided that it was time to halt the journey through the cobbled streets and tie up the donkey, or colt, or "whatever."

For that one Palm Sunday at Wilshire Baptist Church, the triumphal journey ended in near chaos.

After a hurried benediction the Patton boys giggled past me. Albert and Madge just looked at me and managed a weak, supportive smile. The Stinsons, disregarding the "Amen," remained rigid in their pew, looking shell shocked. Flossie did not linger and was one of the first to drive out of the parking lot.

I limped home . . . longing for Easter.

FROM FAILURE TO DEFEATS

I felt downright excited as the hour of the Sunday evening worship drew near.

All week long I had listened to the problems of people, walked with them through difficulties, and suffered with them in their reversals. All of this had "primed the pump" for a sermon that I thought would answer all their needs. I could hardly wait to deliver it.

But, regardless of hours of preparation, there are some last minute checks that need to be made by everyone involved in leading a worship service. Immediately prior to the service staff members and deacons were faithfully moving through the checklist.

Are all the doors leading into the sanctuary unlocked? Are the ushers in place? Is the lighting adjusted properly? Are the microphones in place? Is the room temperature satisfactory?

While this was taking place, choir members gathered in a narrow, dimly lit hallway behind the pulpit area of the chapel. They checked their folders to make sure the special music had been inserted, patted their hair with their hands, and adjusted the stoles worn over the choir robes.

The minister of music peeped through a tiny glass hole in one of the doors and counted for the third time the number of chairs in the choir loft. He then stood on tiptoes, squinted his eyes, peered down the hallway, and counted again the number of choir members who had shown up for the service. The number of bodies and chairs had to match, else some lone soul might be left standing after the choral "Call to Worship."

Others of the ministerial staff scanned the printed program, or order of service, one last time to review their personal duties in the service.

While this was going on around me, I was also busy. I checked my Bible to see that my sermon notes were neatly clipped in place. I also touched my hair to make sure that it was not windblown, cleared my throat, and at the last moment, checked the zipper in my pants. Few things can happen to a preacher worse than bringing greetings to a congregation with an open fly.

After one or two of these painful experiences the creative minister learns to say piously and quickly, "I feel led in this moment to have a brief season of prayer. So, let *every* head be bowed and *every* eye closed." He then hovers closely behind the pulpit, bows his own head and lowers his hand. It's amazing how smoothly this works, providing *every* eye is closed and providing the corner of a white shirt doesn't get caught in the zipper!

At the proper moment we all marched through the doors into the chapel. I smiled to myself in renewed confidence, for I was sure that I had prepared the very sermon that so many people needed: "From Failure to Victory!" My goal was to show the people that any so-called failure, any reversal, any barrier or obstacle can be turned into something positive and victorious.

The congregational singing gave me an opportunity to scan the audience.

There was Herbert, looking alone and desolate. His wife had just thrown him out of the house and was in the process of filing divorce papers. In addition, Herbert had lost his job and had no means of support. He had been forced to move into a one-room apartment over a garage near the church. I noticed that when we all stood to sing, his shoulders slumped and he barely moved his lips. That was understandable; Herbert didn't have much to sing about.

But I had a message for him.

And there was Anthony, a certified public accountant with a brilliant mind and a lousy personality. He was taller than the average person and had a way of making people feel that he was looking down on them as he talked with them. Anthony had an opinion, usually negative, on just about everything. This was accentuated by the hint of a sneer on his face and beady eyes that peered through black horn-rimmed glasses. He couldn't understand why his firm had recently passed over him when promotions were handed out; neither could he understand why so many girls refused to date him.

I could understand, and I had a sermon for Anthony.

Also in the service that evening was Madine. Bless her, Madine tried and tried, but things never seemed to work out for her. She had moved from a small town in east Texas to get away from her parents, but she found it nearly impossible to make it on her own. The best jobs she could get barely paid the rent and bought the groceries. Her old car kept breaking down, and almost every month there was some other kind of emergency. She planned to

---

"Few things can happen to a preacher worse than bringing greetings to a congregation with an open fly."

---

take some night courses at a community college, but semester by semester, those plans just didn't seem to work out. Life appeared to be passing Madine by.

I had a word for her.

All of these with difficulties and struggles challenged me. "From Failure to Victory" was the very message people needed. No one needed to fail continuously. Life could be one grand march from victory to victory.

Asa and Dot Newsom, two of my dearest friends, were living examples of this truth. Asa, a physician, had delivered our two youngest daughters. He had the rare ability to be completely professional and genuinely warm at the same time. He was not a large man, but he stood tall as a leader among the people. With a quiet voice, a wry smile, and a disarming sense of humor he could calm troubled waters in the corridors of a hospital or on the floor of the church during a tense business meeting.

Dot was one of the most attractive and creative persons anywhere. Whether in making a new dress, redecorating her home or in hosting a party (like the one Lawanna and I went to on our first date), she always added a special touch. She was a prolific writer of notes, never failing to remember birthdays, anniversaries, and other special occasions. Beyond that, her sensitivity extended to all kinds of situations where a kind word of encouragement would help. None of this reaching out had even the hint of duty; with Dot, it seemed to spring from the overflow of a gracious life.

Just looking out and seeing Asa and Dot and their three children in a worship service always helped me. On this particular Sunday they might not have needed the message I had prepared, but I needed them.

When I stood to preach, I felt assured and confident. There was not a moment of hesitation or difficulty . . . until . . . until I used as a sermon illustration the world heavyweight boxing match that had just occurred between Ingemar Johannson and Floyd Patterson. Patterson, the holder of the title, was a tough black fighter from the United States. Johannson, the young challenger, was a relatively unknown boxer from Sweden. Oddsmakers gave him virtually no chance to dethrone the champion. In fact, it took a lot of courage for him even to enter the ring with Patton, but he did—fearlessly and courageously. And, to the astonishment of most of the boxing world, he won the bout and became the new champion. It was front page news everywhere.

A timely and perfect illustration for my sermon.

I briefly explained the background of the fight and tried to describe what was at stake. Then, with a strong and vibrant voice, I exclaimed, "And with undaunted confidence that young Swede climbed into the ring with that big black. . . ."

And then I used the "N" word!

I can't explain how it happened, or why it happened. I hadn't used that word in years. I had even spanked my children for using it. Besides, I prided myself in trying to be open and unbiased toward peoples of all races. Why, in the midst of racial tension in Dallas in the early 60's I had insisted that the doors of our church be open to everyone, regardless of color of skin or ethnic background. Furthermore, during that troubled decade our own church had engaged in a partnership program with two different black congregations. I had preached in those churches, and their pastors had preached at Wilshire. We had shared ministries together.

But I had *said* it. It was out of my mouth—never to be retrieved.

From that point on it was downhill all the way. I droned on and on, desperately trying to think of something—anything—that

---

"I can't explain how it happened, or why it happened. I hadn't used that word in years. I had even spanked my children for using it."

---

might redeem the situation and restore any credibility that I might have had. Truthfully, I cried out within to be rescued. I was mortified.

At best, the pulpit is a lonely place; but when you're slushing around in mire up to your knees, with no dry ground in sight, there is no loneliness like it anywhere in the world. To compound the problem, you're on public display, wallowing around in the slush and mire you yourself sometimes create. Agony. Sheer agony.

I knew that time was running out for me, but there was no way that I was going to conclude the service without one last, valiant effort. After all, a miracle could still happen. Only believe. Try. Hope.

Then I remembered the title of my sermon. If this wasn't a classic example of failure, I'd never experienced it. This was the perfect moment to become a living example of how to get out of the slush and mire. Go for it, Bruce!

Pausing for effect, I slowly scanned the stunned congregation. Then, with renewed energy, I breathed deeply, smiled slightly in an effort to exude confidence, rocked back on my heels, rolled forward on my toes, lifted my right hand high over my head, pointed the index finger to the ceiling and into the heavenly beyond, and declared with authority, "And you, too, ladies and gentlemen, with God's help, can turn your failures into *defeats!*"

I just stood there . . . on tiptoes . . . suspended . . . looking helplessly at my finger.

It seemed like half an eternity before my mind told my finger to stop pointing upward. Slowly, painfully, the message finally got through, and the hand came down while the audience watched in shocked disbelief.

We sang a closing hymn. I mumbled a benediction and tried to make my escape. As I exited quickly through the rear door I bumped into Asa. He took me by the arm, drew me aside, and whispered unforgettable words into my ear, "Just wasn't your night tonight, was it, Pastor?"

It was probably the kindest thing he could have said.

Postscript: Herbert's wife followed through with the divorce and married a Dallas millionaire. Anthony lost his job with his accounting firm and moved to another state. He's never married. Madine never did enroll in college. Her old car finally rolled over and died. The last I heard of her she had gone back home to live with her parents.

10

BEDSIGHTS

It was the third day after my major back surgery. After years of moaning and groaning, I decided the doctor was right: It was time to do something to stop the pain. I opened my eyes from a short nap, blinked, and surveyed the room. The special nurse had been dismissed, and Lawanna had gone home for a few hours to check on the girls. For the first time since being admitted to the hospital, I was on my own. I needed to get oriented because this was to be home to me for three more weeks.

The private room was small, but adequate. Every square inch had been utilized. There were two chairs and a small table against the far wall on the far side of the room. A square nightstand was immediately to my right with a telephone and a nurses' call button on it. The telephone was usually just out of reach, especially for the patient recovering from surgery, and the call button kept sliding off the table to the floor.

An adjustable table on wheels had multi-purpose uses. It served as a catch-all for flowers, cards and letters, pictures of family members, magazines and papers, cosmetics, electric razors, and cold water. It also functioned as a serving table for meals, so just before each meal all these items had to be stacked to make room for the tray. It took a lot of dexterity on the part of a patient to sort out all these things.

A television set was mounted high on the wall facing the bed. The bathroom, which I had not seen in three days, was about fifteen feet to my left. I would need to do a lot of picking and choosing along the obstacle course when I made that journey on my own.

In spite of the compact room I was grateful for this hospital and doctors and nurses. And I was grateful that the burning pain in the lower back would subside in a few days. Meanwhile, it was time to close my eyes again and let the pain pill do its work.

ENOUGH IS ENOUGH!

At two-fifty in the afternoon the door opened and a smiling, buxom nurse asked, "And how are we doing?"

The pulsating pain spilled over into my disposition and I wanted to say, "What is there to smile about, and who is 'we'?" But an inkling of prudence restrained me. I was determined to be a good patient, especially since I was serving at the time as a trustee of the hospital.

"We need to take this to get our body functions moving again," she said as she handed me a clear plastic cup filled with chalky liquid. I knew immediately what the medicine was for and protested. And, deep down inside, I definitely resented the "we."

"Please," I begged, "I'm hurting so badly I can hardly move. I haven't done much walking since surgery, and my wife has gone home, and I have a very, very sensitive stomach. Please, I beg you, don't give me that chalky stuff. You don't understand."

"No, you need to take it. It will do you good."

I knew that any other resistance would be futile, so I took the cup with a shaky hand and downed the stuff.

"Thank you, Reverend McIver. We'll feel better in a little while."

I was so weary that I paid little attention to the third "we." It really didn't matter anymore. Just give me rest . . . and quiet . . . and . . .

Twenty minutes passed.

"Reverend McIver? Reverend McIver, please wake up for just a moment."

I blinked, tried to focus my eyes and mumbled, "Who? . . . What is it? . . . What time is it?"

With blurred vision, I saw another nurse standing by my bed.

"I'm Mrs. Wyrick and I'll be your nurse for this shift. It's ten minutes after three in the afternoon. Here, I have something for you."

" 'We need to take this to get our body functions moving again,' she said as she handed me a clear plastic cup filled with chalky liquid. I knew immediately what the medicine was for and protested. And, deep down inside, I definitely resented the 'we.' "

I blinked again and saw, or thought I saw, a hint of a smile. She handed me a plastic cup filled with . . .

"Oh, no! I took that stuff a few minutes ago!"

"Just swallow it, Reverend McIver. It will be good for you."

"But you don't understand! I've already had a cup of it, and my back hurts, and my wife is not here, and this new brace will not let me bend . . . and . . . "

"Please, Reverend, be a good patient and just take this."

My energies were drained and my emotions depleted. The fight in me was gone. I took the plastic cup, like a "good patient," and drank the contents. Nothing seemed to matter any longer . . . except rest . . . and sleep.

Within the hour I was jarred from a deep sleep by a piercing pain in the lower abdomen. It definitely wasn't like the pain from my surgery this time! More blinding than any pain, however, was the urgency to get to the bathroom . . . immediately!

I rolled cautiously, and painfully, off the side of the bed, braced myself against the table, and stood perfectly still until the room stopped swirling. Then, groping along the walls and maneuvering around chairs, I wobbled through the obstacle course toward the bathroom. Fifteen feet seemed like fifteen miles. When I finally reached my destination, I loosened my baggy hospital pajama bottoms and watched helplessly as they fell to the floor. The pain from the low back incision, plus the rigid brace, made it nearly impossible for me to bend. But there are certain moments in life when one finds a way to do what one has to do . . . regardless!

I did. "Necessity is the mother of invention." The genius of my inventive skills really should be written up in medical journals, but I doubt that anyone but us "fellow sufferers" would appreciate them fully.

My problems were not over. Looking down I realized that I could not stoop and pick up my pajama bottoms. I leaned over as far as the pain and the brace allowed, but it wasn't far enough. I tried to grip the bottoms between my toes and lift them a few inches off the floor, but they kept slipping out of the grip. I sat there like the statue of "The Thinker," mumbling over my demise. Finally, I reached up, pulled the emergency cord, and whimpered through the speaker, "Would somebody please come to room 6228 and pull up my pajamas?"

A kind nurse responded, and helped me back to my bed.

But that was only the beginning. Again and again the pains came, and again and again I made the hazardous trek to the bathroom. After the third trip had been completed, all modesty was gone. Whatever nurse or physician or visitor happened by the room had the privilege of assisting me, whether he or she wanted to or not. Necessity is not choosy.

When ten round trips to the bathroom had been made in less than two hours, my entire body trembled in exhaustion. Beads of perspiration dotted my forehead and I panted for breath. Even the stabbing pain in my back seemed secondary to utter and absolute fatigue. All concerns about being a good patient, an encouraging trustee, or a "reverend" vanished. Enough was enough!

Weakly, I reached over and pushed the button next to my bed.

"Yes, may I help you?"

"Would you please ask Mrs. Blanton, the supervisor, to come to my room immediately?"

Two minutes later Mrs. Blanton stood at the foot of my bed. She was a tall, stately, middle aged lady. Her hair was pulled back into a neat bun and her cap sat perfectly straight on top of her head. She was the epitome of efficiency. And she was smiling.

"How can I help you, Reverend McIver?"

"Mrs. Blanton," I began slowly and painfully, "I'm a Christian."

"Oh, yes, Reverend, I know that you are a Christian." (*He's probably hallucinating.*)

"Mrs. Blanton, I'm the pastor of a church in this city."

"Yes, we all know about your wonderful church." (*I need to check his chart to see what he's been taking for pain.*)

"Mrs. Blanton," I said barely above a whisper, "I have a sensitive stomach."

"Yes?" she answered with a puzzled look. (*I have no idea what he's trying to tell me. He might have an elevated temperature.*)

"Mrs. Blanton, I tried to reason with your nurses—*two* of them! One on the previous shift and one on this shift, but they wouldn't listen." (*Goodness, he's becoming paranoid.*)

My body groaned in exhaustion, but my voice grew stronger in exasperation. "I've had two cups of some kind of chalky stuff that has driven me to the bathroom ten times in the last two hours . . . *ten times,* Mrs. Blanton!"

"Well, Reverend McIver . . ."

"Ten times, Mrs. Blanton, ten . . . ten times!" Everybody that has been near this room has pulled my pajama bottoms down . . . and up! . . . (*Heavens, the "Reverend" is beginning to sound angry!*)

I paused to regain my composure and drew a deep breath. The smile on Mrs. Blanton's face was gone.

"Now," I continued slowly and deliberately and with a voice that gained momentum with every syllable, "I don't know what you have to do to stop this problem . . . and I don't care . . . but do it . . . and do it now! . . . Or . . .

"All hell's going to break loose on this sixth floor!"

Mrs. Blanton shot for the door with an ashen, shocked look on her face. (*Reverend McIver is becoming violent!*)

She paused as she opened the door and looked back at me in horrified astonishment.

"One other thing, Mrs. Blanton," I said with a forced smile, "don't call me 'Reverend.' I don't like the term; besides, I don't feel very 'reverent' today!"

She nodded weakly and was gone.

Three minutes later she was back with some kind of shot. I didn't ask what it was; I didn't care. Whatever she gave me worked a miracle for there were no more trips to the bathroom that day.

Before she left the hospital late that evening, Mrs. Blanton came by the room again to check on me.

"I just wanted to see how you were feeling, Rever, . . . er . . . Pastor McIver."

"Better, thank you," I said with a grin. "By the way, what was that chalky stuff I drank twice this afternoon?"

"Haley's M.O."

"No, Mrs. Blanton, it wasn't Haley's M.O. It was Halley's Comet! And it streaked across this room all afternoon!"

She giggled nervously while struggling to maintain her professional appearance.

"I apologize for getting upset," I said quietly. "The physical pain and the emotional trauma were too much. I hope you understand."

"I understand," she responded warmly. "We all get that way at times." Then she straightened the sheets, fluffed the pillow, rearranged the cards and notes on the table, and poured me a glass of cold water. I watched as she busied herself with these tangible touches of concern. When she finished, I thanked her and she moved toward the door.

She turned the handle, paused, looked back and said, "Sleep well tonight . . . Pastor."

We both smiled.

I'm sure I heard another smothered giggle as she closed the door.

" 'No, Mrs. Blanton, it wasn't Haley's M.O. It was Halley's Comet! And it streaked across this room all afternoon!' "

I KNOW EXACTLY HOW YOU FEEL

Custodian John Welch was one of the most delightful persons on our church staff. He was friendly, helpful, and resourceful. There was a small strip of land between the driveway and a fence on Wilshire's north parking lot. John saw wonderful possibilities in this and planted a flourishing little garden next to one of the busiest boulevards in Dallas. In that garden he raised okra, greens, beans, and tomatoes. He loved to cook these and share them with the church staff.

John, a black man, was nearly six feet tall and looked like a beanpole. In fact, he couldn't have weighed more than one hundred and ten pounds, soaking wet. His toothless grin dominated his countenance, and every conversation was accentuated by large, bright, dancing eyes. He was the kind of person who would cause me to go out of my way just to enjoy a brief conversation with him.

One Wednesday afternoon, just a few weeks after my second heart surgery, I closed my office door, picked up my briefcase, walked slowly down the hallway, and headed out the door toward my car.

John saw me and called from around the corner. "Going home, Pastor?"

"Yes, John, I'm moving that way." I knew this was Wednesday, and in a couple of hours this place would be teeming with people coming to the fellowship dinner, prayer service, choir rehearsals, committee meetings, and planning sessions.

John nodded as I continued, "I'm just not up to it today. I'm out of energy and sapped of strength. I feel absolutely fatigued."

"Yes, sir," John replied with an understanding smile. "I know exactly how you feel."

"No, John," I responded, trying to be as respectful as possible, "I don't think you do understand how I feel. It's been only a few weeks since my second heart surgery—a surgery that lasted twelve hours and fifteen minutes—and I'm still trying to . . ."

"Oh, yes, sir, I do understand *exactly* what you're going through."

John's persistence came as a surprise to me. It seemed out of character for him to continue to dwell on understanding how I felt. With mild impatience, if not irritation, I put my briefcase down, looked him squarely in the face, and said, "How do you know how I feel?"

"Well, I can explain that," John replied.

"I'd be interested in hearing about it," I said as I leaned wearily against the wall.

"When I was nineteen years old," John began, "I had some trouble with my heart. My mother took me to the doctor and he said I had a serious problem that had been there since birth. He said I needed to have a heart operation as soon as possible or I would die."

I listened more intently. This was all new to me.

"They put me in John Peter Smith Hospital in Fort Worth and got me ready for surgery," John continued. His eyes got bigger as he talked, and he moved a step closer toward me to emphasize what he was saying.

"They put me on one of those stretchers and rolled me down a long hall. At the end of the hall were some double doors and they parked me there. I knew that I was next in line."

John had completely captured my attention, for now I was oblivious to anyone else passing by us in the hall.

"Go on," I encouraged.

"I lay there on that thing, scared half to death of what was about to happen, but knowing there wasn't much I could do about it. Suddenly the doors of the operating room opened and they rolled this man out on a stretcher. At least," my friend observed, "I think it was a man."

"Pastor," John lowered his voice and said barely above a whisper, "I rolled my eyes to my left to watch them roll the man out. And do you know what?"

"What?" I exclaimed. John had me hanging on to every word.

"His feet came by me first, and they were covered up. Then his body came by me, and it was covered up. And then his head came by, and it was covered up."

"I jumped off that stretcher. . . . I hit the floor and slid right under their arms and dashed out the building. I raced across a parking lot, leaped a fence, and headed for home."

John paused to let me get the full impact of the story, and then continued.

"Well, I stretched my neck, turned my head, and looked over my shoulders as they wheeled that man out—covered from feet to head. As they rolled him past me and on down the hall, someone took hold of my stretcher and started to roll me into the operating room. Pastor, I thought about it for half a second and said, 'Uh-oh! This ain't gonna' work!'"

The whispered tone was now gone from his voice, and he became more and more animated. His white eyes became larger with excitement and bounced in cadence as he spoke. His long arms picked up the beat of his story and all six feet of his body moved in rhythm. I listen and watched, fascinated and mesmerized.

"I jumped off that stretcher," John continued, "and ran full speed the length of the long hall. Two armed guards were on duty at the doors, and they saw me coming and locked arms to block me. I hit the floor and slid right under their arms and dashed out the building. I raced across a parking lot, leaped a fence, and headed for home."

John was now wearing a toothless grin that encircled his face. His eyes sparkled with devilish delight and every statement was punctuated by the slapping of his hands.

"I tell you," John cackled, "it was a miracle—an absolute miracle."

"What was a miracle?" I asked.

"That I didn't get arrested!"

"What do you mean, 'arrested'?"

"Now, Pastor, you've been in those hospitals, and you know the kind of gowns they make you wear. I never could get mine tied in the back. I ran down that hall, out the doors, across the parking lot, over the fence, and two miles until I got home. That gown was flappin' in the wind and my entire backside was bare. I was running so fast I didn't have time to stop and tie it together."

When our laughter subsided, John continued. "I tell you, it's a miracle. I could have been arrested for indecent exposure, but not a single Fort Worth policeman saw me. Yes, sir, it's a miracle."

"But, John," I asked with concern, "how are you doing now?"

"Fine, I guess. That was twenty years ago. My doctor has died, and I've not had a single pain since I leaped off that stretcher!"

We laughed together. "Thanks, friend," I said. "I think you really do understand."

I shook hands with him, picked up my briefcase, and walked toward the car.

I smiled to myself and silently thanked God for another miracle.

Strangely, the fatigue that I had experienced thirty minutes ago was now gone.

A GLIMPSE OF DAISY NELL

Daisy Nell was a character. And she was proud of it.

Daisy Nell had ways of announcing her arrivals that were unmistakable. Eight minutes after a worship service began, rustling sounds could be heard at the back of the sanctuary as ushers tried to accommodate her late arrival. The first seat offered was seldom satisfactory, so the rustling continued for another couple of minutes until she located the place she desired.

While this was going on at the back, people throughout the congregation would whisper to one another, "She's here." Little children would occasionally say out loud, "Mama, Daisy Nell is here."

Daisy Nell didn't intentionally try to disrupt a worship service or any other gathering, for that matter; she just couldn't help it. She was the kind of person whom you heard approaching, who filled a room when she arrived, and whose dust you saw when she left.

She was loud and boisterous and loved a good argument. The subject of debate really didn't seem to matter to her. Among her specialities, however, were the new church budget, taxes, relatives, Paul's missionary journeys, the price of groceries, and the length of hair worn by a church staff member. She would talk as long as anyone listened on any of these matters. I'm convinced that the Daisy Nells of life are sent to keep pastors humble, other staff members nervous, ushers hopping, and Sunday school teachers intimidated.

Daisy Nell was a challenge. Some of us thought—and hoped—that the aging process would soften her, but we were dreamers. Even when she was forced to use a walking cane for support, the steady, staccato banging of the stick announced her arrival. When she could no longer attend worship services or sit in her Sunday school class, she kept the telephone busy, asking questions, making suggestions, and expressing opinions. It was obvious that she was locked into a lifestyle that she could not, or would not, change. It seemed to be the one thing in the changing processes of life that she could hold on to.

Every new staff member, sooner or later, was initiated into the real world of ministry through an encounter with Daisy Nell. That was not in his, or her, job description, but it became a fact of life.

Joe Arganbright learned it the day after his arrival at Wilshire.

Joe was a student at Southwestern Baptist Theological Seminary in Fort Worth. He joined our staff as an intern in the children's ministry, working a couple of days each week and attending school the rest of the time. This was his first job, and he was eager to learn everything he could about the entire ministry of a local church.

"Why not?" reasoned Larry Shotwell, the minister of education at the time and Joe's supervisor. Why not let Joe visit Daisy Nell? It would be a good learning experience for him.

"Joe," Larry requested one Monday morning, "One of our older members has recently had gall bladder surgery. A part of being a church staff member involves working with *all* age groups in the church. Why don't you go with Mark Stanson, our minister of youth, and visit this lady?"

"That would be wonderful!" Joe exclaimed eagerly. "I want to learn everything I can about church work, including hospital visitation. I want to see it *all*."

"Fine," replied Larry. "The lady's name is Daisy Nell. She's a very large woman, and . . . "

"Thank you," Joe interrupted excitedly. "Thank you for this opportunity. I'm sure we'll have a good visit. I'll get Mark and we'll go immediately."

"One other thing," Larry offered, "Daisy Nell is . . . er . . . well . . . Daisy Nell is a unique person."

"I'll be excited to meet her. I'm taking a course in the seminary this semester in psychology and religion. I've been doing a lot of reading, and I'm getting a new understanding of people. This will be a great experience for me, I'm sure."

Larry smiled and said nothing.

Two hours later, Joe, the intern, was back in Larry's office, pale and shaken.

"Did you see Daisy Nell?"

"Did I see her?" Joe groaned. "Oh, brother, did I ever see her!"

"What do you mean?" Larry asked.

"Well, Mark and I tapped on the door, very lightly, and slowly pushed it open. Daisy Nell was on the bed with tubes going everywhere. And Larry, she really is a big woman. I've never seen so many tubes. Mark introduced me and told her that I was new on the staff and that this was my first visit. From what I've learned in my psychology and religion class I thought this would make a good impression on her—knowing that she was the first person I visited."

Larry nodded and Joe continued.

"It did make an impression, a bigger one than I expected."

Joe paused, weighing every word.

"Daisy Nell just looked at me and asked, 'Do you want to see my scar?' I didn't say anything, and neither did Mark. We simply stood there. But in one fling of her arm, tubes and all, she threw back the sheet and she wasn't wearing anything but the bandage that covered the scar! Larry, I mean . . . not a thing!"

"Daisy Nell just looked at me and asked, 'Do you want to see my scar?' "

Joe's eyes were as big as saucers and his face was ashen, but he couldn't stop talking.

"I really do want to do well on this job as an intern, and I'd like to find a permanent place later on to serve as director of children's work. I'll even be glad to visit other elderly people, but, Larry, please don't ask me to go back and see that lady. Please."

"Don't worry, Joe. Some of the rest of us will visit her in the next few days."

"Thank you, Larry. That relieves me, but I do have a problem. I'm supposed to write up all my visits for case studies in my psychology and religion class. What in the world can I say about this visit?"

Larry pondered the question for a moment, looked at poor Joe, and smiled understandingly.

"Just say you made a hospital visit and . . . *saw all of Daisy Nell!*"

11

A CHEERFUL HEART—GOOD MEDICINE!

She signed her name, "Minnie M. Moody," but everybody in my family called her "Punk." The name changing began when Aunt Minnie said to my then three-year old sister, Ella, "I think I'll call you 'Pumpkin.'" And Ella replied, "Then I'll call you 'Punk.'" The name stuck—for more than seventy years.

Punk was my favorite aunt and one of the all-time favorite persons I've known in life.

That may have been because she lived with us while I was growing up, or because she could make the best biscuits ever tasted, or because when I was a boy she paid me fifty cents each week to wash the windows of her dress shop on Main Street in Siler City, or because she would always slip me a twenty dollar bill when I came home from college. That was big money back in '42.

On the other hand, it may have been because she was such a delightful person, and she laughed a lot. She also had the rare gift of helping others learn to laugh.

A CLASSY LADY CALLED PUNK

Punk was Mother's youngest sister. In the 1930s, during the heart of the Depression when there were few business opportunities for women, she determined to own and manage her own store. She paid her dues to accomplish this, working for several years as a salesperson in a variety of stores in the area. By saving a portion of her meager salary each week she was able to put aside enough money to open "Moody's Shoppe," located between Roy Teague's Coffee Shop and the Hadley Hotel in Siler City. As a boy, I thought her spelling of "shoppe" gave the store a real touch of class. That seemed appropriate, for Punk had class also. The way she dressed, the way she threw her head back and sang as she walked the dirt road to work, and the way she helped many people—without anyone knowing—made her very special.

Everybody liked Punk. Her presence—in our home and at her store—attracted people to her. Every day familiar faces would drop by Moody's Shoppe for a brief visit with her, catch up on the news around town, and hear her latest story. On cold winter evenings we would gather as a family around the coal-burning fireplace, blistering on one side and freezing on the other, and she would keep us entertained by recounting humorous things that had happened at the store and "over at town," as we put it, that day. As she talked in her southern accent, she rolled her hair with curling irons heated by the coals of the fire. I sat intrigued, both by the stories and by the way she could roll her hair without burning her scalp with those things. Shoot, to a growing boy, these sharing times were almost as good as the ten-cent Saturday matinees at the picture show—serials included!

There were always beaus, or boyfriends, showing up at our place to see Punk on Sunday afternoons. We all knew that the front room—the one with the mohair sofa that scratched our legs—was reserved for her and her guest from two o'clock until six each Sunday. It was great fun to hide in the bushes to see which beau would show up or to see if he would try to give Punk a kiss when he left.

This spying and giggling was great fun . . . until one Sunday when Albert stayed and stayed—through three pots of coffee. Darkness settled in, and he still wouldn't leave. My twelve-year-old brother, whom we called Sip, and I were in our places under the bushes. I was on one end of the porch and Sip was on the other. We

"This spying and giggling was great fun . . . until one Sunday when Albert stayed and stayed—through three pots of coffee."

were waiting for that good-bye moment, but through the window we saw Punk head for the kitchen with the coffee pot, obviously preparing to brew the fourth pot. Poor Albert had overstayed his bladder and saw Punk's leaving the room as his merciful moment of opportunity. He quickly slipped out the front door, tip-toed to the end of the porch, and in the darkness relieved himself in preparation for the next pot of coffee. The end of the porch that Albert chose, luckily for me, was the end where Sip was hiding. He couldn't afford to cry out for Dad would have taken both of us out behind the barn if he had known what we were doing. So, poor Sip had no alternative but to duck his head and silently endure the baptism from above. He was thoroughly splattered! That ended our spying adventures on Sunday afternoons, and alas, we never even got to see Albert kiss Punk good-bye.

Years later, after Sip and I were grown, we confessed all this to Punk. She laughed until she cried. I couldn't figure out if she was laughing at Sip—or Albert.

In spite of the fact that several courted her, she did not marry until later in life. She and Jesse, an old friend from childhood days, had several good years together before his health failed.

Once on a trip back to North Carolina from Texas, I visited with Punk until late in the evening. Jesse had died; so had my father. Punk had moved back to Mother's house—into the very room that had been hers years ago. It was a good feeling just to see her back home. She had suffered a stroke and had just been diagnosed with cancer. She was also battling Parkinson's disease which slowed her pace and made every step uncertain.

From the recliner in which she rested, she pulled herself to an upright position, held her head high, squared her shoulders, and declared, "Bruce, I've just made me a decision." She emphasized the word, "me."

"What's that, Punk?"

"I'm going to have me some fun in life!"

I smiled and answered her in a teasing manner, "What in the world is a seventy-five-year-old woman in your condition going to do for fun?"

She thought about it for a minute, grinned, and replied, "Well, I think I'll begin by laughing at myself!"

And she did.

I kissed her goodnight and moved toward my own room. "Don't forget," I reminded her, "if you need me during the night just let me know."

I lay down with warm feelings about Punk laughing at herself and helping everybody else to laugh. I chuckled about the good times I had had as a little boy when she let me walk to work with her and the exciting times when she would let me spend an afternoon in my uncle's law office where she worked as a secretary, and the way she introduced me to every law client as her "best helper."

And I chuckled as I recalled the day when she taught me to spell "policeman."

I was five years old and she arranged with Mother for me to spend the entire day with her at the office. This was better than a trip west to the mountains or east to the beach. I could lean out the upstairs window of the office building and watch the traffic below. And twice during the day, I could watch the train from Greensboro to Sanford stop at the station one block away. That was about as much thrill as a boy could stand in one day.

Punk got caught up on her work late in the morning and decided that she and I should work on my spelling. For the next hour she had me memorizing the spelling of "policeman." I didn't realize it, of course, but she had a giggling purpose behind this. By twelve o'clock she was convinced that her five-year-old nephew was ready for what she had in mind.

Then she promised me a nickel if I would go down the steps, find Chief Pickett, the town's only policeman, and spell the word for him. Tightly squeezing the nickel in my hand, I inched toward the corner of Raleigh and Main streets where Chief could usually be found. I peeped around the corner of a building, and there he was, watching an occasional car drive by and chatting with a couple of store owners. There was something about his uniform, his badge, and his cap that overwhelmed me. He was standing beside his Model A Ford that had a siren mounted on the left fender. I figured that Chief must have been the most important person in the whole world. With fear and trembling I slowly inched toward him from the rear.

When I was barely two feet from him, I shouted nervously, "Policeman! P . . . o . . . l . . . i . . . c . . . e . . . m . . . a . . . n!"

Chief wheeled around quickly with a startled look on his face. Then, he looked down at me, shifted the plug of tobacco in his mouth, spat, and grinned. I didn't wait to enjoy the grin. The sight of his uniform and the sound of my own shrill voice startled me. I took off running, like a bank robber trying to reach his getaway car. I circled back around the corner and went up the steps to Punk's office two at a time. I just knew that I would spend the night in the city jail.

Punk soothed my feelings with another nickel and then walked to the corner with me and had a good laugh with Chief. He patted me on the head and told me I was a "right smart" boy to spell such a big word. He then let me look inside his Ford with the siren on the fender. Golly!

A double-dip cone of ice cream at Ed Kidd's Sandwich Shop later in the afternoon made it all the more worthwhile. It had been an exciting day—walking to the office, watching trains, learning to spell, being patted on the head by the most important man I'd ever seen, looking in his police car, and licking a double-dip cone of ice cream at Ed Kidd's. Shoot, there wasn't anything at the state fair down at Raleigh that could compare with this!

I smiled now as I pulled the covers snugly around me and turned out the light. It was good to be back home.

❧ ❧ ❧

At two o'clock in the morning I was awakened by a clatter and a crash. Leaping out of bed I raced through the house and found Punk on the floor under the kitchen table. Chairs were overturned, utensils were scattered across the room, her walker was upside down near the stove, and her glasses dangled from her left ear. A red bump on her forehead had already appeared.

"Punk, what on earth happened?"

"I was on my way to the bathroom, and I slipped and fell."

"Are you hurt badly?"

"No," she answered. Then, with a twinkle in her eye she said, "I fall easy."

A few weeks later I made another trip back to North Carolina. The cancer had spread and Punk was in the hospital and wanted to talk with me. When I entered her room at Chatham Hospital she reached up and hugged me and then motioned for me to close the door. I did and then pulled a chair up beside her bed. I sensed she had some very private and personal concerns that she wanted to discuss.

"It's not fair," she began. "It's just not fair."

Immediately I thought of her cancer and confinement and limitations. But I still raised the question, "What's not fair, Punk?"

"It's not fair for me to lie helplessly here . . . while there are so many people up and down these halls that need my help."

Words failed me as she continued. "I could feed them, read their mail to them, fluff their pillows, and just sit with them, but . . ."

Her voice trailed off and became barely audible. She closed her eyes.

This was Punk, the aunt that I had known through the years—a woman who, in spite of her own reversals, had taught me that life could be fun. And I loved her for that.

I sat by her bed, quietly holding her hand and feeling gratitude for all that she had taught me, including how to spell policeman. She stirred and opened her eyes.

"I'm not going to make it this time," she said calmly. "And it's all right. I've had a good life. We've all got to go sometime."

I choked back the tears.

"Will you come back from Texas and conduct my funeral?"

"Of course I will, Punk."

"Fine. Now here's how we'll do it. We'll sing two hymns, you read Psalm 24, and then make a few brief comments. Have everything over in fifteen minutes."

"I'll try," I said, "but I'm not sure about the time . . ."

"Fifteen minutes!" she ordered.

It was time to leave and drive to Greensboro to catch my plane back to Dallas. "Is there anything I can do for you before I go?" I asked.

" 'Now, can you see better?' I asked. 'No,' she replied with an impish grin, 'but I look better.' "

"Yes," she replied, "get my hairbrush."

"What do you want me to do with it?"

"Brush my hair."

I brushed gently the thin strands of hair on the top of her head.

"Anything else?"

"Yes, get my face powder and put a little on me."

"Fine," I said as I patted it on. "Would you like me to do anything more?"

"Yes, bring me my glasses and put them on me."

I picked them up, took a dry cloth and cleaned them, and placed them on her face. I smiled as I took a step back from the bed, grateful that there are some things that neither age nor illness can take away—completely. The Punk that I had known through the years smiled back at me.

"Now, can you see better?" I asked.

"No," she replied with an impish grin, "but I *look* better."

Three weeks later I conducted her memorial service. It lasted sixteen minutes—from start to finish.

Sorry, Punk. I tried, but the organ prelude was one page too long!

IT AIN'T OVER 'TIL IT'S OVER!

Almost every hospital visit was another story in my pastor's journal. One morning, the word came to the church office that Mr. Hopkins, an elderly man, was critically ill. I laid aside the books I was studying for next Sunday's sermon, canceled an appointment, and drove immediately to the hospital. He was in a private room on the third floor. I quietly opened the door and tiptoed in since he seemed to be either in a deep sleep or in a coma. Not wanting to disturb him, I moved to his bed and stood silently for a moment. A television set was on but the sound had been turned down. I glanced at it and saw that the Texas Rangers were playing another baseball game. A second glance indicated that they were losing, as usual.

Mr. Hopkins stirred, and I leaned over the bed. I was prepared to share a word of encouragement with him or to listen to any last words he wished to say to his pastor.

The old gentleman opened his left eye and looked at me. Then he turned his head slightly and stared at the television set. He sighed, closed his eye, and began to move his lips. I moved in closer to hear what I thought would be his last words.

He took a shallow breath, lifted his right hand from his side, pointed a bent finger toward the television and said barely above a whisper, "They . . . ought . . . to . . . fire . . . the . . . manager."

A week later, to the surprise of everyone, Mr. Hopkins was released from the hospital. He lived to see the manager fired. In fact, he lived to see three more hired—and fired!

LIVING IN THE MIDDLE OF A MIRACLE

It was early in the morning as I drove toward Monty Bower's small, prefabricated office. I wanted to get there before developers and contractors and salesmen arrived. I needed a few minutes with my friend alone. When Monty saw my car he smiled, threw open the door to the office, and waved for me to come on in. That's just like him, I thought—always smiling, always opening doors, and always waving. He was one of the most winsome and optimistic persons I had ever known.

"Welcome to the jungle," he said with a smile, as he closed the door behind us. "If you're looking for a job, I'll put you to work today."

"No thanks, Monty. I've got more than I can handle trying to pastor a church. But if two or three deacons and a couple of old soreheads don't ease up, I may be back in a couple of days."

"Just let me know, and you're hired, Pastor," he joked with a big smile. "But let me warn you, the pay isn't all that great, and it won't be until I get this property developed. Heck, if I tithed my money these days, the church would be paying me!"

We both laughed, and then we were silent.

"How are you, friend?" I asked. "And what can I do to help?"

"I'm not really asking God for a big miracle," Monty said quietly. "I just need two years."

I listened without response. What can one say—even if he is a preacher—to a special friend who has just been told that he has six weeks to live?

"Two years is all I need," he repeated. "I'm not asking for a big miracle—just two years. In twenty-four months I'll be able to complete the development of this tract of land. I can build a new house for Jean and the children, and I can also oversee the construction of a house for you and your family."

"Monty," I protested, "you don't have enough time or energy to think about building me a house. We'd love to be in this new area of the city and in a house with more room, but that's not a priority with us."

"It is with me," he countered with a note of finality. I knew that when Monty talked this way, there was no room for argument.

"Now, put your current house on the market for sale, and tell Lawanna to go to work sketching off the kind of new house she wants. Bring that drawing to me, and we'll start ordering the materials. Tell her to get her plans completed soon, for prices are going up. Also, tell her she can change her mind as often as she desires until we start construction. After that, we make no changes."

"But Monty, I don't think you're in the condition to . . ."

"You leave that with me and the Lord," Monty interrupted. "You just make sure that Lawanna starts sketching some plans."

My friend knew what his goals were and he stated them firmly; but the smile across his face betrayed the sound of his voice. That smile, and the warmth behind it, made Monty everybody's friend.

I drove away from the temporary office on the site of Lochwood Meadows, a new development area near White Rock Lake, confused and bewildered. Lord, why? It doesn't make sense, I cried within.

And it didn't.

A few years before, one of Dallas's leading newspapers had carried a half page story about Monty. He was a native of Dallas and a graduate of Southern Methodist University with a degree in business. Because of his reputation and integrity, he had been able to borrow one million dollars to buy one of the last wooded areas in Dallas for residential development.

This was a major undertaking for a thirty-five-year-old young man, especially in the middle of the decade of the sixties. But challenges didn't bother Monty one bit; indeed, he thrived on them.

I knew this about my friend and was glad to see the stories in the papers. But I also knew him as a devoted husband and father, a faithful churchman, and a sensitive, caring friend. Our wedding anniversaries fell on the same date, and Monty delighted in planning something extra special for the four of us to do in celebration of the occasion.

"Look, Doc, I don't have time to lie up here in bed for two or three days while you take these things out. Just cut it out now, and let me get back to the office."

Then came reversals. First, there was the melanoma, followed by surgery. Then his younger brother who helped him in the development project was killed instantly in an automobile accident. About the same time, a financial recession hit Dallas and construction ground almost to a halt. Through it all Monty's optimism and faith did not waver. Nor did his goals.

Now, this new diagnosis: Both lungs filled with nodules and fluid, and lymph glands saturated with cancerous cells. The prognosis: six weeks, at most.

Monty never slowed down. He was at work every day, pausing only to meet his surgeon in the emergency room of the hospital for the removal of another malignant node from his side.

"Look, Doc, I don't have time to lie up here in bed for two or three days while you take these things out. Just cut it out now, and let me get back to the office."

In spite of his commitment to fulfill his goals, there was nothing frantic or hectic about his lifestyle. He was busy, but there was a calm and quietness within. There was time for his wife, Jean, and their three young children. There was time for his parents and for friends. There was time for God and for worship. There was time to study Lawanna's sketches, coordinate the work of subcontractors, and oversee the building of our new house. There was even time to change the plans once after construction had begun. And he made the change with a smile.

"Monty," I said to him one day, "I'm concerned about you. You're pushing it too hard."

"I don't have time to die, Bruce. Not yet. I'm praying for time to finish these projects."

They were completed, all three of them. And more. Jean's house was built and the Lochwood Meadows development was saturated with construction. When we moved into our new home, one of the first things we did was to invite Monty and Jean over for a celebration dinner. Throughout the evening Monty kept getting up and moving from room to room, grinning, and checking to make sure that every detail measured up to his standards.

Shortly afterwards, his health began to fail rapidly. The last time I visited with him we talked briefly and had prayer together. I thanked him again for his friendship, and prepared to leave the room. He motioned me back.

Weakly, he signaled to me with raised fingers—two, then six.

Two . . . and six? What could he mean by that?

I moved back to the side of the bed, and he quietly said, "God is good. He always gives more than we ask. I asked for two years. He gave me two years . . . and six weeks."

And then he smiled.

So, the McIvers have lived for twenty-three years . . . in the house that Monty built . . . on Ridge Spring Drive . . . in the middle of a miracle called "Lochwood Meadows."

SOFT LEAVES, SUNSHINE, AND LAUGHTER

On a cold, damp November day a few years ago, my aged mother, better known as "Mommie Mac," fell in my sister's front yard in Greensboro and broke her hip. The rolling North Carolina landscape made it impossible for anyone to see her as she lay helpless and in pain on the ground. It was four long hours before a neighbor discovered her. She was taken to Cone Memorial Hospital where a series of X-rays were taken. They revealed a shattered hip, and surgery was performed immediately.

I received the call and flew to Greensboro as soon as possible to be with Mother and with Ella, my sister. When I arrived, the hip operation was over and Mother was awake and able to talk.

"Mother, I'm so sorry you had to lie there on the hard ground for four long hours before anyone heard you calling for help."

"But the leaves were soft." There was a quaint smile across her wrinkled face.

"But Mother, the ground was cold and damp from the drizzle that fell throughout the day," I protested.

"It was nice when the sun came out."

Then she quipped, "Do you know what the worst part of it all was? I was on my way to the mailbox, but I never got there." And with a snap in her eyes, she added, "I had to lie there four hours with no mail to read!"

The next three or four years were severe times of adjustment for Mother. She wanted her independence, but our family was concerned about her living alone. She might fall again and none of us would know it. Also, her eating habits left something to be desired when it came to nutrition. For instance, she loved fresh peaches and watermelons. She could go for two or three days and eat nothing else. Of course, while she was devouring peaches and watermelons, her blood count was dropping.

One day when I was home for a visit, I opened the refrigerator and spied half a watermelon. I pulled it out and prepared to cut a slice off it.

"Son, you'd better not do that," Mother said. "That's been in the refrigerator several days and it might not be good." Then she offered, in a good, motherly fashion, "Let me eat a few bites and make sure it won't make you sick."

I certainly didn't want my eighty-seven-year-old mother to get sick, but she had already taken the watermelon out of my hands and was testing it out.

Several minutes later when most of the melon had been happily tested, I said to her, "Mother, just how long is it going to be before you find out if that watermelon will make me sick?"

She grinned sheepishly and looked down at the thin rind in her hands.

Later in the afternoon, as a kind of peace offering for her forgetting and eating the entire half, she forced me to take some money and sent me off to buy another watermelon for both of us. We shared it this time, and neither got sick.

Who can live on watermelon alone? It's difficult to live alone when the aging processes overtake you. Reluctantly, the decision was made that Mother would move to Greensboro and live with Ella. My sister and her family graciously arranged for Mother to have her own special room, and they provided the best supportive care anyone could hope to receive.

Mother knew this was best, but her emotions lingered around the old homeplace. That's where her heart was.

Four years and two more hip operations later, Mother decided that it was time to make some decisions about the simple, but adequate, possessions that meant so much to her. After all, she was now ninety-two years old, and she knew that time was running out. So, she gathered her three grown children around her and began to take us all on a mental tour of the old frame house back in Siler City—room by room.

"Now, I don't want any discussion about this after I'm gone, so let's get it settled now," Mother declared like a true matriarch. Ella, Sip, and I looked at each other out of the corners of our eyes. We smiled discreetly, glad that Mother still had enough spunk to assert her wishes. She continued, "Who wants the dining room suite? . . . the sofa in the den? . . . the table that Daddy made? . . . the living room furniture? . . . the pictures on the wall?" While she asked the continuous questions, we tried to come up with suitable answers.

"Now you write it down," she insisted. "Write down every item and who gets it. I want all this taken care of today."

It was an emotional experience for us children as we visualized the house and furnishings and scribbled initials beside everything Mother mentioned. It signaled the end of an era, and we weren't ready for it.

But ironically, Mother seemed relieved. It was as if a burden had lifted from her shoulders.

"Now Mother, is there anything else you wish to say to us while we are all together?"

"Yes," she replied. "Sell the homeplace."

"Sell the homeplace? The house? The one that you and Dad built with your own hands? The one we all grew up in?"

"Yes, sell the house. I'll never be able to live there again, and it doesn't need to just sit there. Sell it."

"If that's what you want . . ."

These were somber decisions that touched the very roots of my life. I had been born in that house. I had lived out my boyhood there. I had eaten and slept there. I had gathered with the family around the small fireplace on cold evenings and listened to the stories that warmed my heart. I had played in the yard, climbed the trees, and drunk fresh water from the old well. This was not just a house; this was home. Sell our home? Sell my home?

Yes, sell it.

While I was reliving childhood and mulling through memories, Mother had moved on to other matters and was telling one of her stories. In the process she became tickled. The more she talked, the harder she laughed. Soon she was out of control. Whatever story she was telling was lost completely in the hilarity of the moment.

"Mother," I asked, "what on earth has happened to you?"

She took a deep breath, wiped her eyes, and said calmly, "I was just thinking. I hope all of this fun doesn't stop when I die."

We looked at each other in silence.

It won't, Mother, I vowed to myself. *I promise, it won't.*

Two years later Mother had one last story to tell me. Why she chose to share it at this special time and this particular occasion I'll never know. Maybe she felt that it was just too good to keep.

Her body was weak and swollen. Ninety-four years had taken its toll, but her spirit was strong and her mind was alert. She sat erect in her chair, looked out the window and launched into the tale.

She was thirteen years of age and was playing the piano for the revival services at the Rives Chapel Baptist Church, located out in the country about a mile from where she lived. She wasn't a gifted pianist, she admitted, but she was about as good as anybody else in the community, so they called on her to assist.

There was a woman who lived on a farm near the church named Mrs. McBane. It seems, according to Mother, that Mrs. McBane had a baby every year . . . on schedule. That meant that one was always nursing.

Well, Mrs. McBane came faithfully to the revival services every day. When her baby became hungry, she fed the child as any good mother would do—during the song service, during the offering, during the sermon, whenever. This was just a natural part of having babies and nurturing them, and it didn't bother Mrs. McBane a bit. No one else paid much attention, either, until . . . until the preacher gave the altar call. Mother was playing the piano, the congregation was singing, and the preacher was pleading for people to come down to the altar and confess their sins. As several flocked toward the front of the church, Mrs. McBane got caught up in the spirit of the revival. Mother looked up, and here she came down the aisle, nursing her baby. As she got closer to the altar, she began to shout and dance. In the middle of this excitement, the poor baby got disconnected from his food supply. The baby was bouncing in one direction, and the exposed upper portion of Mrs. McBane's anatomy was bouncing in the other.

One of the older ladies near the front grabbed a shawl and tried to cover Mrs. McBane. But she kept dancing in circles and was hard to catch. Mother tried to concentrate on the hymn that she was playing, but she kept missing notes. No one noticed. There was too much action at the front of the church to be concerned about a few wrong notes.

Mother paused in telling her story and said, "Son, do you know what was more embarrassing to me than anything else?"

"What, Mother?"

"Well, Punk was about seven or eight years old. She was sitting with the preacher's wife, and the preacher's wife didn't always act like a preacher's wife should. Both of them got so tickled that they laughed out loud. I looked out and started watching them, and that's why I kept hitting all those wrong notes."

" 'Mother,' I asked, 'what on earth has happened to you?' She took a deep breath, wiped her eyes, and said calmly, 'I was just thinking. I hope all of this fun doesn't stop when I die.' "

"Mother," I asked, "what was Mrs. McBane's decision that day? What did she come forward to confess at the altar?"

Mother wiped the tears of laughter from her eyes. "Between all that dancing and bouncing and shouting and crying baby, and that old woman chasing her and trying to cover her up, we never did find out."

I dabbed my own eyes, hugged her up, and patted her swollen stomach. It was the size of a large watermelon. She saw the concern on my face.

"Sure hope I'm not pregnant," Mother snickered at me with a ninety-four-year-old grin. And then she added, "Don't forget Abraham's wife, Sarah!"

"You're too much," I said as I kissed her. "I've got to go, or I'll miss my plane back to Dallas."

But I really didn't want to go back to Dallas. I wanted to linger here, near the roots that gave me permission to laugh, even in the shadow of death.

I hugged her again, walked out of the house, and said to my sister who was driving me to the airport, "Ella, that woman will have us laughing at her funeral."

That was Tuesday afternoon. On Friday Mother died. On Sunday we buried her.

As the long blue limousine carrying the family pulled into the cemetery, my sister recalled what Mother had said in Dallas a year before, on the occasion of my thirtieth anniversary and retirement as pastor of Wilshire. We were all dressed and ready to leave our house to attend the special services.

"Doesn't your son look nice?" Ella had said to Mother, who limped toward the door on her cane.

"I reckon so," Mother had replied, "but he would look nicer if he would just zip up his pants!" I had looked down, and sure enough, Mother had been right.

When Ella finished the story—and just as the limousine came to a halt by the grave site—the whole car erupted in laughter.

"Look, folks," I pleaded, "we can't afford to get out of this funeral car laughing. It's just not proper. What will all those folks in the funeral procession think of us? Now everybody, try get hold of yourselves! We're headed for a grave side service, and we need to look dignified."

We pulled it off, but now and then I wonder if "Mommie Mac" wasn't looking down upon us . . . and chuckling.

Her last gift to me was the story of the dancing, half-naked woman at the altar.

And laughter.

I got out of the car, walked with deceptive dignity behind the funeral director toward the open grave, and vowed again, *No, Mother, the laughter won't stop.*

I promise.

12

YOU WANT ME TO DO WHAT?

It was Thursday, officially listed on my calendar as my "day off." But, for some reason, neither the telephone, the hospitals, nor people in need ever consulted my calendar. Thursday was just another day.

This particular Thursday I decided to try to beat the system. My plan was simple: dress in old clothes, have Lawanna take all calls, think positively, and paint the bathroom. My plan worked like a charm for about an hour and a half. Then the telephone rang and Lawanna answered it in the den. I could hear her saying, "yes," and "I'm so sorry," and "he'll want to know about this," and "let me call him to the phone." I heard her coming down the hall, stepping around buckets of paint and ladders.

"Bruce, I really think you need to take this one," Lawanna said. "It's Mrs. McDowell, and she sounds distraught."

Poor Mrs. McDowell had reason to be distraught. Her husband, whom everyone affectionately called Pappy, had been in the hospital several days for a series of tests. The doctors knew that he was seriously ill but were unable to arrive at a clear diagnosis. This had been stressful for both of them. They were caught in the aging problems of life and were having difficulties, physically and emotionally, coping with what was happening.

I took an old rag, dipped it in turpentine, cleaned my hands, and picked up the phone.

"Yes, Mrs. McDowell?"

"Pastor, come to the hospital quickly! Pappy is dying. I need you this minute."

"I'm so sorry, Mrs. McDowell. I'll get down there as soon as possible, but I've been painting, and it will take a few minutes to get cleaned up and dressed and to drive across the city."

"No, Pastor, please come now. As soon as you can possibly get here. I need you badly."

Obviously, this was no time to mention the words, "day off," or "painting" or "family plans." Pappy was dying and Mrs. McDowell needed me. There was no decision left for me to make. I needed to drop everything and go.

"Mrs. McDowell, I'll be there in thirty minutes."

"Please hurry."

I quickly scrubbed my hands again with the rag soaked in turpentine. Thankfully, most of the paint came off, but the reek was awful. I then washed them thoroughly with soap, pulled on some decent clothes, and ran out the door. The twenty-five-minute drive to the hospital gave me the opportunity to think and to put things in perspective:

Crises do not come in an orderly fashion. . . . Personal ministry involves sensitivity to the needs of the moment. . . . Some of life's greatest opportunities are found in interruptions. . . . There are a lot of things more important than painting a bathroom. . . . There will be other Thursdays. . . . This is what ministry is all about.

By the time I drove into the hospital parking lot I was feeling better about my mission, and my day off. There was no question about it; I had made the right decision. Even the turpentine smelled better.

WHITE SHEETS . . . GURNEYS . . . AND PAPPY?

When I entered the corridor of the hospital I punched the elevator button and ended up on the second floor where Pappy was a patient. Mrs. McDowell, an elderly lady, and her middle-aged daughter were in the small waiting room located near the nursing station. They greeted me warmly and, to my surprise, began talking about ordinary things—the weather, the traffic, and the church. They asked about my family and expressed interest in each member. As they continued to talk I had my hand in my coat pocket ready to pull out a small Bible. I had planned to read a comforting passage of Scripture, such as Psalm 23, but I just didn't seem to be able to get my foot in the door. I had come to minister to them in their grief, but they wouldn't give me a chance.

Something didn't add up. While they talked about the rising prices of groceries and how good the food was in the cafeteria where they had lunch, I slipped over to the nursing station.

"Please tell me about Mr. McDowell," I said with concern to the nurse behind the desk.

"Oh, he's fine," she responded.

"Fine?" I questioned. "Then he hasn't taken a turn for the worse?"

"Crises do not come in an orderly fashion. . . . Personal ministry involves sensitivity to the needs of the moment. . . . Some of life's greatest opportunities are found in interruptions."

"Oh, no. In fact he's up on the third floor now—in X-ray."

Unbelievable. I moved slowly back to the reception area, trying to figure out my role in this situation and dealing with all kinds of ambivalent emotions. Before I could sit down, the doors of the elevator opened and a man was rolled out on a gurney, or stretcher. Mrs. McDowell jumped up and exclaimed, "That's Pappy!" She then rushed to the gurney and grabbed the left hand of the man, followed by her daughter who took his right hand.

Now, I knew Pappy; at least, I thought I did. He had been a member of the church for years and had been faithful in attendance until his recent illness. He was a large man—just like the man on the gurney. He was nearly bald—just like the man on the gurney. I looked at the patient with confused hesitation, but thought better about saying anything. After all, a person's appearance does change when glasses and teeth are removed, and when a sheet is pulled up under the neck. Besides, his wife and daughter are both here. Who am I to question?

So, the three of us walked alongside the gurney down the long hall. Mrs. McDowell was on the left, holding the man by his hand, saying repeatedly, "Pappy, we're right here with you; we love you. We love you." The daughter was on the opposite side, clinging to his other hand, saying, "Pappy, you're going to be fine; everyone loves you; we're going to stay right here with you. Isn't it nice that the pastor came to see you?"

More confusion and hesitation. But I had come to the hospital to minister, and though the situation was not what I anticipated, I intended to minister. So, I trailed along behind the gurney, bending over and waving my hand over the man's face. "Sir, we're all here; we're praying for you." My gestures must have resembled an unrefined Baptist "papal blessing!"

The old man rolled his eyes back and forth from Mrs. McDowell to her daughter. Then, he rolled them far back in his head and gave me a bewildering, perplexing look. I just kept on waving my hand and "blessing" him.

This procession continued until we reached the end of the corridor where another set of elevators were located. The attendant pushed the button, and the old man was rolled onto the elevator. As the door was closing he was still looking from the left to the right and at me.

Mrs. McDowell, her daughter, and I went back to the reception area.

Silence. Not one word.

Finally, Mrs. McDowell spoke. "You know," she said pensively, "that didn't look like Pappy."

"Mama, I don't believe that was Pappy," the daughter responded.

I strangled on what I had just heard, excused myself, and moved again toward the nursing station.

"Can you tell me where Mr. McDowell is now?" I asked.

"Sure," the helpful nurse responded as she checked the charts. "He's still up on third floor in X-ray!"

Now, I've often wondered what that old man must have thought as he was rolled down the hall on the gurney . . . with a strange woman on one side holding his hand and professing her love to him . . . and another woman on the other side assuring him that she was going to stay right here with him . . . and some strange preacher, reeking with turpentine, waving his hand over his face and offering to pray for him.

"Please, Doc, don't ever give me another shot like the last one. You won't believe what it did to me! I hallucinated all the way down the hall. There were all these weird people walking alongside me. Just don't ever give me that shot again!"

A few days later Pappy's son telephoned me and apologized for my being called to the hospital that day. Pappy was showing some progress, he said.

"Please, Doc, don't ever give me another shot like the last one. You won't believe what it did to me! I hallucinated all the way down the hall. There were all these weird people walking alongside me. Just don't ever give me that shot again!"

"Mama just gets lonely, and she starts dialing people she wants to see. That's her way of gathering a crowd to keep her company."

It was four Thursdays later before I finished painting the bathroom.

Pappy's progress didn't last long. He took a turn for the worse, and seven Thursdays later we buried him.

At least, I *think* it was Pappy that we buried.

AS THE WORLD TURNS

Ida and Henry Perkins were typical of many people who lived in Dallas. Their family roots were in the rural area of East Texas, and they had never adjusted to city life. After more than a quarter of a century as Dallasites, they still talked about the pasture and the cows, the garden and the "veggies," the little brick church they attended, and "Brother Leroy" who was once their pastor. And, they bragged about how friendly everybody was back home.

They tried to adjust to Wilshire, but there was always something that seemed to bother them about the church. Either the organ was too loud, or I didn't preach loud enough, or the temperature in the sanctuary was too hot or too cold, or we didn't sing "the good ole songs," or the people "jest weren't as friendly as they oughta be."

In spite of all this, the Perkins and I managed to get along. I tried to listen to them, respect their background, tease them, and understand them. I also told them a lot of stories about my roots in the small town of Siler City in North Carolina. They liked that.

Henry's health began to fail, and Ida just ran out of energy. She was no longer able to care for him at home. A difficult decision was made to place Henry in a nursing home across the city. Ida couldn't drive a car, but this should not be a major problem, we reasoned, since there were excellent bus services to the very door of the nursing home.

We reasoned wrong.

Ida didn't like buses. She couldn't think of anything wrong with them; she just preferred to "ride in a car like everybody else." Besides, they didn't have any buses in her small town when she grew up.

So, there. Ida had spoken. Case closed.

The kind and patient ladies in her Sunday school class took turns driving her to see Henry. And a couple who lived two doors down the street from her took her a few times. Some of our deacons who were retired pitched in and helped with transportation when they could. Ida had everybody hopping, and she enjoyed it thoroughly.

One day in November, a cold, wet Texas norther came roaring through Dallas. Frigid air swept down from the Rockies, picked up speed across the panhandle, and gathered moisture as it hurdled across west Texas. By the time it reached Dallas, the wind was blowing in gales, the rain was mingled with hail and pelting the streets, and the temperature was dipping below freezing.

In the midst of this, Ida called. It was ten o'clock in the morning.

"Pastor, I'm worried about Henry. I really am. I'm afraid he's cold over there in that nursing home. I just want to make sure he has a couple of blankets on his bed and that his room is warm. Would you drive me across town to see him for a few minutes? I'd sure appreciate it, and I know he would."

I understood Ida's concern, for the drastic change in the temperature sent icy chills throughout the entire body. It was about as cold as I could remember, and frankly, it warmed my heart to see how much she cared about Henry. So, I juggled appointments, postponed a luncheon, and drove down the already slick streets to Ida's house to pick her up.

She was standing on the small porch waiting for me. Before I could stop in front of her house, she hurried down the sidewalk toward the car. I cringed, hoping that she would not slip and fall. Before I could get out and assist her she opened the back door and climbed in.

"Ida, wouldn't you like to sit up here with me?"

"No, I like to ride in the back seat. Let's go."

I glanced in the rear mirror and she was in the center—the very center—of the seat. I soon learned that she sat there so she could get a better view of the streets and could tell me every turn to make.

"Now turn here, Pastor . . . no, not at this street . . . the next one. . . . Watch that car on your left. . . . You can't trust the drivers in this city. . . . Angle to the right at the next stop. . . . Are you sure the windshield wipers are on full speed? . . . Do you have your headlights on?"

When we reached the nursing home, she insisted that I remain in the car.

"I know Henry would like to see you, but I'll only be a moment. Just want to make sure he's warm. I'll be sure and tell him that you brought me over. Now, you just keep the motor running and the heater on. I'll be back in no time at all."

With those words she opened the door and was gone.

"My," I thought, "Ida sure is in a hurry." I was too cold, however, to try to figure out what was going on in Ida's head. My own cold feet got in the way of any logical thinking. Nine minutes later—by the watch—Ida came out of the nursing home, scooted down the sidewalk, opened the back door of the car, and practically fell into the seat.

Without pausing to catch her breath, she said, "Henry's fine . . . said to tell you 'hello' and 'thanks' . . . he's warm . . . two blankets . . . now we can hurry home."

"Ida," I said, "I have one stop to make on the way back. I've ordered some materials for my office, and they're ready to be picked up. It will only be a few blocks out of the way and shouldn't take more than fifteen minutes. I'd like to swing by and get them while I'm in this area. It will save me another trip over here. Besides, the streets may be iced over completely in a few hours."

Ida didn't respond. I glanced in the rear view mirror and saw that for the first time she was leaning all the way back in the seat. Her arms were crossed, and she had a stern, sullen look on her face. She was pouting.

"Are you doing all right, Ida?" I asked.

"Well, I was," she answered as she glanced at her watch, "but it's 12:05 now, and I'm going to miss my favorite television program, 'As the World Turns,' if we don't make it back home by 12:30."

I drove straight to the place where I was to pick up my materials. My passenger on the back seat no longer directed traffic for me. All conversations ceased. Ida pouted all the way home.

Henry died a few weeks later.

" 'Are you doing all right, Ida?' I asked. 'Well, I was,' she answered as she glanced at her watch, 'but it's 12:05 now, and I'm going to miss my favorite television program, "As the World Turns," if we don't make it back home by 12:30.' "

We held his memorial service at the church at ten o'clock in the morning. Ida suggested the time. The temperature in the chapel was carefully adjusted. The organist played softly, and at Ida's request the vocalist sang "In the Garden" and "Rock of Ages." I spoke a little louder than usual. Ida rode to the cemetery on the back seat of the funeral home's black limousine.

After the grave side service everybody spoke to Ida, and a lot of people hugged her. Ida smiled and whispered to me, "I do believe, Pastor, that this was the sweetest—the very sweetest—service I've ever attended."

She then turned to a small group of friends and said, "You are the friendliest people I know. Thank you for coming. I love you all, but if you'll 'scuse me I really need to get back to the house. I'm very tired. I hope you understand." They nodded that they did.

Ida walked quickly toward the limousine. The door was opened for her and she got in the back seat—alone.

As the long car traveled faster than usual out of the cemetery, I looked at my watch. It was 11:55.

Ida had just enough time to get home to see "As the World Turns" at 12:30!

A HODGEPODGE OF REQUESTS

There have been other strange requests across three decades that left me muttering, "You want me to what?" Here are a few of them.

From an angry mother:

"Pastor, my little girls were picked up early this morning by some members of a church that has a bus ministry. I didn't know anything about the church, but I thought it was nice that they would offer door-to-door service. My children came home following the service soaking wet. The preacher asked them if they wanted to 'go to heaven,' and they said, 'yes.' So, he baptized them right there in the middle of the service. They don't have any idea what it means to be baptized. All they know is that they are cold and wet. They're in the other room sneezing their heads off right now. Pastor, can you please come to my home as soon as possible and *unbaptize* my children?"

From a frightened husband:

"Bruce, I need your help. It's really urgent. My wife is the angriest person I've ever seen. She has already thrown a hammer at me, but she missed and knocked a hole in the wall of the house. She's in her room upstairs now, and she has a gun. If I try to take it away from her, she'll kill me. But if you take it from her, she won't shoot you, because you're a man of God. Please get over here as quickly as you can!"

From an elderly woman whose husband had just died:

"Preacher, you don't have to be concerned about saying a lot at my husband's funeral. Most anything will be all right since he wasn't much of a Christian."

From a young couple that I had never seen before:

"Your name was given to us as someone who would help us. We're not fit parents for our nine-month-old baby. That's why we've come to your office this morning. We've got our bus tickets and are leaving the city. Here, take our baby. We give her to you."

And with those words they handed me a beautiful little girl, carefully wrapped in a worn blanket, and walked out.

I picked up the baby, held her for a moment, and thought of my own children. Then, through tears, I managed to dial one of Dallas's most responsible adoption agencies, one that I had

---

"Pastor, can you please come to my home as soon as possible and* unbaptize *my children?"

---

worked with on other cases. Within three hours the baby girl was accepted by the agency, and later she was placed for adoption.

Today, somewhere in this city—or elsewhere—there's a twenty-seven-year-old young lady that I held briefly in my arms when she was less than a year old. I wonder . . . I hope . . . that she was adopted and nurtured and loved by "fit parents."

From a once-every-five-years church attender:

"Is this the pastor of the church? Do you pronounce your name 'McQuiver,' or 'McKivert'?

"Well, anyway, sir, I'd like to place an order for three chocolate pies, a couple of pound cakes, a baked ham, potato salad, and a couple of green salads. And, we'll need iced tea for about thirty people."

Silence.

"You are pastor of the church, aren't you? The Wilshire Baptist Church, located on Abrams Road? I'm a member there . . . well, . . . I attend services there occasionally, . . . I think it's a beautiful church. . . . You do furnish food when someone in the family dies, don't you? My cousin—she was my very favorite cousin—died this morning, and I just wanted to get my order in so the food could be delivered to my house . . . and . . ."

From a disturbed wife:

"I know it's five-thirty in the morning, but John just left the house, and I just had to talk to you for we are having trouble over our television set 'cause I like to watch it and he don't. Would you and Mrs. McIver please get in your station wagon right now and come to my house and load this set up and haul it off before John gets back so it won't break up our marriage? It's heavy, but I believe the two of you can lift it. I don't care what you do with it; just get it out of our house and save our marriage!"

As I put down the phone, Lawanna—eight-and-a-half months pregnant—rolled over (with no small effort) and asked, "Who was that calling this early in the morning?"

I told her.

"What in the world did she want?"

"Never mind. Try to go back to sleep. You'd never believe it if I told you."

13

BUILDING BRIDGES AND MENDING FENCES

The luncheon at the large downtown Dallas hotel was one of the most prestigious ever held. Notables from all over the city gathered to honor a man who had been named the "Outstanding Volunteer in the Health Field."

Charlie Watson, the honoree, served as a trustee of both Parkland Hospital and Baylor Hospital. He was also affiliated with more than thirty other agencies and boards in the greater Dallas area. In addition to these responsibilities, Charlie was a husband and a father, a vice-president and director of Dallas Power and Light Company, and a deacon at Wilshire Baptist Church. Even more meaningful to me, Charlie was my friend. He was never too busy to listen to my concerns or to reschedule a luncheon so we could have a quiet visit. I leaned heavily on him.

I was invited to lead the invocation for the luncheon and Charlie introduced me. In his introduction he told the story of the three preachers discussing what each would do if he inherited a million dollars.

The Methodist said he would give his money for education. The Presbyterian said he would use his inheritance to build hospitals.

Charlie had the audience in the palm of his hand. Everyone began to sense the conclusion. Knowing looks were exchanged by guests throughout the banquet room and people at every table were smiling. This turned Charlie on even more as he reached for the punch line.

"And the Baptist," Charlie continued after a dramatic pause, ". . . and the Baptist preacher said, 'I'd check to make sure that the money was in the bank, in my own name, and that no one else could get it out. Then, I'd call my deacons together and tell them all to go to hell!' "

The audience roared. But Charlie wasn't through. With perfect timing he turned toward me and said, "And now, *my Baptist pastor* will lead us in the invocation."

That was too much! The dignity of the notables of Dallas went down the drain, and sophistication was forgotten as they pounded the tables and slapped one another on the back. I rose, hesitantly, aware that every person in the large room was watching me, wondering about my reaction. The truth was, I liked the story. As I tried to pray, I heard snickering from all directions.

The luncheon was a great success. The meal was delicious, the music outstanding, and the accolades given Charlie were appropriate. But the hit of the occasion was his story about the three preachers. People left the luncheon saying, "I can't wait to tell my pastor that story."

Charlie hugged me in his characteristic way and said, "I love you, Pastor. Call me if there's ever anything I can do." I'd heard those very words from him scores of times, but they always seemed fresh. He really meant them.

Any hint of embarrassment that I had felt over the story had long faded and I walked away from the luncheon with a warm feeling. *Every pastor needs a friend like Charlie; so does every church congregation*, I thought.

The two of us had been through a lot together and most of the church members were unaware of it. Charlie and his wife, Lufan, had kept Kathie on numerous occasions while Lawanna and I were out of the city. They were the kind of people that looked for special ways they could help without calling attention to themselves. This was most refreshing.

THE DAY LAUGHTER SAVED THE PROGRAM

Charlie also had served on some of the most strategic committees in the church. He and I had recently spent days together trying to find some institution, or individual, who would loan Wilshire enough money to build a new sanctuary. The loan was finally secured, and a congregational meeting was scheduled to discuss the initial architectural sketches.

It was not a good meeting. It was like having five hundred interior decorators designing a house; or twenty lawyers debating the same legal case; or ten surgeons making the same incision. Everyone wanted to design, discuss, and cut.

"How many columns will the new sanctuary have?"

"Three?"

"Why not four? I like four better than three."

"Will we get a chance to vote on three versus four?"

"When can we vote?"

And from that lofty high, the meeting sort of trickled downhill. The people had a right to know; that's the "Baptist way." Besides, they're the ones paying for it, so . . . we listened . . . and listened.

When the meeting was finally, and thankfully, over, Charlie and a few other deacons met in my office at my request. I wanted to talk with them about a personal matter. A committee from another church in Texas had approached me about the possibilities of becoming their pastor. Such a move could affect the new building program because most churches are reluctant to proceed with major programs without pastoral leadership.

My decision had been made to remain at Wilshire, and I wanted to share this with these leaders before any word leaked out concerning contacts made by another congregation. I felt this was only fair to clear the atmosphere and to get on with our building program.

We slowly trudged into my office and plopped down—tired and drained. For the next thirty minutes the conversation was about half a notch above the "three column versus four column" discussion we had just experienced. Things weren't helped when we tried to analyze what had gone wrong in the general church discussion. The more we analyzed, the more we became discouraged; the more we became discouraged, the more we looked for someone to blame. We were all frustrated and emotionally depleted.

As we replayed the same record for the fourth time, I picked up my briefcase and moved toward the door.

"Where are you going, Pastor?"

"Home," I answered tersely.

"But you called us to your office because you said you had something you wanted to share with us!"

"Forget it," I said in an uncharacteristic way as I walked out the door. "Just forget it!"

I drove straight home, told Lawanna what I had said and done, went to bed, and didn't sleep a wink all night. I tossed and tumbled and tried to pray—if you could call it praying.

Lord, how could something like that happen? These men are my best friends, and I'm their friend. What does this do to the building program? Who cares about three columns or four columns? Maybe I should reconsider the offer from the other church. And Lord, I'd apologize, but I don't know to whom . . . or for what. No, I won't apologize for a situation I didn't create. Maybe someone should apologize to me.

On and on it went all through the long night. I thought morning would never come. The whole thing was like a family discussion that had gone sour or a family meal that had ended in tears. There wasn't any one thing that caused it; it just happened.

And it hurt. It hurt because proven friends had disagreed—though we were not sure over what. It also hurt because the church building program was at stake. And it hurt because there were so few people I could share this with. This would accomplish little. Besides, confidences—even among trusted friends—are often hard to keep. So, I talked with Lawanna and wrestled with my own frustrations.

Shortly after daybreak I dressed, left home, and sought solitude in the back booth of an out-of-the-way restaurant. I looked aimlessly at the coffee cup and slowly stirred the contents. I felt trapped—hedged in—and discouraged. The whole thing seemed so ridiculous, so silly. There just had to be a way to solve this dilemma.

"I called Lawanna and told her what I had done. She gasped, and began packing . . . for real! 'I think the Lord will be calling us to another church—real soon,' she said."

And then it hit me. It might work; and if it didn't, I wouldn't be any worse off than I was now. It was worth the chance.

I jumped up, paid my bill, ran out of the restaurant, and drove hurriedly to the office. Fortunately, one of the secretaries had arrived early.

"Quick!" I called to her. "Send a telegram to Charlie Watson, Vice-President, Dallas Power and Light Company, Dallas, Texas."

She looked at me with a big question on her face.

"I'll explain later," I said as I thought, *if there is a "later."*

"Here's the message: Dear Charlie, I've just inherited a million dollars."

"Is that all?" the secretary asked with a bewildered look.

"That's all, except sign it 'Pastor,' and send it *collect!*"

I called Lawanna and told her what I had done. She gasped, and began packing . . . for real!

"I think the Lord will be calling us to another church—real soon," she said. And then she added, "And He'll probably start calling you about the time Charlie receives that telegram!"

The next two hours of waiting were agonizing, sheer torture.

At eleven o'clock a telegram arrived at my office. I signed for it with a trembling hand and ripped open the envelope.

"Dear Pastor," it read. "Congratulations. Suggest you make a generous contribution to our new building program. Charlie."

It was also sent . . . *collect!*

Later in the day I called Charlie. We couldn't do much talking because Charlie kept laughing hysterically and pounding his desk with his fist. I gathered, between his guffaws, that he also had spent a sleepless night trying to figure out how to "rebuild the bridge."

Later, when the laughter subsided, he observed, "Bruce, what happened in your office last night was the silliest thing I've ever seen. Our emotions were drained from the congregational meeting, and we should have gone on home. Instead, we ended up fussing among ourselves, and we're all best friends."

And then he added, "I spent a part of the night, and most of this morning, trying to figure how we could rebuild the relationship. That telegram was the perfect answer."

In a few hours we were all reconciled.

A year later the new sanctuary was completed and dedicated.

Twenty-five years later, Charlie and I still meet for lunch. We talk . . . and remember . . .

. . . and laugh.

I CAN'T REMEMBER YOURS EITHER

The older ladies' Sunday school dinner seemed to be the perfect place to strengthen relationships. Many of the women who would be there were either widowed or divorced and lived daily with loneliness. A pastoral touch could be very encouraging.

"Kermit," I said to my associate pastor, "this is one invitation we should accept. We should be at that dinner. I realize that both of us are tied up night after night in meetings, and all we need is another dinner to attend, but I have a funny feeling about this one. Some of the ladies in that class have felt that we really don't know them, and this will give us a chance to build better rapport with them."

Kermit, gracious as ever, agreed with me. He was relatively new on the staff at that time and welcomed opportunities to become better acquainted with all the members of the church. Small dinners provided the perfect occasion for this to take place.

"I'll pick you up at 6:45," I volunteered. "We'll eat with the class members, visit for a few minutes, and then slip out. They'll understand."

A couple of hours later I pulled up in front of my associate's house, honked the horn for him, and we were soon on our way. As we drove north on Mockingbird Lane I offered what I thought was a helpful suggestion. "Look, Kermit," I said, "I've been pastor here for six years now, and you've been on the field only a few weeks. Don't worry about names. I'll probably be able to call the name of everyone there. Just let me take the lead, and I'll help you through the evening."

Kermit agreed and thanked me for being so thoughtful. Five minutes later I turned right and drove down Camden Street. I was proud that I could show my associate that I was well acquainted with the city and that I knew exactly how to get to the house where the dinner was being held.

We were greeted warmly at the door and ushered into a room filled to overflowing with happy, bubbling women. I knew that for some this dinner was one of the highlights of the year.

"Goodness," the hostess exclaimed, "we must be important for *both* of you to show up." I glanced at Kermit and gave him a knowing smile. We were already making points and building bridges.

Two long tables, borrowed from the church, had been set up side by side in the living room. At the ends of each table were arrangements of fresh flowers gathered from the yards of the ladies attending the dinner. Obviously, the class members had pooled their finest silverware and serving pieces for the occasion. The aroma and presentation of the food rivaled any restaurant in Dallas.

All of this, plus the presence of the pastor and the new associate pastor!

It was predictable that I would be called upon to "ask the blessing." I thanked the Lord for delicious food, for a good church, for wonderful relationships, and for opportunities to get to know one another better. When the "Amen" was said, you could almost feel the warmth of peace and harmony in the room. I was glad I had insisted to Kermit that we attend.

The close arrangement of the long tables in the crowded room enabled everyone to hear what everyone else was saying. Two or three different conversations were going on at the same time, but this didn't seem to bother any of the ladies. On the contrary, it made for a more spirited dialogue. The one speaking just raised the level of her voice and plowed on through the conversation. No one interpreted this as rude; it was a part of happy dialogue and sharing time.

I listened to all of this for several minutes, waiting for the right moment to add a word. Kermit was also silent, since it had been agreed that I would take the lead in the table conversation, and he would listen carefully to learn the names of the people. Finally, near the end of the first course, there was a lull in the table talk and I sized this up as my special moment.

I had noticed throughout the meal a woman at the far end of my table who seemed isolated from the group. She had not entered into the conversations, nor had she made any comment about the food. I felt a strong urge to help bring her into the circle of fellowship. When the lull came, I looked at her and asked in a loud clear voice, "And how are you feeling these days, Mrs. Brown?"

The silence in the room was deafening. Forks laden with food stopped in mid-air, mouths that had been busily chewing food remained locked open, and arms lifting glasses of iced tea were paralyzed. All eyes turned toward me, including those of the woman at the end of my table.

"My name's not Brown; it's Jones," she replied coldly.

More silence. Deadly silence—followed by a cough and a nervous suggestion by the hostess that there was "plenty more food for everyone."

"I haven't had a husband for thirteen years. If I had a husband at home, do you think I'd be at this crummy Sunday school dinner?"

Kermit glanced at me and I slid down a couple of inches in my chair. It was awkward and embarrassing, but there was still hope.

Leave it alone, Bruce, a voice within pleaded.

"But I can't just leave it hanging there," I reasoned silently.

You'll be sorry.

"But the whole purpose of coming to this dinner was to build better relationships."

Let it rest. Leave it alone.

"What will Kermit think? I'm supposed to be a shepherd who knows his flock."

Just finish your meal, the voice continued, *and let it be.*

But my mind was made up. I had to do something to make up for the error that I had just made. So, I took a deep breath and I plunged ahead.

"And did you leave your husband home tonight to fix dinner for himself, Mrs. Jones?" I said the name "Jones" clearly, letting her and everyone else know that I was covering my mistake.

She looked at me with steely eyes and said, "I haven't had a husband for thirteen years. If I had a husband at home, do you think I'd be at this crummy Sunday school dinner?"

There were gasps around the tables, Kermit choked on a piece of bread, and I suddenly lost my appetite. The agony was almost unbearable. I longed for the floor to swallow me, or for someone to wave a magic wand and make me disappear. Mrs. Jones's (or

Brown or Whatever) eyes had not left my face. They were fixed, unmoving, in a deadly stare. I squirmed and sank lower in my chair, but there was no place to hide.

Then some lady at the far end of the second table giggled. This was followed by a "tee-hee" from the kitchen. A dignified lady next to me began to cough, and somebody else snickered. Soon it was out of control as the senior adult women giggled like teenagers. I sat in an embarrassed stupor while Mrs. Jones (or Whatever) continued to stare at me. After what seemed like half an eternity, she looked down at her coffee cup, slowly picked it up and took a sip. As she lowered the cup, the muscles in her jaws relaxed and the eyes softened. When she looked at me again there was a hint of a forgiving smile on her face. I smiled back . . . weakly.

After a respectable amount of time, I looked at my watch and mumbled something about an "emergency at the hospital." Kermit and I rose to leave, declining the dessert.

We thanked the hostess and walked to the car silently.

As I started the engine Kermit turned to me and asked, "What emergency, Pastor?"

"Mine," I replied, and headed toward home.

THE NIGHT THE CHEERING STOPPED—FOR NEARLY AN HOUR!

It was a cool, crisp spring evening when I finally arrived home after a busy day at the office. I parked the car in the driveway, glanced at the firewood neatly stacked against the fence, and wondered if it was too late in the season for one last fire in the den. The warm, dying embers would provide just the atmosphere I needed for complete relaxation.

My longings for such a quiet evening were quickly derailed as Shannon, then an eighth grader, dashed out the door, hugged me, and exclaimed, "Guess what, Daddy?"

"What, honey?" I answered, wondering why so many greetings seemed to begin with "guess what?"

"I think I'm going to run for cheerleader at school."

"That's great," I responded. "Go for it."

"Everyone's telling me to do it," she continued excitedly. "We'll have uniforms and we'll get to go to all the football games and basketball games and baseball games and we'll have pep rallies and I'll have a jacket in school colors that has 'Robert T. Hill Junior High School Cheerleader' on it and . . ."

"Whoa," I interrupted as I put my arm around her and walked past the stack of firewood. "Let's talk some more about it inside the house."

But I knew deep down inside that there wasn't much to talk about. Shannon had leadership abilities, and I wouldn't squelch them for anything in the world. Besides, when I was her age I had been a cheerleader back in Siler City, North Carolina. I remembered pep rallies, and yelling myself hoarse at games, and hugs when we won and tears when we lost. I also remembered a white sweater with the monogram "SCHS." And in small print just below the letters was the word, "Cheerleader." No quarterback on a winning team was ever more proud of a school letter than I was of that cheerleader emblem.

I opened the door and entered the house, wondering whatever happened to that white sweater.

"We're having a poster party here tomorrow night," Shannon continued. "Mother said it was okay."

"A poster party? What's a poster party?"

"I'll invite a few of my friends over and we'll spend the evening making posters about my running for cheerleader and asking students to vote for me. We'll put these up all over the school the next day."

"Sounds like a good idea," I responded. "How many will be here to help make the posters?"

"Oh, about ten or fifteen have said they will show up and help. But I'm going to ask a few more."

The next day Lawanna asked that I try to be home earlier than usual at the close of the day. "There might be a few last minute things to do before the party," she suggested. And Shannon asked me if I would mind picking up a few of her friends who were without transportation to the party. I didn't mind at all and was glad to see that this was becoming a family project. I had often preached on home and family relationships and had underscored the very things that we were experiencing in getting ready for this poster party. In an exciting way we were practicing what I had preached, and this made me feel good.

I arrived home early, drove to the grocery store to purchase soft drinks, dips and chips, and then carpooled for more than an hour picking up some of Shannon's friends. When I arrived back at the house, several dozen junior high students were already there. And the party wasn't scheduled to begin for another fifteen minutes.

Lawanna had a worried, almost panicky, look on her face.

"Quick," she said in an aside to me. "Head back to the grocery store and purchase some more drinks and chips. They've already gone through everything in the house, and kids are piling through the front door from every direction. For heaven's sake, hurry!"

I bumped and pushed my way through a maze of students as I struggled to get out of the house and into the car. I felt like a salmon swimming upstream, leaping through treacherous rapids. Twenty-three "hello's" and "nice to see you's" and "'scuse me's" later, I slumped behind the wheel of my car, took a deep breath, and pressed the button, listening with relief to the "click" that automatically locked all the doors. For a moment I was tempted just to roll over, lie down, and stay there. But fatherhood and parenthood and an old white sweater with school letters and "cheerleader" stitched on it motivated me back to the store. Little did I know then that five more return trips would be made before the evening's party was over.

As I returned with more drinks and chips, I had to pause before I drove into the driveway behind our house. There were kids everywhere—in the driveway, in the backyard, under trees, behind trees, in the Wingers' yard, in the Suttons' yard, behind the

Suttons' house—wherever I looked there were junior high kids. We had been invaded!

It wasn't easy getting from the car to the kitchen, but I maneuvered carefully and managed the obstacle course. Lawanna and the

"I bumped and pushed my way through a maze of students as I struggled to get out of the house and into the car. I felt like a salmon swimming upstream. . . ."

three mothers who had volunteered to help were pressed against the sink and cabinets at the far end of the kitchen. The looks on their faces registered something between panic and terror.

As I "'scuse me'd" my way through the body-to-body crowd, I managed to get within hollering distance of Lawanna. "How many?" I shouted.

"Two hundred and sixty-eight at the last count," she yelled across the room. "And they're still coming!"

"I'm going to my study," I shouted back.

"Don't dare leave the premises," she pleaded.

Thoughts of the solitude of the study motivated me through the kitchen, across the packed den and down the crowded hall. This was my one place of retreat. Here my favorite books lined the shelves that encircled the small room, my special pictures hung on the walls and my kind of music played softly in the background. The room contained everything that I needed for sermon preparation, restful reading, or quiet solitude. My name wasn't on the door, but everyone knew that the study was off-limits for everybody, including the kindly maid who occasionally cleaned the house.

Everybody, that is, except six or eight students who were enjoying their own kind of retreat in the small room. And they weren't reading books! As I opened the door, they looked up with startled expressions, blushed, and disentangled their arms. I didn't have to ask them to leave; they were glad to slip out and get lost in the crowd.

My respite lasted less than ten minutes. Lawanna opened the door and breathlessly gasped, "Come quickly. We need you now."

"What's wrong?"

"Chris Winslow has been throwing water balloons across the fence at the kids in the back yard. A bunch of the boys are on the way to his house to beat him up."

"That's great," I replied. "I've been waiting for a long time for someone to teach that boy a lesson." Chris, a high school senior who lived in the neighborhood, was having a difficult time moving through the teenage years. He could be charming and clever at times; at other times he could be irritating and irksome. He seemed forever to be in some kind of "stage," and most of the people in the area had to endure the stages with him.

"Yep," I added with a chuckle, "it's about time some of those boys taught Chris a lesson."

"But you don't understand," Lawanna protested. "His parents apparently aren't home. He has a gun—a deer rifle—and is threating to shoot anyone who sets foot on his property. He's standing on his porch now with the rifle in his hands. And about twenty boys are headed toward his house!"

This was serious. Serious and dangerous.

"I'm going out the back door and down the alley to Chris's house. I'll try to talk him down," Lawanna continued. "You get Chief and some of his buddies and try to hold back the boys who want to whip Chris!"

With those words she was through the crowds and out the door. I looked in all directions for "Chief."

Del Wesley was a 220 pound high school sophomore who played both offensive and defensive tackle on the football team. He was half Choctaw Indian which accounted for his nickname. Chief was likable and polite—a favorite with both students and parents. He had been to our house many times and had shown up on this occasion with some of his high school friends because he heard that Shannon was having a party. I was thrilled that Chief had crashed the poster party.

"Chief," I shouted over the crowd, "I need you right now. This minute."

He nodded at me from across the room and walked through the students like Moses marching across the Red Sea. When Chief moved, people gave him a lot of space.

"What do you need, Mr. McIver?"

"Some younger students are headed down to Chris Winslow's house to beat him up. Chris has a gun and somebody could get hurt badly."

Chief nodded without a word.

"Lawanna is on her way to try to reason with Chris. I need you to get a dozen of your biggest friends and form a barricade in the middle of the street so those kids can't get to Chris's yard. And I need them now!"

"Done," said Chief. He then turned to some of his buddies and said, "Let's go." They followed him out the front door without a word or a question.

"Keep the younger students back," I hollered to Chief as I hurried down the street toward Chris's house. "I'll go ahead and check on Lawanna."

Chief nodded and said again, "Done."

When I reached Chris's house, I froze in fear.

He was standing on his porch with his rifle pointed toward students in the street. Lawanna was ten feet in front of him and walking slowly toward him.

"Put the gun down, Chris." she said sternly.

Hold them back, Chief, I urged.

"I'm gonna defend my property," Chris snarled.

"Put the gun down," she repeated as she walked straight toward him and straight into the barrel of the gun.

Please. Don't let them through, Chief.

"I said I'm gonna defend . . ." Chris tried to continue.

"And I said," Lawanna interrupted, "put the gun down!" The gun was almost pressing against her body as she eyeballed him.

The hush of the drama was shattered with one last piercing emphatic command. *"Put it down now, Chris! Now!"*

I held my breath as the rifle was lowered as if in slow motion. I breathed a sigh of relief and moved toward Lawanna, just as a Dallas Police car careened around the corner and stopped in front of our house. Obviously, someone in the neighborhood had called them. Chris took advantage of the momentary distraction and quickly opened the door and set his rifle inside his house where it would be out of sight. It was a clever move.

Two officers got out of the patrol car. The one nearest me took off his cap and slowly scanned the block filled with students. Nearly three hundred kids were in the streets and in the yards of neighbors. The officer did a complete circle, a 360 degree turn, scratched his head and asked, "How many students do you have at this party?"

"The officer did a complete circle, a 360 degree turn, scratched his head and asked, 'How many students do you have at this party?' 'Two hundred sixty-eight at the last count.' I replied."

"Two hundred sixty-eight at the last count," I replied.

"And how many sponsors?"

I gulped and swallowed hard. "My wife and myself, and three mothers."

"Well, that's your problem," he said as he looked at me in amazement.

"Sir," I replied, "I don't want to be disrespectful, but I know what my problem is. I've been living with it for the last couple of hours. Now, I'll be happy for you to blow the whistle and call this party off. Or, if you like, put me in your squad car and take me away from this. I'm at my wit's end. Or help me figure how to regain control of this crowd?"

He continued to scan the area, sighting students in the most unlikely places. Slowly, he mustered a smile—a bewildering smile—but a welcomed one.

"Okay," he said, "here's the deal. You'll have to round up all the kids and get them back into your house or in your backyard. They'll have to stay there without leaving your property until the party is over. Meanwhile," he added, "we'll walk down the street and have a talk with the young man who seems to be causing some trouble."

My heart sank as I glanced at my watch. Nine o'clock. Since it was Friday night, the party was scheduled to last until twelve. Three more hours with nearly three hundred kids.

Somehow, we were able to corral all the students in the back yard for an update on what the policemen had said and what the ground rules would have to be if the party continued. They were strangely silent as I called the session to order.

"All of the McIvers are glad you're here tonight," I began. "I regret that we've had some problems with some neighbors and that the police were called." The students stood like zombies, hardly daring to breathe. Not a person moved.

"But I've got some good news," I continued, hoping to liven things up, "The nice policemen said that the party could continue on the condition that you remain here in our house or on our premises." There was a brief sigh of relief and a slight shuffle throughout the crowd. I mustered a weak smile, betraying my feelings about facing the next three hours and wondering how many posters three hundred students could turn out in 180 minutes.

"Have a great time," I added, "and make yourselves at home."

That last invitation was a mistake. They did.

Sometime after midnight, after the last student had been picked up by his parents, we began to survey the damages. There were broken lamps and broken tables and broken chairs. The stereo speakers were no longer attached to the wall. Lawanna and I looked at each other, shook our heads and tried to smile as we waded through the debris. It was obvious that none of this was done maliciously. A reclining chair is not designed to hold nine persons, even if those sitting in the chair are young students. And lamps and tables are bound to break if enough people press in on top of them. And stereo speakers will fall off walls when so many bodies bump up against them. It was several days before the clutter was cleared, and several months before all the furniture was repaired.

Meanwhile, Renie, a year younger than Shannon, began quietly taking her own survey at Robert T. Hill Junior High.

"Shannon will win," she declared when she got home from classes Monday after the party. "No doubt about it."

"How do you know?" I asked.

"It's simple," she replied. "The kids said it was the most exciting party they'd ever attended. They especially liked the police showing up."

Renie's confidence did little to reassure me. I was still grasping for a good answer just in case some member of the church inquired why the police were called to the pastor's house.

"But, Dad," Renie continued, "did you know that our friends were scared to death when you called everyone together in the back yard?"

"Why in the world would they be scared, Renie?"

She hesitated, then grinned and said, "They know you are a preacher, and they were afraid you were going to pray!"

A week later Shannon was elected cheerleader, just as Renie had predicted. She received her colorful jacket with letters emblazoned across the front and wore it proudly. The students kept coming back to our house again and again, but thankfully, in smaller numbers. Chris settled down and moved more quietly through the other stages of the teenage years. No one seems to remember how many games the Hill team won that year.

Postscript: Fifteen Years Later

Most of the furniture broken that memorable evening was eventually repaired or replaced, although the house still bears a few scars of "the most exciting party ever held in junior high school."

Today, "Chief" is a banker in Dallas and also a licensed preacher. He ministers on weekends among his own people, the Choctaws, who live in Oklahoma. The neighbors remain friendly . . . and forgiving, and nice policemen wave at us as they slowly patrol the area. Shannon and Renie are both married and have made us grandparents *twice* while I have been writing these stories. Other once-upon-a-time junior high students drop by occasionally to introduce their spouses or to let us see their new babies. Life moves on, and there are times when "the party" is only a distant memory. . . .

But, on quiet, cool nights, when the dying embers in the fireplace glow warmly, Lawanna and I think we still hear laughter in the walls.

14

GIFTS—AGONY AND ECSTASY

The numerous hospital visits had been made, and I entered my office, or study, relieved that I had a few moments of relaxation before I began to return telephone calls and meet appointments. I sat down in my favorite chair, breathed a sigh of relief, and picked up a hot cup of coffee that had been graciously put on my desk. It was good to be alone again in a place that I had come to know as my second home.

As I slowly sipped the coffee, I surveyed the room and its furnishings. There was so much about this place that was soothing and restful, even in the midst of hectic schedules and tense conferences. The books that lined the wall-to-wall shelves were some that I had collected through the years. Others had been given to me by friends. In a strange way, these books that surrounded me had become not only my tools for sermon preparation, but my daily companions. They were a part of my life.

On the shelves, in the spaces between some of the books, were personal mementos—pictures of the girls and Lawanna, objects collected from trips to other parts of the world, and a variety of trinkets shared with me by children and adults through the years. Most of these were inexpensive, but they were valuable and meaningful to me personally.

On my desk was an ingenious little wooden gadget that Dad had made for me. He called it a "bullgrinder." When you turned a little handle round and round, two small strips of wood slid back and forth in grooves without touching. Dad wrote on the back of his gift: "Bullgrinder. Use when they talk too much." Throughout the years as I sat through tedious committee meetings or listened to rambling, boring monologues, I turned that little handle idly round and round—grinding the "bull."

On the wall to my left was an original photograph of the Middle East taken from one of the first Gemini space flights. To my right was a walking cane collection that I prized dearly. There were canes from Japan, Brazil, Uganda, England, China, and other parts of the world. There were other canes that had been used by people whose lives enriched mine. One belonged to my father and was passed on to me after he died. This room was filled with a lot of memories.

And inspiration.

A MISSING PICTURE AND A STORM OF CONFUSION

Over the fireplace in the corner of the study was my favorite painting—a seascape. The rolling waves in the picture seemed to be either majestic or turbulent, depending on my particular mood. The colorful rays from the sun beyond the horizon portrayed sunrise or sunset. The translucence of the painting was mystical—almost eerie. I often felt that, regardless of the situation on a given day, the picture over the fireplace lent understanding and encouragement to me. That painting and I had a bonded friendship.

I took another sip of coffee, glanced toward the painting, . . . and gasped.

Gone! My favorite painting was gone!

I stared in disbelief, put down the coffee cup, jumped out of my chair, and moved quickly toward the fireplace. Maybe my eyes were playing tricks on me. Maybe I was just imagining things. After all, it had been a difficult day. A second lingering look confirmed my worst fears. My seascape was gone. That was bad enough, but worse was what had replaced it. I couldn't believe my eyes.

On the entire wall above the fireplace was a hideous painting, the most "gosh-awful" thing I had ever seen. Apparently the so-called artist, or artists, had attempted to portray Jesus on the cross. At least, that's the conclusion I reached as I backed away and viewed the picture from several angles.

***"I took another sip of coffee, glanced toward the painting, . . . and gasped. Gone!* My favorite painting was gone!"**

I've never claimed to be a critic, or even a serious student, of art. But I know what I like, and I think I know enough to recognize if something is good or bad. And believe me, this was *bad*!

How bad?

Well, it looked like something some restless fourth grade kids had drawn on the last day and in the very last hour of Vacation Bible School so their parents could see that the week had been productive. I was convinced that no one person could possibly draw that badly; it had to be a group effort. Of course, I couldn't prove my theory, but it was the only thing that made sense as I continued to stare at the "thing."

While struggling to collect my thoughts I noticed a small note under the picture on the mantel of the fireplace. A strange place for a note, I thought, but no stranger than other things that had happened in my private office that very day. I ripped open the envelope and read the scribbled content.

"For my dear pastor," it said, "in gratitude for your faithful ministry." It was signed, "An anonymous friend. Your enjoyment of this picture is all the thanks I need."

I read the note again, and then looked at the picture carefully. I backed further away for a better perspective, studied the picture, and glanced at the note for the third time. Could it be that I was missing something here? Could this really be a valuable painting? Perhaps a masterpiece?

Confusion. Absolute confusion.

The word "anonymous" had me trapped. I needed to be careful about expressing my reactions, for I might be talking to the donor without realizing it. Even if the picture did not appeal to me personally, I had no desire to hurt anyone's feelings. And, whoever gave it to me would doubtless make his way into my office to make sure that it was hanging here. And to study my reactions! I could never again relax through any committee meeting or personal conference. I was trapped.

And, where in heaven's name was my seascape? Wherever it was, the waves were bound to look "turbulent" by now, and the lingering glow beyond the horizon was sunset, not sunrise.

This was more than I could take. I needed a friend, and Barbara was just the person who could help me.

Barbara Boyd (now Floyd) was our attractive, charming, and delightful minister of youth. Along with these characteristics, Barbara had a lot of class. She was well-read, understood the finer things of life, and had a genuine appreciation for art. I called her immediately on the intercom and asked her to please come to my study.

When she walked through the door, she listened patiently to me as I rattled on and on about what had happened.

Finally, I ran out of steam and asked, "Am I missing something here, Barbara? Could this be a great work of art?"

"It is impressive," she replied studiously.

"But Barbara, you know I don't respond positively to most paintings of Jesus. I just have a hard time agreeing with the artist's interpretation, and . . ."

"Let's stand over here and look at it from another angle," she suggested as she moved across the room.

She looked at it intently for a couple of minutes, punctuating the silence with some "hmmms," "ahs," and "a little more light here."

She then sat down, folded her hands, and observed thoughtfully, "Pastor, there's definitely a message hidden in that painting."

My heart sank. Barbara had found a "message." If she had found one, that meant one was there. I was the dummy. My minister of youth had class. And culture. And, above all else, she could be trusted.

"She then sat down, folded her hands, and observed thoughtfully, 'Pastor, there's definitely a message hidden in that painting.' "

"Let's call Exial Mae and get her reaction," Barbara suggested.

"Great idea. I need all the help I can get."

Exial Mae Krevis served on our church staff as director of children's ministry. She had worked for more than thirty years in several churches in the Dallas area and was an authority on ministry to children. She was also an excellent conference leader and was frequently asked to participate in seminars across the nation. Her experience and maturity had given her insights and understandings that the rest of us staff members did not have. We valued her wisdom. I was glad to learn that she was free to confer with us immediately.

When Exial Mae entered my office, I let Barbara explain the problem. I was drained emotionally and slumped into my chair. The two of them studied the painting close-up, turned down the lights, turned up the lights, moved to two or three different spots in the room to get proper angles, and talked quietly among themselves. I didn't care. I just wanted someone to help me out of this sticky situation. Finally, Barbara shared with me their impression.

"We really think you should leave it up for a couple of days. The painting has a way of growing on you. Every time Exial Mae and I look at it we see something new."

"Barbara, there's nothing about that painting that will ever grow on me. The more I look at it, the more I want to take it down. And will someone please locate my seascape? I think I need it now more than ever."

"On the other hand," Exial Mae added, "you don't know who the donor is, and taking it down could be risky. I've been around long enough to know that people can get their feelings hurt over something like this."

Exial was right. I was grateful for her wisdom and maturity.

Pondering what I had heard I moved slowly to the corner of the room. "You know," I mumbled cautiously, "from this angle it does look different. Maybe . . ."

Exial Mae and Barbara smiled to one another, and then to me.

"Keep studying it, Pastor," Exial Mae said. "It may grow on you yet."

I studied that thing the rest of the afternoon. I studied it in my mind as I drove home for dinner. I woke up in the middle of the night thinking about it. I hated it, but I could be wrong. Maybe it was a masterpiece. And, what if the chairman of deacons had been the one who gave it to me? Or the chairman of personnel? Or? . . .

Throughout the next day I vacillated. Is it hideous, or is it a masterpiece?

Was it painted by children or by a genius? Do I want someone to carry it off, or does it really grow on me? Could I be wrong, and could Barbara be right?

By two o'clock in the afternoon my mind was settled. I didn't like it, but the painting would stay. There were just too many risks in taking it down. Besides, the challenge of finding the hidden message was intriguing.

"I've made my decision," I said to Barbara and Exial Mae. "There doesn't seem to be any other choice. Besides, the two of you have helped convince me. You'll never know how grateful I am to have friends like you."

They rose to leave, nodded to me, and looked at one another. Not a word was spoken as they left the room. *Wonderful people,* I thought as they exited, *wonderful people.*

Two hours later, after another trip to visit members at the hospital, I entered my office, sat down in my favorite chair and prepared to look diligently for Barbara's hidden message. I looked over the fireplace and the painting was . . .

Gone!

Gone? Who's messing with my paintings? It can't be gone; I haven't even found the hidden message!

Barbara and Exial Mae had been huddled in an adjoining office. When they heard me sputter, they opened my door, took one look at me, and cracked up laughing.

"Gone!
Gone? Who's messing with my paintings? It can't be gone; I haven't even found the hidden message!"

In a flash the truth was out.

"Pastor, we happened upon it at a bookstore in downtown Dallas. We knew your strong feelings about certain kinds of religious art so we talked the store manager into letting us take this out on approval. It was a great joke . . . until you decided to keep it. Then the joke was on us. You see, there's a substantial price tag on the painting, and we were afraid we'd end up having to buy it. It's now back at the store."

They turned and reached just outside the door and handed me my seascape painting. Barbara hung it back in its place over the fireplace. She then moved to one corner of the room and Exial

Mae went to the other. Both of them studied the painting intently. I sat and watched and wondered.

With a twinkle in her eye Barbara said, "Pastor, don't you think there's a hidden message somewhere in? . . ."

"Get out! Both of you! Out! Now! And please," I added after taking a deep breath, "Don't try to give me anything else. I just might keep it!"

They looked at each other, giggled, and walked out the door.

I looked for a long time at my seascape. The waves were subsiding, and the sun was rising. It was turning out to be a beautiful day.

THE FIG LADY

Mrs. Bledsoe was a remarkable person. She was a diminutive eighty-three-year-old woman who looked frail and feeble. But she could slither through a crowd quicker than any child I'd ever seen.

Sunday after Sunday when the worship services were over, Mrs. Bledsoe would wind her way through the crowded aisles of the church and be at my side before the third note of the organ recessional. She would then take my hand, pump it vigorously, look up at me through the dark shades that she wore over her glasses, and give me an all-knowing grin. It was a game that she played with me, a secret between the two of us, and she wouldn't turn loose my hand until the game was played out. There were times when I would be so drained after delivering my sermon that I would forget our secret.

This happened one Sunday morning. Mrs. Bledsoe caught me as I stepped off the platform to greet some new members. She reached out with her gnarled arthritic hands, pulled my head down, and whispered in my ear, "It won't be long now."

What in the world is she talking about, I wondered. *The end of the world? An omen? Does she know something we don't know?*

Mrs. Bledsoe looked around to make sure no one else was listening, squinted her eyes, smiled proudly, and prompted me, "The fig tree, Pastor, the fig tree!"

"Oh, of course, Mrs. Bledsoe. The fig tree."

"It's going to be the biggest crop in years, and I'm going to bring you a big sack of the best figs you've ever eaten."

"Thank you so much. You're kind. Now you take care of yourself, and please drive carefully."

I watched her as she moved out of the sanctuary. Her slip was two inches longer than her dress and her hose sagged loosely on her tiny legs. But her head was high as she exited—all five feet of her. Her fig tree was about to bear fruit, and few things mattered more to her than this. Not even my sermon!

Less than a week later our phone rang, and Mrs. Bledsoe announced that she was on her way to our house with a sack of figs—the first off her tree.

"Please, let me come by your house and pick them up," I suggested. I had heard horror stories about her driving and made this offer in concern for her as well as in the best interests of my neighbors.

"No, Pastor," she insisted, "it's a nice day and I'll enjoy the drive."

Heaven help us all! She may enjoy the drive, I thought, *but she'll be the only one. If she slithers through our neighborhood like she slithers down a church aisle there's trouble ahead.* I tried to keep these concerns to myself and not alarm the family, but apparently six-year-old Renie read the situation clearly.

Twenty minutes later, there was a yell from the front porch, "Dad," Renie cried, "she's on her way! She's rounding the corner and heading up the hill toward our house. Oops, she almost hit the Ledbetters' car. . . . She's made it past the Gregorys' house . . . and . . ."

The front door opened, and Renie announced in a loud whisper, "She's parked out in front, on the wrong side of the street—a long ways from the curb, Daddy."

I moved through the house and out the door to meet Mrs. Bledsoe. But Renie was way ahead of me. By the time the car door slammed, my six-year-old was standing beside her. She took the dear lady by the hand and guided her up the sidewalk toward the house.

"Oh, Mrs. Bledsoe, I'm sure glad you came to see us. And you brought us figs? My daddy will be so happy. He just loves figs. He said he couldn't wait for you to get here. He said he remembered eating them by the buckets full on his granddaddy's farm way up in North Carolina. That's his favorite fruit."

I couldn't believe what I was hearing Renie say. I'd eaten *a fig* on Grandpa Moody's farm. Well, maybe two or three, and I didn't like them. But "buckets full"? "Favorite fruit"?

Mrs. Bledsoe stopped in her tracks and looked down at what she thought was an angelic smile on Renie's face. She then put her arm around my six year old, hugged her up close, and said to me, "Isn't she sweet?"

I didn't answer Mrs. Bledsoe. Instead, I stared at Renie, but I didn't see an angelic smile; I saw a devilish grin.

Mrs. Bledsoe lingered for a visit, and then we all walked the elderly lady back to her car.

"Now you just go ahead and eat all those, for there are plenty more where they came from," she admonished as she slid under the steering wheel and adjusted her dress.

"Thank you very much, Mrs. Bledsoe," Renie volunteered. "I just know that my daddy will be eating them all afternoon and all evening and . . . "

"Renie, Mrs. Bledsoe needs to be going. Say good-bye to the nice lady."

"Good-bye, Mrs. Bledsoe, and please bring my daddy some more figs soon."

We all breathed a sigh of relief when she made it back down the hill and rounded the corner without hitting any of the neighbors' parked cars. When she was out of sight, I turned to Renie and asked, "Honey, what on earth made you say all that? Buckets of figs? And favorite fruit?"

"Daddy, she seemed like a nice old lady, and I thought it would make her feel better." I wasn't sure whether to discipline my little "angel" for outright lying, or to hug her for being so considerate of the "nice old lady."

But, apparently what Renie had said did make Mrs. Bledsoe feel better, for she drove to our house from across the city a half dozen more times—bringing buckets full of figs. Figs were everywhere—in buckets, in sacks, and in containers in the refrigerator.

"I couldn't believe what I was hearing Renie say. I'd eaten a fig on Grandpa Moody's farm. Well, maybe two or three, and I didn't like them. But 'buckets full'? 'Favorite fruit'?"

Happily, I discovered that our neighbor, who lived across the alley from us, really did like figs. We kept the path between our houses worn as we supplied him with more figs than he had ever seen!

This went on for ten more years until the "fig lady" died. I was grateful for her kindness and her gifts.

But she never realized how much she made me long for Grandpa Moody's farm . . . and just *one* fig. Well, maybe two; but no more!

SOMETHING SPECIAL FOR GOD

It was Saturday evening and I had just walked into the house after conducting two back-to-back formal wedding ceremonies. The first was held in Wilshire's small chapel at seven o'clock; the other took place in the larger sanctuary an hour later. It was an unseasonably hot day, and moving from one building to another, plus trying to keep the names of the brides and grooms straight, had drained me both physically and emotionally.

It was great to be home where I could relax for a few minutes. But tomorrow was Sunday, and later in the evening I would slip off to my study for a last look at my sermon notes. It had been a busy day, and it wasn't over. For a pastor, Saturdays and Sundays have a way of showing up every week, with amazing regularity.

I took off my perspiration-drenched tuxedo coat, loosened my bow tie, and kicked off my shoes. At that very moment the telephone rang. Lawanna moved quickly to answer it.

"It's for you," she said sympathetically, "and it sounds important."

"Hello," I said, working hard to conceal my fatigue.

"Bruce, this is Blanche. Can you come to our home tonight? Dean and I want to talk with you about something important."

"Well, Blanche, I think I can. I've just led in a couple of wedding services at the church, and I haven't eaten. I'll need to change into some dry clothes but I'll try to get over a little later . . ."

Blanche lowered her voice and whispered over the phone, "Bruce, come now. It's very important."

"Is something wrong, Blanche?"

"No," she replied in a low voice, "there's not anything wrong, but Dean wants to talk with you about something very important. Just trust me, and come as quickly as you can."

"I'll be there in fifteen minutes."

I was puzzled. During my years of ministry in one church in a large city, I had received many urgent calls throughout the day and at all hours of the night. The needs reflected in those calls covered every facet of life—domestic crises, runaways, accidents, abuse, financial reversals, mental instability, serious illness, and death. I had learned to listen carefully, not only to what was being said, but to the tone of the voice of the one calling. This usually helped me understand the nature and the urgency of the problem.

Blanche's call was hard to figure out. She sounded urgent, but she assured me that nothing was wrong. Unusual. Very unusual.

I pushed the light snack aside, slipped on my shoes and coat, and headed out the door to the car. As I drove west on Mockingbird Lane and passed White Rock Lake, my mind was racing for answers. Why the urgency? Why now? If there was no problem, why did Blanche whisper into the phone?

The lighted steeple of Wilshire could be seen from a distance as I continued the drive to their house. I recalled that Blanche and Dean had become members of the church less than six months before. They were gracious and supportive members, but they preferred to stay in the background. They would slip into the worship service, sit near the back, and quietly leave when the service concluded. Dean's health was a factor in this. He had undergone seven major surgical procedures, including the removal of most of his stomach and his spleen and open heart surgery. This seventy-two-year-old man was a walking miracle. I knew, through quiet conversations with him, that Dean was struggling to live, and searching for some fulfilling purpose for living.

I pulled the car to the curb in front of their house and walked to the door. Before I could ring the bell, Dean called out, "Bruce, come in. Come on in."

"We hesitated to call you out tonight," Blanche offered, "but Dean and I both felt strongly that we wanted to share something with you."

I listened silently, still without a clue as to the purpose of the call.

"We were reading today in the Wilshire church paper about the plans to renovate the church buildings and add a third story to the educational unit," Blanche continued.

"Yes," I replied. "Our last major building project was completed several years ago with the construction of the new sanctuary. Many of our buildings are old and in dire need of remodeling and we need additional educational space. The congregation voted last Sunday evening to proceed with the projects on a pay-as-you-go basis."

"How much will it cost?" Dean asked.

It wasn't an empty question. Dean knew the value of a dollar. He had told me more than once about quitting school when he was in the eighth grade and moving to Dallas. He made it on his own in those early days by working in a drugstore and delivering prescriptions to the homes of people on a motorcycle. Later, he enlisted a group of boys who would make the deliveries on their bicycles. Of course, as a budding entrepreneur, Dean got his share from each delivery made by his boys. By the time he was thirty he owned the drugstore.

He moved into other enterprises. He and a friend were the first owners of the now world-famous Mesquite Rodeo, located just east of Dallas. He decided to get out of the rodeo business when he was thrown from a bull and suffered a broken shoulder. It was one of the few times that Dean ever backed away from any challenge!

He owned two wholesale drug supply companies, oil wells, and numerous pieces of property near downtown Dallas. But he remembered his roots, and he remembered the value of a dollar.

He was shrewd and tough, and he wasn't engaging in idle conversation when he asked me the cost of the projects.

"The renovation of three existing units and the adding of a third story to our educational wing will cost about two million dollars."

My friend listened thoughtfully.

"But this is something we plan to do over several years—maybe ten or fifteen," I added. "I'm just glad that the church has a long-range plan."

"I've been doing a lot of thinking about my life," Dean said. I'm seventy-two years old, and I haven't done as much for God as I would like to."

He paused, and then continued slowly, deliberately. "As you know, I've had several major surgeries, followed by complications. My health is not good. There isn't a reason in the world why I should be alive today . . . except God."

His eyes became misty. So did mine.

There was a choke in his voice, but he struggled to continue. "I don't know why He has left me here, but I'd like to do something special for God, and thank Him."

Dean then straightened up, cleared his throat, looked me straight in the eyes and said, "I'm going to give the church a million dollars!"

I listened to the words in disbelief. Astounded.

In the emotions of the moment I felt that I needed to give some response to what he had said. So, I asked, "Are you sure?"

As soon as the words were out, I realized that they were probably the dumbest ever uttered! Here I was talking with a man who

---

" 'You'll have to excuse me, Dean,' I responded with a weak smile. 'I haven't had much practice in this kind of situation.' "

---

had made hundreds of deals in his lifetime involving thousands, even millions, of dollars. The transactions were made over cups of coffee, in pickup trucks, in the middle of oil fields, at rodeos, and in plush executive offices. Many were sealed with steady eyes and a handshake. If somebody blinked, the deal was off.

And I was blinking all over the place and stammering, "Are you sure?"

"Yes, I'm sure," Dean replied. "Blanche and I talked it over this afternoon. We're both sure."

But I wasn't through with dumb questions. Out came the second one. "Wouldn't you like to think it over, and we can talk again tomorrow about it?"

Why in the world I asked that question, I'll never know. It made no sense at all. It was just out before I knew it.

"No, Bruce," Dean reassured me, "I don't need to think about it overnight. My mind is made up."

"You'll have to excuse me, Dean," I responded with a weak smile. "I haven't had much practice in this kind of situation."

Dean and Blanche both laughed—at me and with me. The tension was broken.

"Now, here's the deal," Dean stated firmly. "There are some conditions attached to the gift."

Uh-oh, I thought.

Dean clicked them off like the executive that he had been through the years. "First of all, you can't tell anybody who's making the gift. It's to be anonymous.

"Second, I'd like for it to be a matching gift. I'll give a million, the church will raise a million, and the project will be completed. But between you and me," he added, "if the church doesn't raise its million, I'll still give mine."

"Third, you can never treat me any differently from the way you treat me now. If you do, the deal is off. We'll be the same kind of friends that we've been all along."

Dean studied me carefully, trying to read my reaction.

"Agreed?" he asked.

"Agreed," I replied. "Except for one thing. There's no way I can live with Lawanna and not share this with her. We're too close. I'll go crazy trying to keep this secret from her."

"That's fine," he replied. "Tell Lawanna, but tell no one else who is making the gift."

"One other thing," Dean added. "Blanche and I will be in the church service in the morning. We'll be sitting near the back where we always sit. I want you to announce this gift to the people. I'll be listening." There was no intimidation intended in his last statement. He was just letting me know that he cared about how the gift was announced and how the people responded.

I led in a brief prayer, hugged them both, and started toward the door. Blanche followed me with a twinkle in her eye and a sly grin on her face. "Now you understand," she whispered, "why I insisted that you drop everything and come over here immediately. Dean is a tough businessman; but when he's ready to talk, he's ready to talk!"

Neither Lawanna nor I slept much that night.

"A million dollars! Did he really say a million dollars? Things like this just don't happen! How much is a million dollars?" At three o'clock in the morning we were still asking the same questions, repeating the same exclamations, and wondering how I could best make the announcement to the church. No words seemed adequate—for us or for the congregation.

The next morning at eleven o'clock I stood behind the pulpit with my knees shaking and my voice trembling. "Folks," I pleaded, "I hope you will bear with me as I try to share a word with you. There are times when we stand back and watch a miracle take place. That has happened in the last few hours. We voted last Sunday night to move forward with our building and renovation program. The vote itself was an act of faith. Last night two of our members made a commitment to give one million dollars to the program."

There was stunned silence as the magnitude of the announcement settled in the minds of the people. This was followed by spontaneous applause that grew into a thunderous ovation. The congregation then stood and sang in unison the Doxology, "Praise God from Whom all blessings flow. . . ."

At the conclusion of the singing, the people were seated and I continued. "The donors are hoping," I said, "that you will match their gift. If this is done, what we thought would take several years to accomplish can be completed in three years. And we'll be debt free when we finish."

They responded. Positively and optimistically. The congregation pledged $1,150,000. Construction was begun immediately. On faith!

A few months later, in the month of October, Dean asked me to meet with him and Blanche at his accountant's office. He wrote out a check for $250,000.

He handed it to me and said, "Tell the church next Sunday about this check. Tell them, also, that on Sunday morning, December 19, the remaining $750,000 will be given."

In the weeks that followed I watched the renovation and construction of the buildings. I watched, also, a renewal in the life of my friend, Dean. He would call to ask about "*our* building program." He began bringing his friends by to show them the progress being made on the facilities and glowed with pride as he talked about "*our* church." Like a delighted and gleeful child, the shrewd, and sometimes tough businessman was becoming a part of his own gift. And the thrill was too much for him to keep to himself. Anonymity no longer mattered.

A week before Sunday, December 19, Dean called me. "I don't want any credit for anything I've done," he said. "But do you think it would be okay if Blanche and I came forward at the close of the service next Sunday and handed you the check for $750,000 dollars? It's the Christmas season," he added, "and I'd like the check to be a Christmas gift to my church and to the Lord."

"Dean, I think it is a wonderful idea. I'll meet you at the front of the sanctuary as we sing the closing hymn next Sunday."

The sermon had been preached and the congregation stood to sing. Down the aisle came Dean and Blanche. I watched them, overwhelmed with emotions, realizing that Lawanna and I were the only ones present who knew why they were responding. Dean's declining health made his walk unsteady, but his head was high and there was a smile on his face. Blanche walked by his side, radiating charm and grace.

When they reached the front, Dean handed me the check, sat down, and wiped a tear from his eyes. I had a feeling that the check was his way of saying "thank you" to the Lord.

I introduced them to the congregation and explained what the piece of paper was that I held in my hands. Now others wiped tears of gratitude from their eyes.

We sang "Joy to the World." It was Christmas—a week early.

Two years later Dean died. He never stopped bragging about "*our* church."

And he never stopped laughing about my dumb question, "Are you sure?"

I'm thankful that he sealed the deal, even though his pastor blinked!

15

LIVING WITH THE UNEXPECTED

It happened at Wilshire several years ago. The music division of our church, under the leadership of Bill James, had worked long and hard to inspire us with a presentation of "Amahl and the Night Visitors."

The story of the one-act musical drama is an inspiring one. Three wise men follow the star that will lead them eventually to the manger. On the journey they stop for food and rest at the home of a lame boy, Amahl, and his widowed mother. The hosts are poor but gracious, and with the help of others in the village, the needs of the visitors are more than met.

The Magi explain the reason for their journey and, to the delight of the poor villagers, display gifts they are taking to honor the newborn King—gold, frankincense and myrrh. Amahl is so impressed that he gives his most valuable possession, his crutch, to the visitors to take to the Christ child. In the process of making this sacrificial gift, he experiences the joy of healing. It's a beautiful and moving story, designed to stir the coldest of hearts in the dead of winter.

THE PARROT WHO STOLE CHRISTMAS

One of the delightful characters in "Amahl" is Casper, an elderly, bumbling wise man. Casper is hard of hearing, constantly out of step, and a second late in everything that he does. He is proud of his gifts—a small box containing some special offering and a colorful parrot in a cage. Throughout the play Casper sings proudly, "This is my box," and mumbles numerous asides to the parrot while trying to keep up with the other two wise men.

In addition to directing the drama, Bill, the minister of music at Wilshire, was also cast to play the role of Casper. This was an ironic twist because Bill James is a perfectionist. He's always punctual, always in step, and never mumbles to anyone, especially to birds in cages. Neither will he settle for anything that smacks of the artificial.

In most productions of "Amahl," a stuffed parrot is used for obvious reasons, but Bill and the others responsible for the drama saw this as an opportunity to be authentic. No stuffed birds for them. So a search was begun for a live colorful fowl with a hooked bill. After looking most of the day, they found one in a suburban pet shop, but the owner of the shop had reservations about loaning, or even renting out, one of his prized possessions.

"It's a valuable bird. We don't usually let one like this out of the store except when a purchase is involved. It could be injured or lost."

"I understand," Bill responded, "but we need it badly and you have my word that this parrot will be returned safe and sound."

"Your word and a three-hundred-dollar deposit."

"Three hundred dollars!" Bill gulped. This was back in the seventies and three hundred dollars was a lot of money.

"That's what I said. That's the deposit for two days or no bird."

Bill listened to the pet shop owner in disbelief and then turned to walk out. At that very moment the parrot let out a low, throaty squawk as if pleading for a chance to prove itself in the performance. The squawk must have been in perfect pitch, for the perfectionist in Bill caused him to pause and reconsider. Within an hour three hundred dollars was found in the music ministry's budget under the line item, "Guest Performers," and a nervous minister of music drove down crowded Central Expressway with his squawking bird. When he arrived home he called for his ten-year-old son who loved any kind of bird or animal.

"Terry," Bill pleaded, "I've got my hands full these next two days. There are costumes and props and rehearsals that will be taking all my time. On top of everything else I've got to learn my own lines. I need you to be responsible for this parrot. Take care

"It's a valuable bird. We don't usually let one like this out of the store except when a purchase is involved. It could be injured or lost."

of him, and for heaven's sake, don't let him get hurt or lost. We've got to recover a three-hundred-dollar deposit early Monday morning. Can you handle him?

"I'll take good care of him," Terry responded with delight while the parrot nibbled at his fingers. Bill was pleased to see that a close relationship was already forming between the boy and the bird. For the next two days Terry hardly let the parrot out of his sight.

On Sunday evening the congregation began to gather early in order to get good seats. Ten minutes before the performance began, the downstairs was crowded with people and the balcony was opened. Little children, between last minute trips to the restrooms, scampered and jockeyed for the best view available. Nervous parents glanced at the movements of those same children, making sure that they settled into seats close enough to remain under watchful eyes. Cheerful ushers moved up and down the aisles checking to see that everyone had a program for the performance. There was a buzz of excitement throughout the crowd, and I glowed with pastoral pride at what was surely destined to be a highlight of the approaching Christmas season.

At exactly seven o'clock, right on schedule, the house lights were lowered and the drama began. The buzz of excitement faded into a hush that blanketed the congregation as the three wise men prepared to enter the sanctuary from the foyer. In the stillness of this moment a piercing squawk echoed from that direction, as Terry handed over his feathered tropical friend to his father, now dressed for the role of Casper. Unfortunately, the make-up artists had done such a good job disguising Bill that the parrot didn't have the foggiest idea who he was. Besides, the bird didn't like the idea of being shoved into a bamboo cage.

The doors at the back of the sanctuary opened, the wise men entered, and a spotlight focused on our dignified minister of music, carrying a black box in his left hand and a confused parrot in a cage in his right hand. As he moved down the aisle and began to sing, "This is my box," the bird joined in, squawking after every phrase. To his credit, the perfectionist in Bill kept him on key, and he never missed a note in his solo.

About half way through the performance the script called for Bill to sing again. By now the feathered fowl had had enough. In some unexplainable way he slithered through the bamboo slats that imprisoned him, paused to study his surroundings, and flew out of the cage. Fluttering momentarily over the startled cast, he then swooped out over the congregation. For the next few minutes there would be a "swooooshh . . . swoooosh . . ." as he swept low over the heads of people, squawking all the way. Each "swoosh" and each "squawk" found people dodging and ducking lower and lower in the pews.

Finally, the tired bird lit on a chandelier in the rear of the sanctuary, directly above where Terry, his bonded friend, was sitting. Only then did the squawking stop. From that position he watched the rest of the production while the members of the cast watched him.

When the drama was over the real drama began. Following the benediction the congregation was asked to evacuate the building "quickly, quietly, and prayerfully." They did. Most people were not in the mood to tangle with a confused, noisy bird. Those leaving were told to be careful since the lights would be slowly dimmed. Within minutes the church staff and the production crew huddled in near darkness at the front of the sanctuary and

"The miracle that night was not the healing of a lame boy named 'Amahl'; the real miracle was catching that squawking bird."

discussed in whispered tones how to retrieve the bird from that brass chandelier. Everyone agreed that Terry was a key to any success that we might have.

Terry was encouraged to remain seated under the chandelier—and under his feathered friend—which he did, while a couple of the men climbed a long ladder to the attic of the sanctuary, crawled along the floor, and lowered by a hand crank the large lighting fixture. As it descended slowly and gently, the parrot eyed Terry with a fixed stare while we held our breaths. When the chandelier was even with the pew where the boy was seated, the bird gave a happy squawk and hopped on Terry's shoulder. With soft and reassuring words, he was placed back in a reinforced cage. Someone found a small towel and covered the cage in the hope that it would help calm the bird. As he was gently carried out of the sanctuary he twisted and angled his head, stuck it through the side of the cage and yanked off the towel. In the subdued light his glassy eyes sparkled and I would have sworn that he had a smile on his face . . . er . . . beak.

Finally, all the lights were turned out and we went home.

The miracle that night was not the healing of a lame boy named "Amahl"; the real miracle was catching that squawking bird.

THE CHANDELIER THAT STOLE A WORSHIP SERVICE

It had all the ingredients needed for a warm, inspiring worship service: parents and little children, grandparents and friends, joyful introductions and beautiful flowers, affirmations and dedications . . .

. . . and chandeliers.

That's right, chandeliers. Those brass Georgian fixtures, with tall glass globes and lengthy arms, hung majestically over the congregation as if to symbolize a blessing upon all who were present. The soft light from the chandeliers and the sunlight that filtered through the shuttered windows accentuated the beauty of the colonial-styled sanctuary. There were many edifices in our city that were more elaborate, but the architectural design of this building, simple as it was, spoke to me.

My emotions were stirred as the congregation began to sing, "Jesus loves me." During the singing of the second verse, eighteen sets of parents, with beautiful babies in arms, entered the front doors of the sanctuary. They were led in by the lovely and gracious Merle Harrell, minister to preschool children. People looked up from their hymnals and sang from memory while shifting positions and stretching their necks for a better glimpse of the babies. Without a doubt, this parent-child dedication service was a favorite with the congregation.

Before the parents could be seated in the reserved section at the front, one of the babies decided that he, or she, didn't like "big church," and began to wail. The poor parents of the child turned red in embarrassment while the other parents faked nervous smiles and gently patted their own babies. Fortunately, Merle and I had prepared the parents for this in a brief meeting prior to the service.

"Now, don't worry; everything's going to be fine," I had assured them in the earlier session.

"But, Pastor, what if our baby begins to cry?"

"It's natural for babies to cry," I had replied paternally. "I have three children of my own, and I had to get used to it a long time ago. Besides, you'll find our people to be very understanding. Scores of them have been through this kind of dedication service themselves."

"But, Pastor . . ."

The words came from a young couple new in the church. They were extremely uneasy.

"Look," I had emphasized in a soft voice directed toward them. "I know you're a little nervous. But Merle and I will take good care of you. Just follow her into the sanctuary and sit where she indicates. I'll guide you through the simple dedication part of the service. It'll be over in ten minutes and you can then take your children back to the nursery area. Okay?"

"Okay," they had nodded, but it had been obvious that they had nodded with some hesitation.

Now the parents were in the sanctuary—babies in their arms—hoping and praying that a chorus of crying would not begin. It didn't, and we made it through the brief commitment part of the service without difficulty. As each family unit was recognized, a flower was presented in honor of every baby. The parents and the congregation read aloud statements pledging mutual support of families, and I led in a prayer. Merle then guided the young parents out the doors toward the nursery where the babies would be left in good hands for the remainder of the service. During the singing of the next hymn the obviously relieved parents reentered the sanctuary and sat again in the pews reserved for them. Every now and then one of them would look up at me and smile, as if to say, "Pastor, you were right. We can trust you."

I beamed with pride.

Following the special music by the choir, I stood to preach. I read the Scripture and moved through a brief introduction to the sermon. The young parents near the front, together with the entire congregation, seemed to give me undivided attention.

Everyone, that is, except a man who sat on the back row. It was obvious four minutes into the sermon that his attention was elsewhere. It didn't take a lot of intelligence to figure this out for he was standing, waving his hands wildly and pointing toward the ceiling. He was also saying something, but I couldn't understand him.

My first impression was to ignore him. I reasoned that the ushers would assist if he were having emotional problems. It didn't seem right to stop a worship service because one man was having difficulty, and besides, others could be of more help to him at the moment than I could. I was convinced that the best course of action was to press on with my message.

I tried, but the man at the back kept interrupting me. He was urgently trying to communicate with me, but I still couldn't hear him. By now the undivided attention of the congregation had shifted from me to him.

Amazingly, people all over the sanctuary, including the parents at the front, had turned in their pews and had focused their attention on him. When more than a thousand people turn away from you and look elsewhere while you are trying to preach, it's a good sign that you've lost your audience. So I gave up and spoke to the man.

"Sir, I sense that you're trying to tell me something, but I can't hear you."

There were more gestures, more waving of the arms, and more pointing.

"I'm sorry, sir, but I still can't hear you."

Then a remarkable thing happened. Like smoke signals delivered from mountain peak to mountain peak, his words spoken at the back of the sanctuary were relayed section by section to the front. People would turn around in their pews, listen to what was being said, and then repeat it to the group in front of them. It took four or five of these relays before the man's frantic message finally reached me. By that time, all across the large room the words reverberated, "It's the chandelier! It's the chandelier!"

I was still confused, but some members of the choir who sat behind me interpreted the message to me. "The chandelier is spinning, Pastor!"

I looked up and saw that majestic brass Georgian fixture turning round and round, immediately over the place where the young parents were sitting.

In an attempt to regain control of the service, I announced, "The chandelier is spinning," as if everybody there had not already heard those words.

From behind me I heard the calm voice of Bill James, our minister of music. "Tell them it's all right. It does that all the time."

"Folks, the chandelier is spinning, but Bill James tells me that it's okay; it does that all the time. And to our friend at the back who gave us the warning signal, I'd like to thank you for your concern for the safety of . . ."

There was a gasp from the choir and a loud whisper from Bill. "No," he exclaimed, "It's slipping. It's going to fall!"

"I'm sorry, folks. Bill now tells me that it's slipping and it's going to fall! Please. Let me have your attention. Will all of you seated under this spinning chandelier please move!"

Not a person moved an inch. They were paralyzed.

"Please, ladies and gentlemen, would you move to the outer aisles. For your own safety. Please!"

Still no action. The chandelier spun round and round erratically, dropped suddenly about four inches, jerked to a halt, and then began to spin again.

"In an attempt to regain control of the service, I announced, 'The chandelier is spinning,' as if everybody there had not already heard those words."

"Now!" I screamed. *"Move now!"*

That did it. They fell over one another getting out from under that whirling fixture.

I was drained. Empty. People were standing everywhere. Every eye was on that crazy chandelier that had now lost its stately magnificence. If it could have made a sound, I'm sure it would have looked down . . . and laughed at the commotion it had caused.

In the silence of that confusion I surveyed the situation. I glanced down at my sermon notes, coughed nervously, and prepared to finish the message. Out of the corner of my eye I saw the frightened young couple whom I had reassured prior to the service with the the words, "Everything's going to be fine. Trust me. Okay?" They had bewildered, anything-but-trusting looks on their faces.

I didn't have the nerve to ask them to trust me again. My watch read eleven-fifteen.

"Ladies and gentlemen, I think we've had about all we can absorb this morning. The best thing I can say is Amen, God bless you, leave quickly, and stay out from under that chandelier."

They filed out obediently and gratefully. Not a person criticized me for dismissing a worship service forty-five minutes early, nor has a single person asked for a copy of the sermon I did not preach. The man who sounded the alarm from the back row was visiting Wilshire for the first time that morning. He never came back. The spinning chandelier was fixed the next day and has slowly regained some of its Georgian grace. The frightened young couple and their growing child are still actively involved in the church. And a congregation survived *not* listening to a sermon.

Things sometimes do have a way of working out.

Trust me.

16

BEST FRIENDS

While I was trying to prepare myself for my first open heart surgery, one of our church members was trying to figure out how she could best help her pastor. With genuine excitement she shared with Lawanna her answer.

"Bruce needs a dog," she said. "And I've got the very one for him. I breed miniature French poodles, and we've just had a new litter. I've picked one out that would be perfect."

Lawanna loved the idea and talked it over with the girls. Each one of them agreed on what I needed (they were good at that), but they couldn't figure out how to tell me, for they knew my reservations about having another dog.

Finally, a day or two before surgery, Lawanna shared the news with me. "Diane wants to give you a miniature French poodle."

"She wants to give me *what*?"

"A miniature French poodle. She raises them and has a new litter. She's picked one out just for you. His name is Napoleon Bonaparte, but we can call him Nappy for short, and the girls all agree that this will be good—"

"Hold it. Wait just one minute. The last dog we had, Chrissy, was nothing but trouble. A car hit her in the middle of Trammel Street—where she wasn't supposed to be—and broke her tail. She walked all over the neighborhood for years with that broken tail dragging the ground. That dragging tail was an embarrassment to the McIver household. Then the dog ran away and was gone for six weeks in the cold of winter. Don't you remember how it nearly ruined our Christmas? And don't you remember that I spent hours walking and driving all over this part of the city trying to find her? If that wasn't bad enough, by the time the kids seemed to be getting through their own grieving process, Chrissy decided to come back home, dragging her tail behind her. We finally had to give her away because she squatted on the carpet in our new house. Nope, I've had enough of dogs."

"But this is a special breed," Lawanna protested. "Diane says they are sold for good money . . ."

"Another thing," I interrupted, "most poodles that I've seen are nervous and dainty and yap all the time. My nerves won't take that. If we ever do get another dog, I want it to be a real dog, not some delicate little thing with a ribbon tied in its curly hair and with painted nails."

"Diane says these are very expensive dogs, and she's trying hard to give one to us. But actually, it's a gift to you. She thinks it will be good for you during your recuperation."

"If they're that expensive, let Diane sell the dog and tithe the money to the church. Besides, I'll get well a whole lot faster without a yelping poodle under my feet."

"The one she has picked out is black with one tiny white spot under his chin. He's cute, and he's so small I can hold him in one hand. And the girls promise to take good care of him."

Lawanna didn't give up easily, and I knew her and the girls well enough to know that any more protesting would be a waste of time. For all practical purposes, the deal was done and the transaction was finished. I wouldn't have been surprised to have heard that miniature poodle barking at that very moment in the garage.

"Okay. Okay," I sighed, "I know when I'm defeated. This vote is four to one. Now, since all of you are intent on this, I have only one thing to say: he's your dog. You feed him, walk him, shut him up when he's barking, search for him when he gets lost, and clean up after him. Understand?"

"I understand," Lawanna grinned. She knew all along that she would win this one—as always. I smiled back, for it was a game we played. In a house with four women, I would howl and growl and protest while they worked me like putty in their hands. Through the years they learned to play the game with remarkable skills.

Three weeks later the surgery and hospitalization were over, and I returned home to be formally introduced to Nappy. They brought him to me in one of my white walking shoes. The little mutt stuck his head over the top of the shoe, studied me for a moment, and then stuck his tongue out to give me an affectionate lick.

From that moment we were friends.

THE LITTLE GENERAL

Nappy would huddle near me under my feet, curl up in my lap, and sit on the floor next to my chair at the table. He loved Lawanna and the girls, but I think he sensed that he and I were

"Nappy really thought he was a person. When the table was set, he came and sat with the rest of the family."

the only two "men" in the house. Of course, I could have led him to think that as we talked together on our walks through the neighborhood. He would waddle along after me with his little feet constantly churning as he took four steps to my one. His tiny red tongue would be hanging out and he would be panting for breath, but he was always ready for a walk and seldom ready to return home. He loved these outings so much that I had to be careful not to use the words, "leash" or "walk," unless I was ready to go. Nappy would be at the door, begging and whining to get on with it. It got so bad that we started spelling those words when we talked. This worked well until Nappy learned how to spell. We then had to resort to sign language.

Nappy really thought he was a person. When the table was set, he came and sat with the rest of the family. He lingered in the kitchen while the meal was being prepared and ate the same food that we ate. The height of insult was to offer him plain old dog food. That was stuff for dogs—not him. When people came for a visit, Nappy was sure they had come to see him. He would gather into the den with the rest of us and watch and listen throughout the conversation. There were times when people came to the house to share their hurts and problems. Nappy listened quietly and sympathetically. He knew more about family problems and church problems than any ten deacons in the church knew. But to his everlasting credit, he never once broke a confidence.

When the Christmas tree was put up each year, that dog was a part of the trimming of the tree. He loved it when we hung peppermint candy canes on the branches. Those on the lower branches had a strange way of disappearing from the tree during the night. The next day bits of cellophane wrappings could be found all over the house; there was no doubt in anybody's mind who the culprit was. Nappy also had his own stocking hung over the fireplace, and he expected it to be filled with goodies on Christmas morning.

One year Lawanna found and purchased a magnificent manger set that covered at least a third of the space in the den. Sofas and chairs were rearranged and lamps and tables were pushed against the walls to accommodate the carved figures of wise men and shepherds, cattle and sheep. A bundle of hay was brought in to make the scene look even more authentic. When every figure was in place and the lighting had been adjusted, the entire family stood at the other end of the den admiring the beauty of the scene. The next morning we found Nappy sound asleep . . . on the hay . . . between Baby Jesus and the sheep. He looked right at home.

That tiny black poodle had access to the entire house. Nothing pleased him more than to go from room to room, receiving pats on the head from the girls and rummaging through clothing that they had discarded, usually in the middle of the floor. He especially liked bras and panties, and around a house that was alive with three teenage girls, there were always plenty of these. He liked to lie on his back, put one end of a bra in his mouth, stretch the elastic, and then roll over and wrap himself up in it. Or he would take panties and stick his head through the leg holes. Occasionally, he ended up dressed in bras and panties at the same time.

This happened one evening while Lawanna and I were hosting a meeting of the deacons and their wives. Out of nowhere Nappy strolled proudly into the crowded den with a bra around his neck and colorful bikini panties draped over his head. Most everybody cracked up laughing except two or three who didn't understand Nappy, bras and panties, laughter, or their minister. It was obvious what they thought: The pastor's dog is a transvestite!

But that wasn't the worst.

THE MYSTERY OF THE EMPTY PIE PANS

Our premises were being invaded each night by an army of snails. They weren't causing a lot of problems, but they were leaving unsightly, slimy trails all across the patio. I shared this problem with Wayne Miles, the deacon who had helped us fence in our back yard.

"What in the world am I going to do?" I asked Wayne. "Those slugs are everywhere."

"It's simple." he said. "Get some aluminum pie pans and sink them in soft dirt even with the ground. Then, get some beer and fill up each of the pans."

"Beer?" I asked. "Wayne, where in the world do I buy the beer? I am a Baptist preacher, you know."

"That's no problem," Lawanna said. "I can take care of the beer. Just leave it to me." I decided that I would rest easier that night not knowing how she planned to get the beer.

"Okay, Wayne, when we get the pie pans sunk into the dirt and when we get the beer, what's the next step?"

"Fill the pans with the beer, and the next morning the snails will be dead. Just believe me; it will work."

For the life of me I can't remember if Wayne said they would die from drinking the beer or if they would just fall in and drown. Anyway, it really didn't matter for it looked like my snail problems would be solved.

The next afternoon Lawanna came in with a six-pack of beer.

"Where did you get this?" I asked with genuine concern.

"At the 7-Eleven store across the street from the church."

"You didn't!"

"I did."

"Did any of the church members see you?"

"I don't know, but the clerks were nice and helpful. They asked me what kind of beer I wanted, and I told them any kind would do. So they picked out this brand for me."

"For the record," I said while shaking my head in bewilderment, "you're probably the only person in Dallas today that's purchased a six-pack of beer and had the store clerks decide for you what kind to buy."

We opened a couple of cans and poured a generous amount into the shallow pie pans. Later in the evening, Wayne and his lovely wife, Dort, dropped by for a visit. We sat in the den drinking coffee and visiting, and then Wayne asked, "How are you doing with your snails?"

"We just got the pans filled with beer a couple of hours ago. Let's step out on the patio and see what's happening."

To my amazement the pans were empty. Not a drop of beer in any of them.

"I don't understand this at all," I mumbled in confusion. "The snails couldn't have drained those pans this quickly. Besides, there's not one of them to be seen anywhere—dead or alive." I scratched my head, perplexed, and exclaimed, "It just doesn't make sense."

We made our way back inside, pondering and analyzing the case of the bone-dry aluminum pie plates. After another cup of coffee I saw Nappy under a chair on the other side of the room. This was unusual since he liked to be in the center of everything going on.

"Nappy," I called to him, "come over here and sit by me." His normal response was a quick wag of the tail, three leaps across the room, and a bounce into my lap. This time he made a running start toward me and then his hind legs buckled. Drooling at the mouth and eyeing everyone suspiciously, he wobbled round and round, sometimes on four legs, and sometimes on three or two. There was no wagging of the tail.

Nappy was drunk!

"For heaven's sake," I exclaimed to Wayne, "that's the answer to the empty pans. Nappy has been in the back yard."

"We may have a problem on our hands," Lawanna said with concern as she tried to guide a weak and wobbly poodle out of the den and off the carpet. "Remember when Nappy drank half a cup of coffee and nearly died. This could be serious. I'm going to call Dr. Melton." Lawanna had already dialed his number when she covered the phone with her hand and exclaimed in a loud whisper over her shoulder, "Goodness! How am I going to explain this to? . . ."

"Hello. Dr. Melton? This is Lawanna. . . . I have . . . we have . . . Dr. Melton, Nappy has a problem. You see, he drank a lot of beer out of some pie pans. . . . That's right . . . pie pans . . . and beer . . . Look, Dr. Melton, it's a long story. I'll explain it to you tomorrow, but what do you think we should do now? He's very . . . well, sir, he's very drunk."

There was silence while dear Dr. Melton patiently outlined what we needed to do, step by step.

When she hung up we all chimed in, "What did he say to do?"

"He said it could be serious since Nappy is so small. He told me to get some Pepto-Bismol down him immediately. He said it will help absorb the alcohol. But we don't have any in the house, and it's nearly eleven o'clock. Come on, Dort, we've got to get to the 7-Eleven before it closes in ten minutes."

It was nearly midnight before the four of us stopped struggling with that tiny mutt. We came to the conclusion that you can't pour anything down the throat of a drunk dog if he doesn't want to swallow it.

"He'll just have to sleep it off," I said wearily, "providing he can live long enough." It took Nappy three days to recover, and even then his eyes were roadmapped and bleary. It took me a little longer.

A couple of days later a reporter for the Dallas Morning News heard about the incident and splashed a story on the front page under the bold-faced caption: "Baptist Preacher's Dog Gets Drunk." Radio station KVIL, one of Dallas's most popular, chatted about the Baptist preacher and his drunk dog throughout the day. When we finally told Dr. Melton the whole story, he suggested with a chuckle, "Pastor, if it happens again, don't call me; call Alcoholics Anonymous."

And for months after that experience, Nappy would get a silly grin on his face every time he saw an aluminum pie plate!

AGE TAKES ITS TOLL

One of Nappy's favorite sports was to kick ping-pong balls, marshmallows, grapes, or little square pieces of dog food across the floor. He would back up to the object, get into position, and kick the daylights out of it, soccer style, with his left hind foot. He would then turn around and chase it across the room. No one taught him to do this; he just came up with the idea himself. On more than one occasion, when the Dallas Cowboys were floundering, I thought about calling Tom Landry and telling him about Nappy.

"Hey, Tom, my dog not only has a great leg, but he's willing to chase the ball downfield. That's more than can be said about some kickers you've had. I'm his agent if you want to discuss this further."

Somehow, I just never got around to calling Tom. And besides, Nappy's knee gave out. Dr. Melton's associate called it a trick knee, or a football knee. Honestly. We talked about surgery, but decided that we'd let Nappy tough it out.

As the years wore on, other poodle parts began to wear out. In addition to his bum knee he developed arthritis. His body began to creak when he walked and he would occasionally moan in pain during the night. We began taking him to Dr. Melton's clinic for steroid shots. Looking back, I suppose it was just as well that I didn't call Coach Landry. Nappy would have probably been kicked off the team for using drugs.

"We came to the conclusion that you can't pour anything down the throat of a drunk dog if he doesn't want to swallow it."

Sixteen years of a full life had finally caught up with him. His hearing failed, and at times he became disoriented. We knew things had reached a critical state when he walked straight into the swimming pool and nearly drowned. Sure enough, both eyes were covered with cataracts.

"What do you think we should do?" I asked the veterinarian.

"Bruce, he's getting old, just like all of us will be some day. But this is the holiday season, and Christmas is just around the corner. This is not a good time for the family to have to make this decision. Get through the next few weeks and then we'll discuss it again." It sounded like wise counsel to me. I was in no mood for trying to make it through the holidays and not having Nappy stealing candy canes off the Christmas tree.

MILLIE COMES TO TOWN!

Early in December one year, our daughter Shannon called and said that she and George, her husband, wanted to drive to Alabama and visit briefly with Lawanna's parents, and then drive on to North Carolina for a visit with my mother, who was still alive then.

"And Dad," Shannon added, "Kathie says that she can go with us."

"That's a great idea, Shannon," I said. "The grandparents will be thrilled to see you. And," I added with excitement, "Kathie has worked hard for several years pursuing academics and deserves a break." With three college degrees behind her—two from universities in North Carolina and one from Texas A&M—she had just begun her career as a college English teacher. It would do her good to get away from books and students for a few days.

"Dad, we thought it would be nice for you and mother to keep Millie for us while we're gone."

"Well . . . er . . . sure . . . I suppose . . . I guess. . . ."

"That's wonderful, Dad, thanks so much. That will solve our problem. You'll love having Millie around."

I wasn't sure—not at all. Millie is their bouncy, feisty two-year-old dachshund. She has her own personality, her own routines, and her own idiosyncrasies. For instance, every time the doorbell rings, Millie lets out a shrill, high-pitched yelp. That bark is her way of greeting people, just as wagging his tail is Nappy's way of saying hello. I immediately thought of the yelp and calculated in my mind how many times I would hear it during the busier-than-usual holiday season. But I had said "yes" to Shannon's request, and a deal is a deal.

Millie was left at our house, and we walked outside to tell Shannon and George good-bye.

"Thanks a lot for keeping Millie," Shannon said as she patted the whimpering dachshund and hugged us. "By the way, she sleeps with us every night under the sheets at the foot of the bed. And she likes to snuggle against our feet."

"She does *what?*" I asked as George started the engine.

"She likes to sleep in the bed with you, but don't worry; she won't bother you. And one other thing," Shannon hollered as they drove out of the driveway, "She's in heat, but she should be over that in four or five days. Merry Christmas. Love you. Good-bye!" And they rounded the corner and were gone.

The next few days before Christmas nearly drove me into post-holiday depression. Sure enough, Millie crawled into bed with Lawanna and me and burrowed her way under the covers to the foot of the bed. Later, I rolled over in my sleep to pat Lawanna and found myself embracing a bewildered, cold-nosed, growling dachshund! Obviously, she had decided that she liked my pillow better than the foot of the bed. I spent the rest of the night downstairs in my recliner.

Nappy had been oblivious to Millie at first. That's understandable for he couldn't see her or hear her. On the second day, however, the poor old thing became acutely aware that a frisky little female was in the house.

He would lift his head when she passed by and follow her with his nose. Soon his arthritic bones began to creak and he was on his feet chasing her, football knee and all. For an entire week we coaxed, corralled, and chased those animals. We had a lot of cheap advice from friends who learned of our plight.

Deacon Charlie Watson had a dachshund, and he suggested putting doggie panties on Millie. "It will solve your problems, Pastor," he said. "You can pick some up at the pet store." I brought some home, and Lawanna and I tried; boy, did we ever try! We worked at it until we were exhausted, and after forty-three minutes we finally gave up. We discovered that it's mighty hard to get two short, kicking hind legs and a long wagging tail into three tiny holes that look alike. And it complicates matters when a poor blind and nearly deaf poodle is dancing under your feet while you're trying to solve the problem. I'm just glad that Grandpa Moody, who always had a pack of hounds around and under his house back in North Carolina, was spared seeing his grandson trying to put panties on a dog.

It's nothing short of a miracle that we managed to keep Shannon and George from becoming "grandparents" of a curly-headed dachshund pup.

The holidays were over and Millie went home. I consoled Nappy by patting him on the head and whispering real loud in his left ear: "Old man, there's still some life in those creaking bones!"

I declare, I do believe he looked at me . . . and grinned.

MEMORIES

But old age had finally won the battle with my furry friend. I patted him on the head for the last time, thanked him out loud for being one of my best friends ever, choked back a tear, and walked out of the kitchen onto the patio.

For a brief moment everything in the back yard seemed to come alive with memories—the pool around which he raced, barking for joy at the top of his lungs while I swam laps; the half empty water bowl that seemed to gurgle as he gulped until he was satisfied completely; the worn spot on the patio carpet where he snoozed away many an afternoon; the empty dish that was replenished with dog food each morning; the tiny sparrows, watching from tree limbs and fences, waiting for me to leave so they could fly in, hop across the patio, perch on the edge of his bowl and eat their friend's food. I filled the dish for the last time, knowing that it would be empty within an hour. Somehow, I longed to tell the little birds that this was the last meal I would be serving them also.

I basked for a moment in the warm memories of long walks and quiet talks. There were times when he seemed to ask so little; yet, he gave so much. I wished some people I knew could be more like that. Reaching down, I touched and turned over in my hand the tag that hung around his neck. It read "Napoleon Bonaparte (Nappy) McIver." I smile when I read the word, "McIver," for he never doubted for a single moment that he was part of the clan. Neither had I.

The luxury of warm memories gave way to the crispness of early morning air, and reality set in—the reality of chronic pain, deafness, and near blindness . . . the reality of aging . . . the reality that every life, even that of a dog, has a cycle involving both birth and death . . . and, the reality of the loneliness and pain in saying farewell and thank you to my furry friend.

I closed the patio gate quietly . . . and wondered.

What now? Are there dogs in heaven?

I don't know; I really don't. But I remembered the day the Lord God said, "Let the earth bring forth living creatures," and it happened. And God said, "That's good."

And, I remembered the promise that one day "The wolf . . . shall dwell with the lamb" (Isaiah 11:6).

"I'm just glad that Grandpa Moody, who always had a pack of hounds around and under his house back in North Carolina, was spared seeing his grandson trying to put panties on a dog."

Admittedly, at times like these my theology may seem shallow and my emotions may be tender. But could it be that the Lord's, "That's good," is a part of his creative, redemptive purpose? And could it be that furry poodles and feathered friends shall continue to eat from the same dish? I don't know, but the child in me would like to think so.

By the way, somebody ought to watch those pearly gates. If Nappy McIver makes it there, the first thing he'll do is hike his leg and try to claim them!

17

HINDSIGHTS

Years ago, Kermit Whiteaker, my associate and friend, was standing in the aisle talking with Allen Jackson following a Sunday morning worship service. Allen was an electrical engineer who weighed, pondered, and analyzed every statement that he heard. In fact, he was so exacting that it was difficult to conclude a conversation with him. When time or energy—or both—would run out, Allen would still be absorbed in contemplation and reflection. Life for him was a gigantic jigsaw puzzle, and he was forever searching for another missing piece. Allen was also a bachelor.

Shannon, then nearly five years old, had just gone through a minor surgical procedure to correct a bladder problem. This was her first Sunday back in church after being in the hospital. She rushed up to Kermit, interrupted the conversation, and excitedly exclaimed, "Kermit! Kermit! Guess what?"

Kermit looked down, patted her on the head, and asked, "What, Shannon?"

"I sat all the way through big church and didn't wet my pants once!"

Kermit knelt down beside her, hugged her up close to him, and said, "That's wonderful, Shannon! I'm so proud of you."

Shannon smiled proudly and danced off to share the good news with others.

Allen watched and listened to this interchange without a word. The wheels of his mind were turning round and round, and the analytical process was in motion. Then, his brow furrowed and his eyes narrowed. Slowly, deliberately, he moved his lips and observed:

"I've had that experience myself, but it just never occurred to me to tell anyone about it."

There are some experiences in life that one grows to understand . . . and appreciate . . . and celebrate . . . only through the gift of hindsight.

One of the good things about growing older is the opportunity to pause, look back with gratitude, and say, "I've had that experience myself."

TWENTY-TWENTY HINDSIGHT

In the middle of the fifties, before I came to Wilshire as pastor, I worked for the Baptist Convention of Texas in the Department of Student Work. One of my responsibilities was to enlist outstanding, promising college students who were capable of preaching to conduct youth revivals in churches throughout the state. In the search for the most gifted students, I would visit campuses and conduct personal interviews. I also depended on good referrals from responsible people.

The name of one student, a senior at North Texas State University, surfaced again and again over a period of several months. I was told that he was a dynamic leader on the campus, an excellent student, and a superior communicator.

"In addition to those qualities," a mutual friend observed, "he's planning to enter the seminary as soon as he graduates from college. He's thinking seriously about becoming a minister."

Then my friend added, "Bruce, you just can't let this student get away. I know he's interested in ministering to youth and leading in youth revivals. He's told me so. Believe me, he's the kind of person you're looking for."

"Tell him to come see me," I responded eagerly, "or I'll be happy to drive to North Texas State and visit with him on the campus there."

"That won't be possible. He's doing some special study in Europe this semester, but he'll be back home before the summer youth revival program begins."

"I regret that," I replied. "I'm afraid I won't be able to use him."

"Why not? He's the best."

"Well, I . . . er . . . we . . . have this policy that I need to meet and interview personally every student who works in the program. It's for the advantage of everyone . . . and . . . "

I didn't finish the sentence. My friend was no longer listening. I could almost see the wheels turning in his mind, and I could almost hear his thoughts: *Dumb, dumb, dumb.*

I walked away from the conversation with mild frustration. I would have liked to have had the young man work in our program. From what I could hear, he seemed to have the talent and characteristics needed, but rules are rules, and policies are policies.

Besides, I reasoned, with his talents, he should find other opportunities somewhere.

Two or three letters came from the young man in Europe, asking that I reconsider the policy and that I grant him the opportunity to work in the program. I answered each one, underscoring the needs for guidelines and regulations.

At the beginning of the summer, after our youth revival program had already been launched, he returned from Europe and showed up at my office. He was neatly dressed, wore a warm smile, and extended a gracious hand toward me.

"I just wanted to meet you personally," he said with a twinkle in his eye, "just in case something like this comes up again."

It didn't. The youth revival program moved on without him.

And he, somehow, managed to move on without our program.

In fact, he moved on and on . . .

He studied at the seminary, became the director of the Peace Corps, served as press secretary to the President, edited a leading daily newspaper, wrote several books, lectured on numerous campuses, worked as a member of a major network news team, and is now one of the most respected public broadcasting producers and journalists in the entire world!

Several years ago, he and I chatted in the Rose Garden at the White House.

"The greatest favor I ever did for you," I said, "was to turn you down for our youth revival program!"

Bill Moyers and I both grinned.

FREE TO FLY

Renie and Shannon bounced out of bed early one Saturday morning, ran down the hall and into our room, jumped on the bed, and exclaimed with excitement, "Get up, Daddy. This is the day you promised to take us on a walk through the woods. Get up . . . right now!"

I groaned, rolled over, and pleaded for another ten minutes of sleep, but they wouldn't hear of it. Those little girls, then ages four and five, had minds of their own, and they never forgot any promise made to them about a special activity.

"You told us that we would go today," they insisted. "So, let's go."

Reluctantly, I got out of bed and began to dress slowly while Lawanna packed a snack for us. In my heart I knew that nothing I could do this day was more important than the two or three hours we would spend together walking through the woods—not visiting people in the hospitals or calling on prospective church members or adding the final touches to the sermons I would preach tomorrow or soothing the ruffled feelings of Mrs. Swenson, whose mother had been sick, and I hadn't called on her because I didn't know the poor mother was sick, because Mrs. Swenson hadn't bothered to tell me.

Nothing was more important than that promised walk in the woods. I knew this in my heart, but my body had a difficult time reacting swiftly to what my heart said. The second cup of coffee helped, and we were soon out the door and on our way.

An hour later we were walking through a wooded encampment area twenty miles south of Dallas. The November morning air was crisp and the fallen leaves crackled beneath tiny feet that moved quickly in all directions, searching for another wonder of creation. With every pause there was a barrage of questions.

"What's this, Daddy? . . . And this? . . . How old is this? . . . Did God make this? . . . How did He do it?"

I tried to be a good father and answer the questions, grasping for everything . . . anything . . . that I might have learned in high school or college science courses to help me. Some of the questions had to go unanswered, however, for like a child, I was also wondering . . . and asking . . . and remembering.

"Several years ago, Bill Moyers and I chatted in the Rose Garden at the White House. 'The greatest favor I ever did for you,' I said, 'was to turn you down for our youth revival program!' "

I was lost in memories about another November day back home in North Carolina. I was nine years old. The sumptuous Thanksgiving meal had been eaten and Dad and I sat outside by the old woodshed whittling with our pocket knives. We weren't trying to carve anything special; we were just lazing away the afternoon after a full meal.

"Let's go for a walk in the woods," Dad had suggested.

I was thrilled, for this was to be something special. Dad worked long hours in the furniture factory five days a week, and Saturdays were usually spent catching up on numerous chores around the house. I played in those nearby woods almost daily, but seldom walked in them with my father.

My jacket was buttoned up around my neck, my gloves—lined with rabbit fur—were on each hand, and the flaps of my leather aviator cap were snapped under my chin. It was a crisp, cold day, but my heart was strangely warm as we plodded aimlessly along just like two grown men. Dad carried an old, twelve-gauge, double-barreled shotgun. He said he brought it along because we might see a squirrel, but I thought it was just a good excuse to get the old gun out of the closet and handle it once again. We saw several squirrels, but he never bothered to lift the gun or try to get off a shot. I was glad for I was fascinated by those bright-eyed, bushy-tailed little creatures that kept leaping from tree to tree. I don't remember a word of the conversation on the walk that day. Maybe nothing was said, for when a boy and his father walk in the woods together, words are not that important . . .

"Daddy, come over here quick! What's this?"

I was jolted from childhood memories by the excited cries of my own two little girls. They were standing still and looking up at a long, crusted-over thing attached to a twig on one of the lower branches of a tree.

"What is it, Daddy?" Shannon asked.

"Honey, I think it's a cocoon."

"What's a cocoon?"

"Well girls, a cocoon is . . . well . . . a cocoon starts with an egg . . ."

"An egg?"

"Yes, an egg is laid, and it finally grows into larva, or a caterpillar. The caterpillar eats a lot and then makes a shell around its body."

"Why does it do that?"

"It's getting ready for something special to happen," I said, struggling to remember the process, and hoping to make it simple so the girls could understand.

"Before long," I continued, "that hard shell will pop open and a beautiful butterfly will come out."

"Out of that thing?" Renie quizzed.

"It sure will. Right out of that thing there."

"Daddy, can we take it home and watch it happen?"

"Well, girls, I'm not sure how Mother . . ."

"Can we take the thing home and surprise her?"

"Well, . . . all right . . . Mother will be thrilled, I'm sure. Break off the twig."

Before we left the encampment grounds, several bits of free advice from other hikers were given to the girls on how to care for "The Thing," as they now called it. One suggestion was that they should get a glass jar, punch some holes in the lid of the jar, and put the whole thing in the refrigerator. They were told that this would speed up the process. I was skeptical about this whole idea, and then I recalled painfully that my grades in high school science courses weren't anything to brag about. So, when we arrived back home a jar was found and the holes were punched in the lid. "The Thing " was then placed on the second shelf of the refrigerator, right up against the butter dish. Fortunately, Lawanna was out shopping.

An hour later we heard her car enter the driveway and listened as she came through the back door. Shannon, Renie, and I were in the back room, waiting for the dramatic discovery that was about to be made. The girls were giggling all over with excitement. The opening and closing of cabinet doors as groceries were put away only added to the suspense.

And then it came—a shriek . . . followed by a squeal . . . and topped off by a scream . . .

"What in the world is this? Right next to the butter in the refrigerator!"

"She's found it," Renie hollered as both girls ran toward the kitchen. That was definitely the understatement of the moment. Lawanna had found it—no doubt about that—and the tone of her voice sounded like she was anything but thrilled.

"It's a cocoon," the girls exclaimed excitedly, "and it's going to become a butterfly. We're going to watch it happen."

"Well, it's sure not going to happen in this refrigerator!" Lawanna declared.

"Please, Mother, please!" the girls pleaded. "A butterfly is supposed to pop out."

Lawanna looked at each of the girls, gave me a "how-could-you-do-this" look, grinned, and gave in.

"Okay. Okay. You can keep it in the refrigerator, but don't be opening the door every five minutes to check on it."

They were good kids. They didn't open the door every five minutes. Why, sometimes there would be a space of nearly twenty minutes before it was opened. During the next three days the twenty-six preschool children who lived in our block marched through our kitchen at least seven times a day. It reminded me of a small-scaled repeat performance of Joshua marching around the city of Jericho. They came and went, eyes wide open in anticipation, cautiously opening the refrigerator door, peeping at the jar and wondering when the blessed event would take place. No children on the block were more popular than Shannon and Renie, and no parents were more fatigued than Lawanna and I.

As the hours dragged on, and as the children came and went, we both began to doubt that the process, the metamorphosis, would ever happen. On the third day our doubts were dispelled by the the shouts of happy children.

"Mother! Daddy! Hurry! It's happening!"

Lawanna and I ran into the kitchen, peered over the heads of the neighborhood gang, and became little children ourselves as we shared in the event. The squeals and shouts soon settled into "ooohs" and "aahs" as all of us looked on in childlike wonder. Out of that ugly thing—that unsightly cocoon—a magnificent, beautiful monarch butterfly slowly emerged. Right next to the butter dish.

With the help of neighbors and friends an insect cage was found. The beautiful butterfly was gingerly removed from the jar and placed in his new home. For the next couple of days the girls' popularity continued to rise as they carried that cage from house to house, showing their new pet to everyone on the block. They were usually followed by at least a dozen delighted friends and two or three playful dogs. It looked like something right out of a Norman Rockwell painting.

On the third day the girls became quiet and pensive.

"What do butterflies eat?" Shannon asked.

"Well, they eat the nectar—the sweet juice—from flower blossoms or blossoms found on trees."

"There's not any blossoms in the cage," Renie observed.

"How far do they fly?" Shannon asked again.

"Some of them fly a long way," I answered. "Some even fly across oceans. And sometimes so many fly together that they look like a cloud in the sky."

"Well, that one can't fly far while he's in that cage," Renie added.

" 'Mother. Daddy. Hurry! It's happening!' . . . Out of that ugly thing—that unsightly cocoon—a magnificent, beautiful monarch butterfly slowly emerged. Right next to the butter dish."

Lawanna and I both sensed that the girls were struggling through a tough decision, and we didn't want to push them through it. After all, they had found the thing and had been a part of the transformation, and all of this had made our house the favorite gathering place in all the neighborhood. Besides, this thing-become-butterfly was their new pet.

"I think," Shannon began slowly, "I think . . . we ought to set him free and let him fly."

"Yeah, me too," Renie added.

"Let's make it a party," Lawanna suggested. "Let's invite all your friends and their parents to meet on our front lawn, and we'll turn the butterfly loose with everybody present."

The next afternoon twenty-six preschool children and many of their parents gathered for the celebration. Even dogs and cats wandered up to see what all the excitement was about. The movie camera began to roll, and a hush fell over the children. Something very important was about to happen, and they felt it keenly. Every eye was on the cage that Shannon and Renie held in their hands. I helped them open the door, but the butterfly made no move to go through it.

"What's wrong, Daddy?" Shannon asked with disappointment on her face.

"He's never flown before. We'll have to help him."

I tapped lightly on the back of the cage while every child held his breath, waiting for the big moment. The butterfly fluttered to the edge of the door, looked out through it for a second, then spread his colorful wings, and flitted out amid cries of ecstasy from twenty-six kids and applause from their parents. He landed on a limb of the nearest tree, looked down as if to say "thank you," spread his wings again, swept down over the heads of the cheering children, and then soared out of sight. Two or three parents had tears in their eyes. I cleared my throat and began to fiddle with the empty cage.

As the girls prepared for bed that night, there was another barrage of questions: "Did God make the caterpillar? Did He help him spin the cocoon? And did He help the butterfly get out of the cocoon? Will the butterfly come back to see us?" Most of the questions were answered with a simple "yes," or with a nod of the head, or with an honest, "I don't know."

"Daddy," Shannon asked thoughtfully, "God doesn't make butterflies to live in cages, does He?"

"No honey, He doesn't."

"Well, where's our butterfly now?"

"He's free!" Renie exclaimed with a circular swoop of her arm and a jump on her bed. "He flew out the door of the cage and z . . . o . . . o . . . m . . . e . . . d away. I bet he's already found his family and friends."

"And I bet his stomach is about to pop 'cause he's drunk so much of that sweet stuff from flowers," Shannon giggled.

I kissed them good-night and quietly closed the door. As I walked down the hall I found myself praying, "Lord, thank you for the faith and oneness of little children. Thank you that out of cocoons and ugly 'things' something beautiful can develop. Thank you for freedom.

"And, please, dear Lord, don't let me be content to stay in a cage with doors wide open . . . when I'm created to spread my wings . . . and fly."

LESSONS FROM A WALLET

When I arrived back home in North Carolina after Dad's fatal heart attack, I found his well-worn wallet. In it were some identification cards and six crisp fifty dollar bills. There were no credit cards.

"Mother," I asked, "what are all these new bills doing in Dad's wallet?"

"He knew that you and your family were planning to come home in a couple of weeks for your vacation, and he wanted to have some cash on hand so you wouldn't have to spend any of your money while you're here."

I smiled through tears. I should have known, for that was the way Dad was, and it's taken me most of my life to figure it out.

George Sylvester McIver was born in a log cabin near Bear Creek, North Carolina. He and mother left the farm shortly after they were married and made the journey seven miles west to the thriving small town of Siler City. Dad went to work in a furniture factory and lived by the factory whistle for forty-five years. He never made a lot of money by today's standards, but money was never an issue that was discussed around our house.

Except once.

"Ollie," he said to my mother when he came home from work, "I stopped at the grocery store and picked up the items you said we needed. This sack of groceries cost two dollars and sixty-eight cents! We've simply got to cut back on what we buy."

As a seven-year-old boy, I watched and listened in disbelief. Wow! Two dollars and sixty-eight cents—enough to buy just about anything a fellow could ever want.

Looking back, there were times when Dad made two dollars a day in wages, but we had plenty—and more. We lived in a white bungalow that he and Mother had helped build with their own hands. Late at night she would hold the kerosene lamp and Dad would hammer together the finishing touches of the ceiling. We grew our vegetables, milked the cow, churned the butter, raised and killed two hogs a year, made preserves out of blackberries and watermelon rinds, and had fried chicken straight from the backyard any time we desired. My clothing, if inexpensive, was warm and comfortable; and my own mattress, filled with straw or feathers, provided all the luxury a growing boy could hope for as he lay down to sleep.

There was usually a nickel for chocolate candy at Rose's Five-and-Ten-Cents Store, or for a double-dip cone of ice cream at Ed Kidd's Sandwich Shop. A dime could always be found somewhere for a western picture show at the Elder Theater on Saturday afternoon, and Dad always came through with fifteen cents for a Friday night basketball game. Sometimes he gave me a quarter, which meant that I could have a cold soft drink and some popcorn.

Dad somehow managed all this, working hard at the factory and around the house. And he never talked about how tough times were, except the day when he brought home that sack of groceries. I knew we weren't rich, but neither were we poor. We had plenty.

And more.

When I was nine years of age, I was stricken with osteomyelitis, an infection and inflammation of the bone. Three major surgeries were performed on my left hip at Duke Medical Center where I was a patient for sixty-nine days. The cost of the surgeries and the hospitalization were never mentioned in my presence. Several years later, after I had my own family and became more aware of medical expenses, I asked Dad how in the world he managed all the bills while I was sick.

"Oh, it wasn't that bad," he replied. "We managed without any difficulty." And, with those words, the conversation about the costs of my surgeries and hospitalizations was ended.

Years later, after he died and after I found his wallet, Mother and I were driving around Siler City, basking in memories and reliving warm experiences. I turned a corner, drove up a street, and passed a house that looked familiar.

"Mother, didn't Dad used to own that house?"

"Yes, he owned it once."

"Looking back, there were times when Dad made two dollars a day in wages, but we had plenty—and more. . . . There was usually a nickel for chocolate candy at Rose's Five-and-Ten-Cents Store, or . . . a dime could always be found somewhere for a western picture show at the Elder Theater."

And then, almost without thinking, she added, "I believe that's the house he sold to pay your hospital bills."

Tears welled up in my eyes—tears of gratitude. It took forty-two years to get the answer to my question. And I should have known it all along, for that's the way Dad lived . . . and died.

The crisp fifty dollar bills found in his wallet said it all.

He knew we were coming home.

18

THE QUALITY OF LIFE

I stood at the hospital window in Milwaukee late one night and watched the large white flakes of snow gently blanket the landscape. Lake Michigan was in the background, reflecting through the haze, harbor lights and flashing signals from tug boats and freighters. The panoramic scene was a magnificent picture of peace and quiet—the kind of peace and quiet that I had gradually come to experience in recent weeks.

But not at first.

The road to my own personal peace had been a rocky one, draining me physically and emotionally. It had begun with shortness of breath and slight, but recognizable, chest pains. The diagnostic tests had been run, and the sympathetic cardiologist had sat at the foot of my bed to give me the results.

"I'm sorry," he said. "The cardiac catheterization shows extensive disease. The arteries on the back of the heart are almost closed."

"Okay," I said with a note of resignation. "What about angioplasty? Let's try putting a catheter into the clogged areas and pressing the plaque, the junk, back into the walls of the arteries."

"That's a good procedure in many cases," the doctor replied, "but because of scar tissue from your first surgery, your arteries have a lot of crooks and turns in them, and the disease is widespread. I'd say that on a scale of one to ten, it will take a ten just to get the catheter in the arteries and into the right places."

"Then, let's do another bypass surgery. My first one was nearly sixteen years ago, and I'm satisfied with those numbers. Sixteen sounds good at a time like this."

"Several of us have studied these pictures for a couple of hours, and we honestly feel that you're not a candidate for another round of open heart surgery. You have extensive arteriosclerosis, and it looks like you have experienced some damage to the heart itself. The risks are high. We suggest that you go on home . . . and. . . . of course, you may want to get other opinions about this. But, meanwhile, we have nothing further to suggest at this time."

I didn't hear much else that was said to me that afternoon. The shock of the results of the test had blocked out words . . . and thoughts . . . and positive actions. I was locked into a stunned paralysis. Everything about me had felt the impact of the diagnosis—my body, my life, my family, my vocation, my ministry, and my future. I went home to brood and to ponder.

Within a couple of days the shock of the test results had slowly and painfully settled and things were seen in a better perspective. For me, the alternatives had been clearly defined: I could sit at home, become a cardiac cripple, waiting for the "Big One" to hit; or, I could exnlore surgical possibilities, respecting the risks, but choosing to meet them head-on.

One of my mentors and friends in sorting my way through the decisions before me was Dr. Kenneth Cooper, founder of the Aerobics Center and Director of the Cooper Clinic, both located in Dallas. I met Dr. Cooper and his delightful wife, Millie, seventeen years earlier shortly after he retired from the Air Force and moved to Dallas. At a party for a mutual friend he and I talked about some of the orthopedic problems that I had lived with through the years, the stress and demands that everyone experiences when working with people and their needs, my weight and the lack of any on-going physical conditioning program.

Admittedly, it wasn't the most comfortable conversation I've ever had, but out of the genuine concern that Ken showed that evening, I ended up at the newly opened Aerobics Center for a stress test.

As a result, three months later, after extensive consultation with my internist and friend, Dr. Billy Oliver, I had my first heart

---

"I didn't hear much else that was said to me that afternoon. The shock of the results of the test had blocked out words . . . and thoughts . . . and positive actions."

---

surgery—"just in time," they said. Six weeks after the surgery, I led the dedication prayer for the official opening of the Aerobics Center. In the ensuing years, that initial stress test has led to nearly fifty others and to a constant monitoring of both exercise and diet.

In some ways, the diet is the worst part of it. Ken accepts no excuses, shows no sympathy, and refuses to listen to explanations. He's tough. Just before one of the stress tests, I stepped on the ever-present scales for the weigh-in. Ken looked at the figures, pulled his chair across the room, looked me squarely in the eyes and asked, "Bruce, God has spared your life twice. In the light of that, how can you dare come into this office nine pounds overweight?"

It was one of the most awkward moments of my life. Ken was right, I was wrong, and I deserved to squirm. Later I shared this with Buckner Fanning, pastor of the Trinity Baptist Church in San Antonio and Dr. Cooper's former pastor and close friend. He listened to my tale of woe and observed with a grin, "I fear God less than I fear Ken; at least God has mercy!" We both chuckled, and then Buckner added, "Seriously, in many ways I owe my life to Ken Cooper. Had it not been for his focus and constant challenge I would not have stayed with the program which I feel has kept me alive and well since I began running twenty-six years ago." I listened to Buckner with renewed gratitude for the perceptive concern and tough love of our mutual friend.

So, it was natural that I should turn to him as I faced alternatives. I had already revealed to him that I didn't like the idea of just hanging things up and going home to wait for the inevitable. At my request he had begun to talk with heart surgeons across the nation and in Canada about my situation. There was an indication that surgery might yet be an option, but high risks would be involved.

It was Christmas Eve, 1987. Dr. Cooper and I stood just outside his office and talked again about the dilemma.

"Have you made your decision?" he asked quietly.

"I think I have, Ken. Let's go for it. And, let's see if we can schedule it with Dr. Dudley Johnson of the Milwaukee Heart Institute." Dr. Johnson is one of the pioneers in open heart surgery and has a world-wide reputation for excellence in his techniques. Seventy-five percent of his operations were "redo's" and high risk surgeries.

"I'll get on it immediately," Ken replied. "And I think you've made a good decision. Merry Christmas."

I walked out of the building and felt the cold Texas air against my face. But I had a warm feeling inside. At least I wasn't going home just to sit and wait for the inevitable attack to hit me. I was going home to tell Lawanna and the girls that we were all flying to Milwaukee. It was good to feel that I had given myself a Christmas gift—the gift of making a decision.

I found myself humming "Joy to the World" as I started the engine of the car and headed toward home.

So, two months later, here I was in Milwaukee . . . Saint Mary's Hospital . . . looking out a window . . . reflecting . . . pondering . . . and praying. All the tests had been completed—chest X-rays, blood samples and matchings, EEG, echograms, and angiograms. There was nothing to do now but wait until tomorrow.

"Hello, I'm Dr. Johnson."

I turned from the window and faced a pleasant looking, medium-sized, middle-aged man who mustered a hint of a smile as he nodded in my direction. It was ten o'clock at night, and he was still dressed in his green surgical garb. His mask was partially untied and dangled loosely from his left ear. I knew that he had just finished his second surgery for the day. I knew, also, that

"I walked out of the building and felt the cold Texas air against my face. But I had a warm feeling inside. . . . It was good to feel that I had given myself a Christmas gift—the gift of making a decision."

his first operation tomorrow was scheduled to begin at seven o'clock in the morning. It was his practice, so I had been told, to take the easier cases first in the day, and the more difficult ones second, leaving as much time as necessary to work into the night. For some reason, it did not bother me that I was scheduled for the later surgery tomorrow. I was just glad to get on with it.

Dr. Johnson picked up my chart and studied it thoroughly and silently. He engaged in no small talk, and his nurse-assistant standing by him had not volunteered a word. There were no questions about the weather in Texas or the Dallas Cowboys or the kind of work I did. Everything focused for the moment on that chart. When he finished reading it, he turned to the assistant and spoke softly to her, so softly that I could not hear the conversation. He then put the clipboard holding the chart back into the slot at the end of the bed, turned to me as he stepped toward the door and said, "See you tomorrow."

"Excuse me, Dr. Johnson. I'd like to ask you a question."

He paused, and nodded.

"Well Doctor, you've seen the test results, and you've studied the angiogram. My question is, can you fix it?"

"Sure," he replied as he opened the door. And he was gone.

I remained standing in the middle of the room with my mouth half opened. The man didn't say, "Well, I hope so, or "In the light of the situation . . . or "We'll do our best."

He just said, "Sure."

I smiled to myself, for there was something about the clipped way he spoke the four-letter word that exuded confidence. "Sure." It had a good ring to it at ten o'clock on the night before my surgery. I laid down, but I did not fall asleep. I just kept repeating the word, "sure . . . sure . . . sure." There was a quiet assurance in the hospital room that was better than sleep.

Two weeks later. The twelve-hour-and-fifteen-minute surgery was over, the intensive care unit stay was behind me, tubes had been removed, and a mild exercise program had begun. I was walking the halls daily, gaining strength, and preparing for the flight back to Dallas.

Dr. Johnson stood at the foot of my bed again—the night before I was to be discharged from the hospital. He picked up my chart and scanned it carefully while his nurse-assistant stood silently by his side. He completed reading the chart, put it back into the slot, nodded, and moved toward the door.

"Doctor," I called, "you saw the angiogram of my heart when I checked in, and you've seen the results of the one taken last night. You worked over twelve hours on my heart, bypassing vessels and cleaning out arteries. Now, my question is, in the light of the blood supply that I had when I checked in, how much blood supply do I now have as I check out?"

"All you'll ever need," he answered. And he was gone.

After Lawanna and I were back in Dallas we were marveling over these two "conversations" with Dr. Johnson.

"And that's not all," she said. "When your surgery was finally over at 2:15 in the morning, he came out to speak with the family and the friends who had sat with us through the lengthy ordeal. He gave us the preliminary report. Then I said to him, 'Doctor,

Bruce's primary concern is quality of life. That's more important to him—and to us—than anything else.'

"Dr. Johnson listened, deep in thought for several seconds, looked at us, and replied, 'I fixed his heart; his quality of life is up to him.'"

Three years after that last "conversation" with the heart surgeon, I've had other conversations with another Heart Surgeon:

"Lord, there are times when life gets broken. Can you fix it?"

"Sure."

"Well, Lord, how much strength, how much grace, how much of Your power do I have?"

"All you'll ever need."

"But, Lord, I want the best life possible, and I'd like to really experience the 'abundant life' that Jesus promised, and I want to enjoy the fullness that . . ."

And God responds, "I fixed your heart; your quality of life is up to you."

Amen.

ABOUT THE AUTHOR

Bruce McIver, a native of North Carolina, is a graduate of Mars Hill College, Baylor University, and Southwestern Baptist Theological Seminary. During his early years of ministry, he taught and worked with students at Southwest Texas State University, San Marcos, and at Texas Tech in Lubbock.

For thirty years, he was pastor of the dynamic, growing Wilshire Baptist Church, located in the heart of Dallas. He retired as pastor after his second heart surgery but remains active—leading conferences and seminars, speaking and preaching, and writing. His first book, *Grinsights,* was published in 1977.

Although he has spent most of his adult life and ministry in a busy metropolitan area, he still remembers fondly the "hills of home" and his family's favorite recreation—telling stories.

Bruce and his wife, Lawanna, live in Dallas. They have three daughters and two grand children.

JUST AS LONG AS I'M RIDING UP FRONT

More stories I couldn't tell while I was a pastor

JUST AS LONG AS I'M RIDING UP FRONT

Bruce McIver

Guideposts®
CARMEL • NEW YORK 10512

This Guideposts edition is published by special arrangement with Word Publishing.

Library of Congress Cataloging-in-Publication Data

McIver, Bruce.
Just as long as I'm riding up front: more stories I couldn't tell while I was a pastor/Bruce McIver.
p. cm.
ISBN 0–8499–3597–0
1. Christian life—humor. 2. Christian life—Anecdotes. 3. McIver, Bruce. 4. American wit and humor. I. Title.
BV4517.M35 1995
286'.1'092—dc20
[B] 94–44566
CIP

Printed in the United States of America

To Lawanna,
Kathie, Shannon, and Renie—
the four most important women in my life
who have loved me, encouraged me, laughed with me
and helped me to laugh at myself—
thanks.

Acknowledgments

Interestingly, this page—at the very beginning of the book—is the one I wrote last. I waited 'til the end because of continuing gratitude for those special people who have helped me right up to the last moment.

Lawanna—wife, friend, and joyful companion for thirty-five years—has been a constant source of encouragement. She has read every paragraph in this book, offering constructive criticism and positive suggestions. She's a gift to me and I can't imagine life without her.

Daughters Shannon Allen and Renie McCarthy have been most supportive. Shannon and Renie jogged my memory and helped me fill in some of the blanks as I recalled these stories. Unfortunately, in the process they told me a few things about their younger days I wasn't expecting to know—now or ever! Happily, time has a way of making life more mellow, and more forgiving. Besides, I'm not about to get upset now with the mothers of my three grandchildren—Emily, Ali, and John-John.

Oldest daughter Kathie, now a college English teacher, has read and edited most of these stories with a fine, sharp pencil. I had hoped that she might show her old father some leniency, but she has been tough on me as she would be on a freshman student taking one of her courses in composition. I sometimes have the strange feeling that she thinks it's "payback" time!

Barbara Jenkins, a best-selling author and a dear friend, has been a primary encourager from the beginning. Thanks.

Thirty-six years ago I became the pastor of the Wilshire Baptist Church in Dallas. For thirty years and one month we walked together, worshiped together, wept together, and laughed together. It was a great journey, and no retired pastor ever felt more gratitude than I do. Today the pastor, George Mason, is my pastor, and he and the members of Wilshire are the best friends Lawanna and I could have. We are very fortunate and would like to thank our Wilshire family for their prayers and love.

A special word of thanks to the people who are a part of these stories. In many cases they have laughed with me before the stories were ever written down. Now, they have graciously freed me up and given me permission to use their names in sharing their experiences. In a few cases, however, the names were changed—to protect *me!*

Finally, my gratitude to Joey Paul, vice president, Word Publishing, Inc., and to Alyse Lounsberry, editor at Word, for their encouragement, suggestions, and—most of all—patience.

Contents

Introduction

On a recent visit to Dallas, four-year-old granddaughters Emily and Ali raced across the den, climbed up in my lap, and snuggled close.

"Tell me a story, 'Goose,'" Emily said excitedly as she put her arm around my neck.

"Yeah, 'Bwoose,'" Ali giggled, "tell us about the time when you were a little boy and the goat butted you off the porch."

Two-year-old John-John, content to let his sister and cousin do most of the talking, nodded his head, grinned, and climbed on up beside his sisters.

I smiled and wrapped all three of them up in my arms, grateful that after nearly three-score and ten years and two heart surgeries, I was still around to bask in the warmth of this moment. I didn't even mind that Ali had tagged me "Bwoose" or that Emily called me "Goose," although I wondered at times if "Father Goose" or "Granddaddy Goose" wouldn't have sounded a little better. But I had learned early on that when your grandchildren name you, you're branded for life.

So I told them about my pet goat that didn't act like a pet. I told them about my first little dog, Trixie, and how she yelped in excitement each day when I came home from school; I told them about little rabbits that played in our yard and squirrels that gathered and hid nuts in the woods; I told them about my own Grandpa Moody and how I loved to ride his horse, Roberta. I told them all these stories—along with embarrassing experiences I had at weddings that went awry, near-drownings at baptisms, getting lost on the way to cemeteries, and losing my way through sermons. Of course, they giggled with glee, as little children do.

I have tried to tell them about God—how He loves and cares for them—through simple, everyday stories.

Simple stories to explain the profound things of life? Everyday stories to shed light on eternal truths?

Admittedly, I wondered at times whether this was really possible—until I remembered some of the words of the One who came to give us life: "Look at the birds . . . . ;" "consider the lilies of the fields . . . ;" and "a man had two sons." Finally, I pondered, "except ye be as a little child . . . ."

Today, I believe these simple stories of His are called "parables."

So, pull up a chair, and let me tell you a story.

"Once upon a time . . . ."

1

Lost—On the Way to "RIP"

The memorial service concluded at the church and the funeral director invited me to ride with him to the cemetery.

"You're new in the city," he said graciously, "and this will give us an opportunity to get to know one another better. "Besides," he added, "the burial is in a small private cemetery—one of the last in Dallas—and you might have some trouble finding your way back to the church."

"That sounds like a good idea," I replied. "I'll enjoy visiting with you, and I'm still trying to learn my way around this city. Just let me pick up my Bible and my notes and I'll be with you in a second."

"Take your time," he answered with ease. "It will take a few minutes for us to gather up the flowers and see that the family and friends are in their cars. We'll also have to wait until the motorcycle escorts give us the signal to start."

This man is smooth, I thought. *He's got a dozen things on his mind; yet he's the essence of efficiency. He exudes a quiet, calming confidence. And, along with all this, he's taking time to look after my needs.* I was impressed.

"Oh, by the way," he added as he walked away, "we're a little short of help today. This is our fourth service, so I'll be driving the funeral coach myself." Then he looked around to make sure that he was not being overheard, and whispered, "Hope you don't mind riding in a hearse."

"Not at all," I responded in the same whispered tones, *"just as long as I'm riding up front."*

We smiled politely at each other, realizing that it would not be appropriate to laugh openly—not even to grin.

Less than ten minutes later the escorts turned on the flashing signal lights of their motorcycles and we eased out of the church parking lot and headed north on Abrams Road. The director kept one eye on the road ahead, and the other on the rearview mirror, checking to be sure that the thirty cars in the funeral procession were moving at an orderly pace.

As we turned right off Abrams and headed east on Northwest Highway my new friend reached for a piece of paper on the seat between us. He studied it for a minute, muttering to himself and nodding his head.

"Looks fine," he said, "I had the folks in the office draw me a map to the cemetery. We'll turn right again down here on Buckner, pass by White Rock Lake on the right, and move on through the Casa Linda area. Did you know that it's twelve miles around the lake, and did you know that Casa Linda is one of the oldest shopping centers in Dallas?"

I didn't, but I was fascinated by his easy, animated travelogue.

"And from Casa Linda we go to east to . . ." His voice trailed off as he glanced again into the rearview mirror. "No need to worry about directions now," he added as he laid the hand-drawn map down. "My biggest concern at the moment is that all those cars make it safely through that busy intersection back there."

They did, and the motorcycle escorts zoomed on ahead to clear the way at the next crowded crossing.

We continued east, making turns here and there that had me completely confused. The escorts appeared confused also. From time to time they glided up next to the hearse with question marks on their faces. The director smiled through the window at them, picked up the map and instructions from the seat, and gave them an affirming nod to move on ahead. With this reassurance they revved their engines and roared on to the next intersection. It was a good feeling to know that the funeral director had matters so well under control.

And, it was good to talk. We discussed churches, city leaders, and sports. Mostly sports. We shared thoughts about the Dallas Texans, the AFL football team that was the talk of the town. I told him proudly that five or six of the players, including the quarterback, were members of the church that I pastored. We also discussed briefly the "new kids on the block," the Dallas Cowboys. I mentioned that I had gone to a Cowboy game recently and the attendance was less than 10,000. He shook his head, and both of us wondered aloud if the Cowboys and their new coach, Tom Landry, would make it in Dallas—or anywhere else. We were totally absorbed in our speculations—so much so that we failed to realize that by now we were well beyond the city limits of Dallas . . . moving slowly through the suburbs of Mesquite . . . away from busy intersections . . . traveling along some obscure farm-to-market road. . . .

LOST, BUT STILL LEADING

Lost. Completely lost.

The funeral director, his furrowed brow beaded with perspiration, drove nervously with one hand and clutched the now-crumpled map in the other. The procession had slowed to a crawl and the escorts lingered further behind. It was obvious that they didn't want to be identified as the "leaders" of this misdirected caravan. The director didn't say a word; he just glanced repeatedly at the map, then at the farmland surrounding us. I turned and looked back over my shoulder. Thirty cars were still following us. We didn't know where we were, or where we were going, but at least we hadn't *lost* anybody! The meandering procession had remained in tact, the drivers of all thirty vehicles looking to *us* for leadership!

Finally, the director spoke with hesitation. "Bruce," he said, "I think we've missed a road, or maybe several of them. We're already beyond the Mesquite city limits. We've got to turn around and go back."

I was a young pastor and had never considered the hazards of trying to turn a hearse around in the middle of an asphalt, two-lane country road. And how do you communicate your intentions to thirty bewildered drivers behind you? But, as is true with most funeral directors, this man was very resourceful. That's why they gave him the title "director."

We topped a hill at a snail's pace and spotted on the right, immediately before us, a dilapidated "filling station" with two lonely-looking gasoline pumps. The once-white paint on the building had long since peeled, and three or four old cars ringed an area designated: "GARAGE—Mechanic on Duty." Potholes, filled with water from recent rains, punctuated the graveled driveway. An old white icebox, with "COLD DRINKS" hand-lettered on it, leaned to the left of the screen-door entrance.

At the first crunching sounds of tires on gravel and the sloshing of wheels in water holes the lone attendant sitting on a crate next to the icebox, half asleep, yawned and stood. Then without bothering to look up, he moved lazily toward the pumps. In one motion he slowly lifted a hose with one hand and pushed the lever to the "on" position with the other. He then waited for his customers to stop.

We were his first "customers"—the funeral director, the pastor, and the deceased—all in the lead car. But we didn't stop. Without saying a word, the director steered the long hearse around a pothole, skillfully avoided the ice box, made a sharp U-turn, and headed back toward Dallas. Other "customers," including the motorcycle escorts—now at the rear of the procession—obediently followed their leader.

I nodded and waved politely at the startled attendant as we maneuvered our way through his driveway. After we made our

U-turn, I looked back over my left shoulder and could see him standing there—confused, bewildered, and holding a limp, dangling gasoline hose with his right hand.

I never knew the name of the gasoline attendant but I could tell he was a gentleman. By the time we had topped the hill, going back in the opposite direction, he had removed his floppy cap with his other hand, and in a gesture of respect, he had placed it over his heart. I was told later that he held that position while all thirty cars circled through his place of business.

Forty-five minutes later, after numerous other turns, we found the small, private cemetery. I read a passage of Scripture, led in prayer, spoke to the family, and joined the director as we headed back west toward the church. The conversation on the way back was sparse. Even my mention of rumors of the possible move of the Dallas Texans to Kansas City didn't seem to excite the dour-faced funeral director. Instead, he kept looking at his watch and mumbling something about "another service."

When we reached the church parking lot I thanked him, shook his hand, and said the wrong thing: "Maybe we can do this again someday."

He smiled weakly, made no reply, and drove off.

I watched him exit the church parking lot and made a simple decision: I refuse to ride in a hearse again—until they put me in the back of it!

"THAT'S WHAT I DREAD ABOUT DYING!"

"Who cares who the speaker is?" Or, "who cares about the program?" "I'm just interested in Miss Julia's pies."

Those were the attitudes of most of the members of the Kiwanis Club in San Marcos, Texas as they gathered weekly in the early '50s at Julia's Tearoom. Miss Julia, showing unusual entrepreneurial skills, had taken a stately old antebellum house on San Antonio Street, renovated it, and turned it into one of the finest eating establishments in the area. Her business skills, coupled with her culinary abilities, made her tearoom a favorite gathering place for luncheons.

THURSDAY—MEN STILL BOYS

But on Thursdays the tearoom was off-limits for everybody but the Kiwanians. As this day rolled around each week the civic club members lined up early, waiting for the doors to open. It was an occasion for unscheduled and uninhibited fellowship. The men laughed loudly and called out greetings to one another, punctuating their salutations with hearty handshakes and slaps on the back. Some entered into exciting discussions on what the entree of the day would be, and a few took delight in making small bets on the height of the meringue atop Miss Julia's lemon pies.

Thursday was a day in San Marcos when grown men became children again—for a couple of hours.

Promptly at twelve o'clock the doors opened and university professors, professional businessmen, salesmen, representatives of the medical field, and hourly laborers rushed in like kids playing "musical chairs." They scrambled for the best tables—meaning, of course, the tables they predicted would be the first served that day. It was just another part of the weekly game.

And it was great fun—a brief reprieve from the daily routines of lecturing to sleepy students, making rounds at the community hospital, attending committee meetings, promoting sales, and pushing levers and switches on the job. Everybody participated.

Everybody except Roger Shelton.

Roger was a "good old boy," well-liked by the rest of the members of the club, but he was a quiet person—a loner. He would usually arrive late for the meetings, after all the jostling and the backslapping and the scrambling for tables had subsided. He would survey the group and then would slip to an isolated table in a less crowded part of the room. This served two purposes: It kept him from having to talk with people about things he wasn't interested in, and it afforded him the opportunity to slip out of the room if the program didn't appeal to him. He often took advantage of this option.

Roger was a paradox. Deep down inside he seemed to care for people but, like a lone Texan on the prairie, he sought solitude. He contributed to the civic projects sponsored by the club, but he did it quietly—without fanfare. He wasn't much of a talker but, when necessary, he could cut through tangled discussions, get to the heart of the matter, and offer the solution in a terse, straightforward sentence.

When most of the members had gathered, with or without Roger, the president would tap a fork or a knife lightly on the side of a glass in an effort to bring the meeting to order. If this didn't work, others at the head table would help him by tapping on their glasses also. And, if the crowd continued to talk, some uninhibited, self-appointed member would shout out above the noise, "Okay, everybody *shut up!*" No one ever seemed to take offense at being told to "shut up." This, too, was part of the game.

When the noise level had muffled to snickers, the president of the club asked someone to pray or, as he usually put it, to "lead the invocation." Because I was a Bible Instructor at Southwest Texas State University, I was often included in these requests. I learned quickly that grown men—even with Ph.D.s—have limited attention spans when caught up in savoring the aroma of Miss Julia's cooking. So, the principle was simple: the shorter the prayer, the greater the gratitude.

After the brief prayer came the pledge of allegiance, with someone at every table inevitably forgetting the words and mumbling his way to the finish. Finally, before the food could be touched, we would sing a stanza of "God Bless America." Two bars from the end of the song the metal chairs would begin to clang as hungry Kiwanians prepared to "dive in."

When the meal was finished it was time for the program. Topics of these varied with the seasons, the community emphases, the special projects sponsored by the club, and the availability of politicians and others who were "turned on" by podiums and lecterns.

On one occasion a local quartet was invited to sing. This foursome consisted of college professors, all with their Ph.D.s—in subjects other than music! But they enjoyed harmonizing in barbershop-style.

They were good—so good that they were often asked to sing at functions at the university and in the community.

And . . . at the funeral home.

Willard Pennington, a congenial civic leader in San Marcos, owned Pennington's Funeral Home located three blocks down the hill from the college. When a family had no specific requests concerning music for a funeral service, Willard would recommend his four college professors. They could leave the campus, dash down the hill, sing two songs, slip out the back door of the funeral home, and never even miss a class. Besides, a few extra dollars in the early '50s went a long way to supplement the meager salaries earned by college teachers. They sang so often for Willard that they were dubbed the "Funeral Quartet."

THE FUNERAL QUARTET . . . SINGS 'EM QUIET

So on this Thursday, after a glowing introduction, the Funeral Quartet began to sing their first number, "Fairest Lord Jesus."

I'm not sure what happened, but I think the person singing the lead pitched it in the wrong key. It was all downhill from there. Terrible. Never has "Fairest Lord Jesus" ever been so rendered—or should I say "rended." What I mean is, "torn apart." The longer they sang, the worse they got. The Kiwanians in attendance bowed their heads (to keep from having to look anyone in the eye), scratched their eyebrows (to give the appearance of prayerful concern), coughed and cleared their throats (to keep from snickering), and lifted cups of cold coffee to their lips (just to have something to do). It was so bad that most people would have given all they had in their pockets to be able to slip out a rear door, or to be carried out! It really didn't seem to matter which!

When the Funeral Quartet sang the last note, still off-key, they sat down. Unfortunately, there was no curtain separating them from the audience like there was at Pennington's Funeral Home. And there was no back door. Escape was impossible, so they just stared blankly, ignoring the generous pieces of lemon pie left for them at their places around the table. No one reached for his fork. Even the promise of savoring Miss Julia's pie couldn't redeem this situation!

Silence. Not a word was spoken. Even the president was speechless.

Embarrassment and disaster had struck the club.

Then a voice cut through the awkward silence. To everybody's amazement it was the drawling, raspy voice of Roger Shelton. He was still with us. The Funeral Quartet had so paralyzed him that he had been unable to slip out his favorite exit.

So, still seated in his chair, he observed loudly and clearly:

"You know, that's what I *dread* about dying!"

The Kiwanians, it seemed, thought Roger had summed their sentiments up nicely. Everyone broke up laughing.

THE DAY NO ONE LAUGHED

November 22, 1963.

It was a beautiful day in the city of Dallas—just the kind I enjoyed most.

The temperature was 76 degrees and there wasn't a cloud in the sky. Most of the leaves on the trees had changed colors, curled at the edges, and fallen gently to the ground. A few hung on tenaciously as though they were challenging the first "blue norther" that would sweep down from the Rockies, across the Panhandle, and through our city, sometimes plunging temperatures down as much as 40 or 50 degrees in a few hours. The norther would eventually come, and every leaf would finally fall . . . but not today. This was a special day for Dallas.

The thirty-fifth president of the United States, John Fitzgerald Kennedy, was coming to town for a brief visit. Accompanying him on the hasty tour of four Texas cities—San Antonio, Houston, Fort Worth, and Dallas—were his beautiful wife, Jacqueline, Texas Governor and Mrs. John Connally, Vice President and Mrs. Lyndon Johnson, Senator Ralph Yarborough, and other dignitaries of the Democratic Party. The trip was designed to mend fences among Democratic party leaders in Texas and to display unity in elections scheduled for 1964.

FATEFUL DECISION

"The president is scheduled to land at Love Field just before noon," Lawanna said. "Let's call Mary and Frank Wilson and see if they can keep Shannon and Renie for a couple of hours so we can go out and see him."

Lawanna is a "now" person, a celebrative spirit, a "don't-dare-miss-this-experience" kind of individual. I'm more the "wait and see," "let's think about it," "are you sure?" type.

I pondered her suggestion, thought of unfinished sermons, and mumbled something about Sunday coming in two days.

"Look," she urged impatiently, "this is supposed to be your day off from church activities; and we haven't had a lot of time together because of your schedule; and it really is the *president himself* who's coming to town." Then she added with a hint of a smile, "You tell the people to pray for our leaders; it might also help for you to go see them."

That did it. We called the Wilsons, who loved to play grandparents, listened to the excitement in their voices, and delivered Renie and Shannon, ages one and two, to their house. Kathie, our oldest, was in the sixth grade at Dan D. Rogers Elementary School.

"Now, you folks take your time about getting back," Mary said in an assuring tone. "We'll take good care of them." Frank, affectionately called "Gi-Gi" by the girls, beamed. Everybody was happy—Mary, "Gi-Gi," Shannon, Renie, and Lawanna. And in spite of my pastoral "oughtness" about sermons and visits, I was happy too. Lawanna was right—again. It was a good day, and we were on our way to welcome the President of the United States to Dallas.

We turned left on Mockingbird Lane and drove west . . . by the historic Dr. Pepper plant . . . across Central Expressway . . . alongside Southern Methodist University . . . through Highland Park . . . and to the entrance of Love Field. A large crowd had already gathered and cheering people were waving hastily prepared banners and signs—"Welcome to Dallas J.F.K," "Welcome Jack and Jackie to Big D," and "Welcome Mr. President." There was a festive mood as the well-mannered crowd of several hundred quickly grew into a crush of thousands. Lawanna and I parked the car and inched our way through the mob of people to the chain fence that separated the spectators from the airport runways.

Enthusiastic chatter was punctuated with eager glances toward the westward skies over Fort Worth, thirty miles away. Adults were like excited children, each anticipating the sight of Air Force One and each hoping to be the first to spot it.

At 11:37 the wheels of the huge, majestic, blue and white presidential jet touched down amid the cheers of the throng that had gathered. President and Mrs. Kennedy stepped through the door, waved to the crowd, moved down the steps, and shook hands with local civic leaders and politicians. Radiant Mrs. Kennedy, wearing a stylish hot pink suit and a smart black pillbox hat, was presented a large bouquet of red roses. She pushed her dark hair from her face, smiled, and waved in the direction of the admiring crowd. Then she took her place beside the president in the waiting car. Riding along with the Kennedys in the open presidential limousine were Governor and Mrs. Connally.

At 11:50 the motorcade, escorted by the Dallas Police Department's new black and white '63 Ford Galaxies and a dozen Harley Davidson motorcycles, slowly began the winding journey that would lead them through downtown Dallas and on to the Trade Mart where the president was scheduled to speak. As Lawanna and I walked to our car, I said, "I'm glad we did this. It's a lot better than watching a re-run of it on the television news tonight."

Traffic out of Love Field was congested, with cars inching along bumper to bumper, but no one seemed to be in a hurry. Individuals and families were still basking in the warmth they had just experienced in personally greeting the president and his entourage.

"Let's take the back streets," I suggested to Lawanna as we listened to the radio announcers give progress reports on the motorcade. "Gordon Abbott's barbershop is on Oak Lawn Street just a few blocks from here. I can get a quick haircut there while the traffic clears out." Gordon was a deacon in the church that I pastored, a good friend and an excellent barber.

THE PRESIDENT IS SHOT

I parked the car in front of Gordon's shop and reached to turn off the ignition but before I could, there was an awkward pause in the flow of communication—an interruption—as a second radio announcer broke in and said breathlessly, "A report . . . three shots . . . unconfirmed . . . three shots fired at President Kennedy's motorcade today in downtown Dallas. . . ."

Lawanna and I sat in stunned disbelief, straining to hear words like "correction" . . . "mistake" . . . "rumor". . . . But words like those were never spoken. Instead, we heard terms, now familiar to the world, like "Elm Street" . . . "Book Depository" . . . "triple underpass" . . . "grassy knoll". . . "Parkland Hospital" . . . Bits of sketchy information were punctuated by periods of silence—haunting silence—as stunned reporters and announcers scrambled for additional details.

The events that followed are a blur. Lawanna and I leaped out of the car and ran over to the barbershop. Inside Gordon, the other barbers, and the customers were all huddled around a small radio. Their world, like most of the rest of our worlds, had come to a halt, frozen in time and paralyzed by the hesitant, troubled voices of reporters. I don't remember if I ever got a haircut that day; I do remember the anguish I felt in my heart—and in the pit of my stomach.

We left Gordon's place hurriedly and drove quickly to the Wilsons, arriving just in time to hear Walter Cronkite—voice breaking, struggling to frame the words—announce "President Kennedy died . . . Parkland Hospital . . . 12:39 . . . today. . . ."

It was time to go home to our babies . . . time to wait for Kathie to get out of school . . . time to try to explain to her what we could not understand . . . time to be brave like mature adults . . . time to weep like little children.

On Saturday morning, after a sleepless night, I got up, dressed quietly, slipped out the door, and drove slowly toward the church. Strange. The offices were not open on Saturday, but I wanted to be alone. I didn't want to be pastor to anyone on this day. I didn't want to think about sermons, or budgets, or committees, or anything. I just wanted to be alone. When I arrived the other members of the staff were already there. We discovered that each of us had wanted the same thing: to be alone . . . together.

ALONE . . . TOGETHER

We sat together in an isolated room, shared our feelings and concerns, prayed, and wept. We also talked about church members and other friends who were caught up personally in the tragedy: two surgeons—members of our church—who were on the staff at Parkland; nurses who worked in the trauma room; a dear friend who was chief of chaplains at the hospital; policemen and civic leaders who were seeking answers and struggling for solutions; and thousands of people across the city who, like us, wanted to be alone . . . together.

"Let's have a prayer meeting here at the church tonight," someone suggested. "No program, no special music, and no sermon. Just give the people a chance to pray together and share their concerns."

There was no time for newspaper or radio announcements. The staff called some deacons, and the deacons called some teachers and committee members, and they in turn called their friends.

At seven o'clock Saturday evening over four hundred people crowded body-to-body into our chapel. I read a brief passage of Scripture from the Old Testament: "If my people, who are called by my name, will humble themselves and pray and seek my face and turn from their wicked ways, then will I hear from heaven and will forgive their sin and will heal their land" (2 Chron. 7:14 NIV).

"I have nothing else to add to this," I told the people. "You're invited to remain seated, stand, or kneel—as you wish—and pray. Feel free to pray silently or aloud."

Scores of people knelt right where they were in the aisles; others remained in their seats, bending forward with their heads resting on the pew in front of them; some stood in the back and in the foyer, leaning their bodies against the wall.

For nearly an hour there was silence, broken only by the gentle sounds of soft weeping and the whispers of burdened petitions: "O God . . . forgive . . . bless . . . guide . . . ."

When I sensed that the time was right, I stood and said simply, "Amen."

Those who had gathered quietly stood to their feet and walked out without a word.

They had been alone . . . together . . . with God.

THEN CAME SUNDAY

Sunday morning an estimated 500,000 people gathered for worship in the churches in Dallas. Overflow crowds attended each of the services at Wilshire that day.

What does a minister say to a congregation in grief? I'm not sure. I never have been sure. And, I wouldn't have remembered what I said that day—November 24, 1963—had I not found my sermon notes one day many years later as I was cleaning out some file cabinets in the garage:

> "There is no need to recount the tragic details. We are all too well aware of what has happened in our city and in our nation. We are still in a daze, a state of shock, a sense of nightmare—thinking that soon we will wake up. Slowly, the awful reality closes in upon us. It is no nightmare. We are awake. Custom does not dictate it, but we would like to sit down in sackcloth and ashes and weep our hearts out. If our city had a wailing wall like Jerusalem of old, we would lean against it and weep."
>
> "We come to this service with remorse, and repentance, and (dare I say it?) Thanksgiving. Is this the epitome of irreverence? Is this pious talk? Yet, I am reminded that the very spirit of Thanksgiving is born in suffering, trial, and adversity. The writer of Ecclesiastes said, 'In the day of prosperity be joyful; but in the day of adversity consider . . .' (Eccles. 7:14 KJV). This is a good time on the eve of Thanksgiving to stop and consider . . . that . . . out

> of the depths of this tragedy perhaps good can come. Pray God that it shall."
>
> "We will do what we must—in spite of obstacles and dangers and pressures. And, with God's help, through our remorse and repentance, blended with a spirit of thanksgiving, we will try to build a better city and a better nation. This is the essence of Christian courage."

Just before the benediction, as we prepared to leave the worship service, one of the ushers walked down the aisle and handed me a note. I glanced at it and with a trembling voice read it out loud to the congregation: "Lee Harvey Oswald was just killed at the police station."

I managed some kind of brief closing prayer, and the people filed out wordlessly. There were no back slappings or light-hearted greetings in the aisles or hallways. No "good sermon, Pastor," and no "how 'bout those Dallas Cowboys?" Nor did anyone say, "Have a nice Thanksgiving holiday." The people walked out in stunned silence.

Monday was declared a day of mourning by the now thirty-sixth president of the United States. Schools closed, businesses shut down, office buildings stood dark and vacant, the streets were empty as people stayed home, glued to their television sets, watching every facet of the memorial service. When the day was over we were physically and emotionally drained.

WE MUST GO ON

That was thirty years ago.

Kathie now teaches composition and literature courses to college students who were not yet born in 1963. Renie and Shannon are married and have children the ages they were thirty years ago. Lawanna and I are grandparents, and I have retired from pastoring. Mary Wilson is with the Lord, and "Gi-Gi" is still our special friend. Had John Fitzgerald Kennedy lived, he would be seventy-six today. He died at forty-six.

"Hail to the Chief" has been played for seven other presidents since that fateful November day in Dallas.

So, life goes on. The grieving—which knows no partisan politics—eventually subsides, although at times it returns . . . unexpectedly . . . and without invitation.

It lingers for a moment, and then we get on with life and "do what we must . . . with God's help."

2

Old Folks at Home

Years ago . . .

Ethel and Jake, newcomers to Dallas, attended worship services at Wilshire one Sunday morning. Following the service they lingered to introduce themselves to me and to visit briefly.

"We're looking for a church home here in the city, and we like what we see at Wilshire," Ethel said warmly as she shook my hand. Jake stood in the background and silently nodded his head.

"I'm grateful," I responded with a smile while breathing a silent sigh of relief that we had at least passed the first test. I knew from experience that there were other tests we'd have to pass if Ethel and Jake joined our church. These often included the number of parking spaces, the length of services, the comfort of the pews, the kind of music and the loudness of the organ, the friendliness of the congregation, and the preparation and varieties of foods served each Wednesday evening at the "fellowship dinners."

"Would it be possible for you to drop by our house later this week?" Ethel continued. "This will help us get to know each other better and will give us the chance to ask you some questions about the church. Jake and I would appreciate that very much, wouldn't we Jake?"

Jake nodded.

JAKE'S CURIOUS ABSENCE

"You just call us, Pastor, and let us know when it's convenient for you to drop by," Ethel glowed as she shook my hand a second time. "We'll be mighty glad to see you."

Then she turned and walked away. Jake followed her.

The visit was made and apparently most of their, or her, questions were answered adequately, for they joined the church the next Sunday. Both were regular in their attendance for several weeks, and then Jake became less and less involved.

"How's Jake?" I would ask Ethel.

"Oh, he's fine. This has been a difficult week at work for him, and he's worn out;" or, "he's not feeling well today;" or, "something came up unexpectedly." Ethel would always have an answer like one of these readily available, anytime I questioned her about Jake's absence.

Then one day I received an urgent telephone call. "Something's wrong, seriously wrong with Jake," Ethel cried. "He's in the hospital now and they plan to operate in a couple of hours. They say it's an emergency and has to be done. I . . . we . . . need you. Can you come to the hospital immediately?"

"Of course I can, Ethel. I'm on my way."

By the time I reached the hospital most of the relatives had already gathered. They filled Jake's room and overflowed into the corridors. Concern, accentuated by tears, was written across their faces.

"The doctors say they've found a mass, Pastor—a huge mass in his intestines. They say they'll be taking him to surgery in fifteen minutes. Please pray for him," Ethel pleaded as she reached down and took Jake by the hand. I could tell by the glazed look in his eyes that he had already received his pre-operation injection, sometimes called the "happy shot," or the "don't care shot." Poor Jake didn't look happy, but neither did he seem to care. The shot was partially working, at least.

I took Ethel by one hand and Jake by the other. Relatives crowded back into the room and I prayed briefly for Jake, for the surgeon, and for the entire family. When I finished, Ethel wept, the relatives hugged each other, and Jake snored. The "happy shot" had done its work.

Normally after having prayer with the patient and the family, I would leave to make other hospital calls or perform other pastoral duties. I would usually check with the family either during the surgery or after the operation. This time, however, I had a feeling that I needed to stick around. Ethel seemed emotionally depleted and everyone was concerned about that mass in Jake's intestines.

So I lingered. Relatives paired off or sat in small groupings, drinking coffee and struggling for encouraging words to say to one another. One older man identified himself as Jake's cousin and invited me to walk down the hall with him. As we slowly moved out of the traffic and away from the conversations, he spoke softly.

JAKE PICKS BEER

"Sad about Jake, isn't it?"

"Could be serious," I whispered.

"Sad about Jake and Ethel too," he added.

"Sad? What do you mean?"

"You don't know?"

"I have no idea what you're talking about," I replied in confusion.

"Preacher, Jake likes his beer."

"Yes?" I responded, sensing there was more to the story.

"Well, Ethel gave him an ultimatum. Told Jake, 'it's me or beer.'"

"What happened?" I asked innocently.

"Jake chose beer and moved out. Hasn't been home in over a month. Don't know where he's been living, but he's sure not been with Ethel."

Slowly the picture was coming into focus for me. That's why I hadn't seen Jake in church, and that's why Ethel had been making excuses for his absence. Apparently he had allowed her to take the initiative, be aggressive, and make all the decisions—until she gave him one ultimatum too many.

The waiting moments dragged into an hour, then two hours. The conversations in the hospital corridors lapsed into hushed comments and whispered expressions of concern. Every door that opened and every person in surgical garb who rounded the corner heightened the shared anxiety.

PASTOR, WILL YOU PRAY?

Finally, a weary surgeon with a mask dangling from one ear walked slowly into the room. You could feel, almost hear, the hush of the moment.

"Ethel," he asked with a sigh, "where has Jake been living in recent weeks?"

"Well . . . ah . . . he's been living away from our house," she answered hesitantly with eyes lowered. "I don't know his address but I've been told it's in one of the lower income sections of the city. He has a new job and it's hard to make it on one income, especially when you pay rent on two places, and . . ."

"And where has he been eating?" the surgeon interrupted impatiently.

"I really don't know," she replied uncomfortably as she glanced at me. "I guess he's been eating at some of the diners and dives near where he's been living. Why do you ask?"

"Because, Ethel," the doctor answered in frustration, "I've just removed from Jake's intestines a mass—a mass . . . a mass of undigested . . ."

The surgeon took a deep breath and Ethel gasped.

"A mass" he repeated through clinched teeth, "of undigested *chicken dumplings!*" He then wheeled around and without another word, stalked out of the room.

Silence. Stunned silence.

"Pastor, will you lead us in prayer?" someone asked.

I muttered some kind of answer, asked everyone to bow his head, and for the first—and only—time in my life, thanked the Lord for *chicken dumplings*.

So, you're not feeling well today?

Cheer up—it could be chicken dumplings!

"AIN'T GONNA HAVE NO MORE!"

I parked my car alongside the curb, turned off the ignition, and sighed. There was something sad about the visit I was about to make. Dear old Mr. and Mrs. Darby, faithful members of our church through the years, were confined to their home. The aging process and the frailties of life had finally caught up with them. He was ninety-four years of age and she was ninety. Both had been in the hospital recently and neither was able to adequately care for the other. He had suffered a stroke, leaving his right side paralyzed, and she battled a cancer that sapped her energies. They were little more than shells of their former selves.

I got out of the car and glanced around as I made my way up the steps to the front door. Everything seemed to be aging right along with the couple who lived inside. The lawn, once manicured and immaculate, was brown and thirsty for water. The scattered patches of grass were dry and brittle. Only the weeds grew. The window boxes designed for colorful blooming flowers were filled with tired, withered stalks of what had once been. The old car in the driveway, idle and unused for weeks, was powdered all over with dust and grime. Two rocking chairs on the front porch had been turned backwards and leaned against the wall, a silent signal that late evening chats with friendly neighbors had finally come to an end. The paint around the door facing had peeled, and taped across the doorbell was a handwritten note that read, "Out of order." Somehow, that little sign, obviously written with a shaky hand, summarized everything.

It's not fair, I mused. *It's just not fair! It's not right for good people like these to come to the end of life with so many things "out of order."*

How on earth can I hope to say anything at all that might help this elderly couple?

But pastoral duty called, and for the moment I laid aside my own frustrations and knocked lightly on the door.

IT HAPPENS TO EVERYONE

"Mr. Darby . . . Mrs. Darby—it's Bruce, the pastor of your church."

I pressed my ear near the door and listened as a weak voice invited, "Come to the back door."

I walked around the house, climbed some rickety steps, and raised my hand to knock again.

"Come on in, Pastor; the door's not locked."

I hesitated, then stepped through the door, wondering again what in the world I could say or do to minister to their spiritual and emotional needs. This was unexplored territory for me. I was a young minister and these folks were walking slowly and painfully down paths that I had never traveled.

"Good to see you, Pastor," Mr. Darby said as he slowly waved a trembling hand at me from his recliner chair. "I'd get up to greet you but I'd probably fall, and you'd have to try to pick me up. And I don't think that's in your job description," he added with a chuckle.

I was relieved to hear the chuckle. So familiar. So encouraging. I had heard that chuckle of his in tedious committee meetings at the church, and had felt with others the immediate easing of tensions. I had heard it in the crowded hallways as I threaded my way toward the sanctuary for the worship service, wanting to be friendly to people but feeling the urgency of being on time. I had heard it—that special chuckle of friendship—at the close of a sermon when I knew better than anyone else that I had failed miserably in my attempts to get my point across. That chuckle and a pat on the shoulder helped pick me up and kept me going on more occasions than anyone could ever know.

Mrs. Darby, lying on a bed on the other side of the room, greeted me with a smile and a nod of the head. Her illness made speaking difficult, but the slight gestures and the kindness in her eyes expressed the warmth of friendship and welcome that I had felt so many times when I had visited with them. The world needed more people like the Darbys. For that matter, *I* needed more people like them.

"Yes sir," Mr. Darby continued, "it's so good to see you. Thank you for visiting an old, worn-out couple like us."

His greeting jarred me. It was hard, almost impossible, to think of this couple as "old," or "worn out." For a quarter of a century they had been involved in all aspects of the ministry of our church. They had unselfishly given their time, their money, and their prayerful support. The words "pillars of the church" had an authentic ring when applied to them.

"Now you just pull up a chair and have a seat," he continued. "Sorry we're not dressed for the occasion but the wife and I are being kinda lazy today. Hope you don't mind."

"Not at all, Mr. Darby. I just wanted to drop by and let you know we're all thinking of you and praying for you."

For the next few minutes we talked about the church, mutual concerns, and my family. They asked about each of the girls—Kathie, Shannon, and Renie—and wanted to know every little detail about their lives. I shared some of the latest "stories" from the McIver household and they responded with smiles and more chuckles.

This was not the time for a lengthy visit. I didn't want to tire them out and knew they both needed rest, so I suggested that it was time for me to leave.

"I'll be back in a few days," I promised as I stood. "Meanwhile, let's have a prayer together before I go."

"That'll be fine," Mr. Darby replied, "but first I want to talk to you about something."

A WISE CONCLUSION

"Of course," I answered as I sat back down. I wondered what was on the mind of this ninety-four-year-old man. Did he want to talk about his health? His will? The church? Some unfinished business? Death, or dying? Maybe plans for their memorial services?

"Pastor," he began seriously, "my wife and I had a discussion this morning."

"Yes, Mr. Darby," I responded in genuine concern. "Would you like to talk about it?"

"You know, Pastor, that we've had three children."

"Oh, yes," I replied. "I know them well."

"Now, since you know them well," he continued, "you also know that none of them turned out right."

Gulp.

How in the world was I to respond? My pastoral care class in the seminary didn't prepare me for this. The truth is I *did* know his children and, although I would never have dared say it, they really *didn't* turn out right. Thankfully, the old gentleman didn't wait for any reply from me.

"So, the wife and I talked it over this morning, and we came to a conclusion."

This time he did pause for my reaction.

"Yes? And what was your conclusion?" I asked.

He straightened up in his recliner, lifted a bony finger for emphasis, and declared with finality . . .

"WE AIN'T GONNA HAVE NO MORE!"

And then he looked across the room at his wife . . . and chuckled. She mustered a faint smile—tender and affirming.

I doubled over and fell out of my chair—right there in their den—pounded the floor with my fists, and guffawed! Then, in absolute ministerial disarray, I picked myself up from the floor, held my sides, and laughed my way out the door. I was so rattled, I had forgotten to pray! I laughed all the way to my car, and I admit that at that very funny moment in history, I wasn't worried that I hadn't prayed with this beloved couple, or even concerned that the whole afternoon had failed to go as planned. All I could think about was the neighbors—and hope they weren't watching.

3

And the Two Shall Be One. . . .

It was a wedding service never to be forgotten and, hopefully, never to be repeated. Once was enough.

I glanced at my watch and noted that it was seven-fifty in the evening—ten minutes before the organ fanfare would be followed by the traditional bridal processional. I knew that excited bridesmaids were adding final touches as they nervously checked their dresses in front of full-length mirrors, lightly sprayed their hair again . . . and again, and eagerly made last-minute searches for the flowers they would carry when they soon walked down the aisle.

I knew, also, that the groom and his attendants were secluded in another room, making fun of one another as they tried to don ill-fitting tuxedos and wondered which way to turn the cummerbunds. Having participated in hundreds of wedding services, I knew that it was time for the conversation among the fellows to become louder and more intense as the "countdown" to eight o'clock began. Often in the midst of this verbal melee, someone would yell, "Quiet! Everybody listen up!" This would be the cue for the groom to check again and be sure the best man had the license and the ring. And it was time for everyone to check his zipper for the tenth time!

All of this is predictable. It's all part of the ritual of any wedding service. It seldom changes.

THE FATHER OF THE BRIDE

On this occasion I made my rounds. I tapped lightly on Angelia's dressing room door, told her how beautiful she looked, and wished her "God's blessings." I then headed down the hall to speak with Timothy when one of the church staff called, "Pastor, there's an urgent call for you."

"I can't take a call now," I answered impatiently. "I have a wedding service to perform in five minutes."

"You'd better take this one, Pastor. It sounds urgent."

Timothy would have to wait for the moment. Something serious could have happened to one of the members of the church. An accident? A death?

Maybe something was wrong at home. Lawanna? The girls?

I picked up the receiver and heard someone ask, "Pastor McIver?"

"Yes."

"I'm a friend of Angelia's family, Pastor, and I thought you needed to know that Angelia's father is on his way to your church."

"But Angelia told me he had refused to attend the wedding," I replied quickly. "She said he's a very angry man with a lot of deep problems, but he won't let anyone help him. Apparently he's been out of touch with her and her family for several months. That's why her uncle is giving her away tonight."

"I know all that, Pastor, but he's headed that way now."

"That's fine, but I hope he gets here in the next five minutes or he'll be late."

"No, Pastor, you don't understand. He's drunk—very drunk. He's a big man and says he's going to "shoot up" the wedding.

He's mean, sir; and when he gets drunk he gets *real* mean. If I were you, I'd be very careful."

I thanked the caller for alerting me, glanced at my watch—two minutes to go—and trembled all over.

"Lord," I mumbled, "when I told you I would preach, I thought that's what you wanted me to do. Frankly, Lord, there's enough tension in performing a wedding ceremony without having to look over my shoulder to see who's going to shoot me!"

Time was running out. One minute to go.

I dashed down the hall (as fast as a man with a bad hip and a chronic limp can dash!), opened the door next to the organ loft, and whispered to the organist, "Not yet; keep playing!"

He looked at me in surprise, nodded that he understood, and then uttered under his breath, "When?"

"I don't know," I whispered back. "We've got a problem. Just keep playing."

"PASTOR, HE'S MY BROTHER!"

I ran out the door and raced around the building to the rear of the sanctuary, hoping to intercept the bride and her attendants before they began the procession down the aisle. I was in luck. The bride was a couple of minutes late and had not yet arrived. But her uncle who was to give her away was standing there, dressed in his evening clothes and smiling ear to ear. I motioned for him to meet me outside the door.

"Something wrong?" he asked, noticing the obvious concern on my face.

"We may have a problem," I replied. "I just received a call that Angelia's father is on the way to the church. He says he's going to 'shoot up' this wedding. Do you think he'll really cause trouble?"

"Is he drunk?"

"Yes, very drunk."

"Well, Pastor, he's my brother and I hate to say this, but if he's drunk, he will cause trouble. Big trouble."

"What do you think we ought to do?"

"Call the police and have him thrown in jail. He's tough, and he weighs over two hundred and fifty pounds. I think you need to call the police right now. By the way, tell them he'll probably be driving a two-tone red and white Buick."

"I'll do what I can," I promised weakly. "I'm on my way to make some calls, but don't tell Angelia. She's got enough on her mind without having to deal with this."

"I won't tell anyone," he agreed as he stepped back inside the building. "I'll not let on to Angelia or any of the family that he's on his way here. Just make sure the police get here in a hurry."

"Lord," I mumbled again, "did he say two hundred and fifty pounds? And he's drunk? Please, Lord, I've got a sanctuary half-full of happy well-wishers, and I've got Angelia and her bridesmaids ready to march down the aisle. . . . and I've got a groom who would pass out if he knew what's going on. . . . and I've got an organist who's probably sitting up there whispering to himself, "When?" And I've got to make these calls. . . . and . . ."

I turned quickly and headed toward the office area to make the calls. Fortunately, Lieutenant Wayland Fields of the Dallas Police Department was in his office. I got through to him immediately. He was a good friend and a faithful member of Wilshire. Just the sound of his voice made me feel better—for the moment.

"Look, Wayland," I exclaimed excitedly, "I've got some problems out here at the church." I told him briefly what had happened, described the father of the bride, and gave him information on the car he would be driving.

"You go ahead and begin the ceremony," he replied. "I'm dispatching three units immediately. They will be there in ten minutes. I'm also on the way myself. This will be a priority code, but we'll not have the lights and sirens on. I don't want what we do to add to the disruption."

I thanked him and breathed a prayer of gratitude for all policemen—especially those who protected ministers at weddings!

I then scurried out the office door and headed down the hall to whisper to the organist, "NOW."

Ten paces later I bumped into John Bowen, one of our church custodians. John was a delightful black friend about thirty years of age. He was tall, fine looking, well-built, and had salt-and-pepper hair that made his appearance even more distinctive. He had a warm spirit and a kind, soft voice. John was always ready to do anything anyone asked of him, and most of the time the asking was not necessary. He was a valuable member of the staff.

"John," I blurted out without thinking, "There's a big man . . . two hundred and fifty pounds . . . he's drunk . . . and he's on his way to the church right now. He says he's going to shoot up this wedding. Now, John," I continued without taking a breath, "I've just called the police. Lieutenant Fields is on his way and he's dispatching three other units."

John's eyes got bigger and bigger and his mouth fell open.

"John, I want you to go to the back of the sanctuary. Don't tell anybody you know what's happening, but for heaven's sake (and mine!), don't let any two hundred and fifty-pound man with a gun in his hand through that back door!"

John didn't say a word. He just looked at me, mouth wide open.

"I gotta go now, John. I'm telling the organist to begin the processional. Thanks for helping."

"LORD, PLEASE PROTECT US!"

Ten minutes later the bridal procession was finished and fourteen smiling attendants surrounded the nervous but happy couple. Angelia and Timothy had never looked more radiant. Somehow I managed to get through the introduction of the ceremony and through an opening prayer. How I prayed!

For blessings, and for guidance . . . and for protection. Especially for protection!

Then someone sang the "Lord's Prayer." While others bowed their heads and closed their eyes, I peeped. To my delight I discovered my prayer for protection had already been answered. Through the glass in the doors at the rear of the sanctuary I saw Lieutenant Fields. He was wearing his dress uniform and his braided white cap. He was standing tall and erect against the double doors with his arms folded across his chest in an authoritarian stance. He must have had a feeling that I was peeping for he nodded ever so slightly in my direction and smiled at me. I do believe he looked like an angel that night!

The rest of the ceremony went off without a hitch. The rings were exchanged and the vows spoken. I pronounced Angelia and Timothy "husband and wife"—to the joy of those in attendance. The recessional was celebrative. I exited through the side door—with hardly a limp.

The two hundred and fifty-pound father was apparently so drunk he never found the church.

Angelia and Timothy never knew about his threat.

Thirty years later, they still don't know.

The crowd had dispersed. The bride and groom had dashed to their car in a traditional shower of rice. The family and most of the wedding party had gathered up tuxedos and other garments and headed for home. The organist, with a sigh of relief, had closed the console. I made my way through the small kitchen adjacent to the reception hall, hoping for a cup of soothing coffee or a hot punch. The drama was over. I was grateful and ready to get on with life.

A LIKELY STORY

At that very moment, I spotted John, the custodian, sitting on the floor next to the stove with his legs drawn up and his chin on his knees, looking like he was in a helpless, semi-fetal position.

"Hi, John," I said.

Not a word. Not even a glance upward.

"Something wrong, John?"

Slowly, ever so slowly, he raised his head and looked at me with eyes as big as saucers.

"Pastor," he said, barely above a whisper, "don't you . . . don't you *ever* do that to me again."

It took a moment for his words to sink in.

"I'll do anything you ask," he said in measured tones, "except guard doors at weddings."

I laughed, and after a long moment, he managed a weak smile.

Still later that night, after I had gone home. . .

John and the other custodian, Denver, were turning out the lights and closing up the building. It was nearly midnight.

"John," Denver said, "I've been having trouble with my car lately. The batteries seem to be weak. Would you mind waiting on the parking lot until I see if it will start?"

"I'll be glad to."

Denver got in his car, put the key in the ignition, but nothing happened. Sure enough, the battery was dead.

"I've got some jump cables in my car," John offered. "Let me pull up next to you on the parking lot and see if we can get it running."

John walked across the lot, got into his own car, and drove it over next to Denver's. He raised the hood, connected the battery cables, and froze as he heard the squeal of tires as three Dallas police cars—with red lights flashing this time—screeched to a stop and surrounded them!

It took a lot of tall talking for John to convince the policemen that he was not the man they were looking for—even if his own car *was* painted two-tone red and white!

It wasn't long afterwards that John resigned as custodian and began selling insurance.

I figure he found it easier to deliver death benefits than to risk his life guarding doors at weddings.

"Grow Old Along with Me!"

Jean, my first wife and Kathie's mother, died at the young age of thirty. Polio. Our only child, Kathie, had just turned four, and I was unprepared—woefully unprepared to be a "single parent." By the way, this was long before they had discovered the term.

A few days after Jean's memorial service, it hit me: Kathie and I were on our own—alone—in our duplex in Dallas. It wasn't that family members didn't want to help. They did, but distance and health conditions and a variety of other situations made it inadvisable, if not impossible, for them to step in and assist on a day-by-day basis. Their moral support, prayers, and loving concern meant more than they could ever know.

A lot of things hit me without announcement in this "single parenting" role that had been so suddenly thrust upon me:

- sitting in the surgery waiting room with fourteen mothers while my child was having a tonsillectomy

- rearranging work schedules so I could attend PTA or "Bluebirds"
- looking the city over for a blue Christmas tree just because Kathie wanted a blue one, and trying to explain that to neighbors who have never had, or even seen, a blue Christmas tree
- standing outside a toilet in a public place, hoping some kind lady would understand and help retrieve my little girl who refused to come out
- explaining to Kathie that I couldn't marry that nice lady—because she was already married . . . to a deacon in my church.
- and dreading holidays, vacations, family gatherings, and even "family suppers" and "family fellowships" at the church.

But with God's help, I learned quickly that life is lived day-by-day and the "dailiness" of it, as Mother used to say, is overwhelming.

"Daily" meant fish sticks and beef potpies and, for a change, chicken potpies. "Daily" meant rolling hair, trimming hair, and finally cutting hair—real short. "Daily" involved selecting clothes for a little girl (with the help of some dear friends), buying clothes, and washing clothes. "Daily" meant walks to the park, reading stories, and saying prayers at night. "Daily" also involved a rollercoaster ride through all the five-year-old childhood diseases—every one of them, or so it seemed!

But most of all, after the pangs of grief subsided, and after friends began talking about other things, "daily" meant experiencing the loneliness of existing in a suspended frame of time, with no clear perspective of the future. There was neither the time nor energy to talk about next year, or a new house, or a new job, or even new furniture.

Everything was daily; everything was on hold; life was pregnant with "meanwhile."

Then as time passed, friends began to talk . . . and tease.

"What about her?" or, "I know a friend;" or, "I saw her looking at you;" or, (worst of all) "You know, of course, Kathie *does* need a mother. . . ."

So like a little schoolboy, you begin to think . . . and wonder . . . and wait.

And wait.

The dating game finally begins, and for the most part it's a downer. You're too old to play games and too proud to run the risk of rejection and too independent to rely on well-meaning but sometimes unreliable friends.

And too tired to stay out late . . . and too poor to afford fancy dinners and expensive musical productions.

So you date . . . and hope . . . and wait . . . and pray. You pray a lot. And Kathie prays, to your chagrin and frustration, "Lord, give me a little brother or a little sister."

And you think you want a miracle but, "Lord, I'm not sure even *You* can pull this one off!"

Things don't work out once . . . twice . . . more. . . .

And you're glad.

"Lord, if it's not in Your will for me to find the right one—not just a mother for Kathie, but someone I can love with all my heart—then I'll try to understand . . . and adapt . . . adjust . . . and become the best 'single parent' ever."

And then came Lawanna. A gift. A gift from God . . . with an Indian name meaning "By the still waters."

As I was soon to realize, there's nothing "still" about her, but strangely, she calmed my heart . . . my life . . . and my home . . . more than anyone could ever imagine.

And she took the toil out of all those "dailies" and gave me a future.

DAD'S VOTE OF CONFIDENCE

When I called Mother and Dad on January 2 and told them that I had met the *very* girl and would be marrying, Mother asked, "What's her name?"

"Lawanna," I answered.

"When are you getting married?"

"February 13th."

Then Dad spoke up, interrupting with, "Son, why on earth are you waiting so long?"

(Frankly, if I had known then what I know now, I don't think I would have waited the six weeks until February 13!)

"Son, I'm happy for you," Dad continued. "Now, tell me, what's she like?"

"I'm not sure, Dad; but she's not like anyone else I've ever known."

"Marry her, Son. Don't you let her get away. Marry her!"

Dad's been gone a long time, and I discover each day new answers to his question, "What's she like?"

- She's a free spirit . . . but she's anchored to the basics.
- She's a wife who cares . . . but doesn't coddle.
- She's a mother . . . who knows how to play with her children (and now grandchildren).
- She's independent . . . but she's a gracious part of the whole.
- She's creative . . . without being strange.
- She's a concerned Christian . . . without a pinched look.
- She's "Lawanna" . . . still waters . . . and rippling currents.

And Dad, wherever she is, things have a way of "happening."

LAWANNA'S GREAT BANK ROBBERY ADVENTURE

Lawanna was on one of her trips back home to Anniston, Alabama, to check on her elderly parents, Walter and Delba House, and to enjoy a good visit with them. Her sister, Susie, lived in the area and was in touch with them daily, but Lawanna would spend three or four weeks a year with her parents to lend her own support. These were usually "working" visits for Lawanna—taking inventory of the pantry, cooking and storing foods in the freezer, and assisting with practical needs.

A couple of days before she was scheduled to return to Dallas she ran some errands in the downtown area of Anniston. As usual, she had more to do than she had planned and, as usual, time ran out. Late in the afternoon, after the sun had gone down and after darkness had settled in, she called to tell her parents that she would be a few minutes later than she thought.

When she finally reached home about six o'clock she was met by a concerned eighty-five-year-old father who said anxiously,

"Sister, it's dark outside; I don't like for you to be out on the streets after dark."

Lawanna, who has traveled the world over—in daylight and dark—humored her father by reassuring him that she had been very careful.

"But you never know what can happen out there after dark," he countered. "You just can't be too careful these days."

"I understand, Daddy; and I appreciate the love and concern you've always had for me. But I don't want you to worry about me. I'm nearly sixty years old and . . ."

"But there's all kinds of mean things happening out there after dark."

"Okay, Daddy, I promise I'll be very careful," Lawanna smiled, realizing that even as a grandmother she would always be a "little girl" to her father.

The next day there was another errand to run. Walter had a small Certificate of Deposit that had matured. Happily, he had learned that a bank in the adjoining town of Oxford, just over the mountain, was paying 2 percent more interest than he had been receiving. So he cashed the CD in, got a cashier's check for the amount, and asked Lawanna to drive him and her mother to the new bank. They agreed to leave late in the morning, transact the business, and then have lunch together at Morrison's Cafeteria. Shortly after 11:00 A.M. they were on their way. As they approached the bank, Delba sat quietly in the backseat while Walter watched for the entrance to the parking lot.

"Turn the car right here—right here, Lawanna," he said.

"But, Daddy, are you sure? The sign says 'exit.'"

"I'm sure. I've been to this bank before."

"But the sign says . . ."

Oh, well, rather than prolong the discussion from the middle of the street, Lawanna made a turn into the parking lot of the bank, entering with the arrow pointing in the opposite direction.

AN OMEN . . . WASN'T IT?

That should have been an omen of what was to follow.

"Mother, we won't be long," Lawanna said as she parked the car in front of the door and got out. "Why don't you just sit here while Daddy and I do our business? We'll only be a few minutes and then we'll go to lunch."

"Sounds good to me," Delba replied. "Take your time. I'll be fine out here."

Lawanna and Walter opened the front door and walked into a nearly empty lobby—empty and silent. Strangely silent.

"Looks like everybody's gone to lunch," Lawanna commented as she surveyed the room. There was one bank officer at her desk, assisting a customer in filling out forms, and there was one teller behind the counter, apparently taking care of a young man. "Daddy, you wait here. I'm going over to the counter and ask the lady if there's a place where you can sit and be more comfortable while you wait."

Walter protested mildly, insisting he was fine and did not need to sit down. Lawanna smiled, ignored him, and began walking across the lobby. The young man at the window finished his business, placed his things in a black backpack, turned, and walked straight toward Lawanna on his way to the door. Their eyes met and he stared at her boldly for several seconds. Then he continued walking casually out the door.

Before Lawanna could reach the counter the terrified, ashen-faced teller screamed, "We've been robbed! We've been robbed!" She then dashed across the lobby, ran past Walter who was still holding his cashier's check and still waiting for a "comfortable seat," locked the door, and sounded the alarm.

Within minutes the building was teeming with bank officials, security officers, policemen from both Anniston and Oxford, and FBI agents. As the first came through the door Walter whispered nervously to Lawanna, "I didn't see a thing; and if they ask you any questions, you didn't see anything either."

"I think I've already seen more than I bargained for!" Lawanna replied, wondering how in the world one could be on an errand of mercy for elderly parents and end up in a real-life "Bonnie and Clyde" adventure.

The officers and agents methodically and professionally went about their business. They dusted furniture and doors for fingerprints, removed and reviewed film, frame-by-frame, from the video cameras, and secured the building.

Meanwhile, Delba sat in the car . . . on the parking lot . . . wondering why the doors to the bank had been locked . . . and why all those bank customers were lining up outside the building . . . and why Walter and Lawanna had apparently been locked inside.

"My mother has been waiting outside in the car," Lawanna said anxiously to one of the officers. "She's not in good health, so you'll either have to let me out or you'll have to bring her in here."

DELBA'S FIRST BANK JOB

Two officers graciously escorted Delba in, ushered her to a plush leather chair, and brought her a soft drink. Delba was pleased. It was her first bank robbery.

Later, Lawanna was questioned at length by one of the FBI agents. "Lady, just relax and tell us what you can," he said in a calm voice. "The terrified teller followed carefully the man's note of instructions but couldn't give us any concrete information. The robber was very professional. He kept his head down and the bill of his cap covered most of his face, so the bank video camera isn't much help. We need any information you can give us. It appears that you are our only witness. Did you get a good look at him?"

"We stared each other in the eyes for what seemed like half a minute, eyeball to eyeball," Lawanna replied, "and then he ambled past me to the door. He was Caucasian, about thirty years of age, medium build, approximately five feet, ten inches, and I remember vividly . . . brown eyes."

"Can you give us a description of the clothes he was wearing?"

"He had on a loose-fitting green shirt—the same color people wear who work in medical centers."

"Anything else?"

"Yes, he had a dark backpack over his shoulder and he had a full, neatly trimmed mustache. For some reason by the time he reached me he had taken his cap off, so I could see his dark brown hair pulled into a pony tail, about collar length."

"That helps," the agent responded as he took notes.

"Now Mrs. McIver, is there any other general impression that you had that might be helpful to us?"

"As a matter of fact, there is," Lawanna answered. "I hope you'll understand what I'm about to say, but to a 'little old lady in tennis shoes' nearly sixty years of age, he was—well, he was rather good-looking."

The agent forgot that he was an agent. He lost it professionally as he collapsed across the desk, doubling up with laughter.

While he was still laughing, beepers, "walkie-talkies," two-way radios, scanners and whatever else policemen and agents carry with them went off.

"Armed bank robbery in progress! Armed bank robbery in progress! Colonial bank . . . just off Quintard Avenue . . . . . behind Wal-mart!"

The officers and agents raced out the door, dashed across the Wal-mart parking lot, and were just in time to give chase to the robber. They nabbed him as he attempted to escape in his stolen vehicle.

Same robber.

"How can you know he's the same one?" Lawanna asked the agent later.

"Your description helped, Lady," he said with a grin. "And by the way, he *is* sorta nice looking."

Nice looking or not, he was an escapee from a prison in Florida. He had been convicted of armed robberies—ten in all—and was serving a sentence of life without parole, so he had nothing to lose! He was being investigated for six other bank robberies—and now he had been caught in two more in one hour! Obviously, he worked fast.

Later Lawanna, Delba, and Walter sat over a delayed afternoon "lunch" at the cafeteria, compliments of the bank. As they finished dessert, Lawanna looked out the window and watched the sun sink slowly behind the mountains.

"It's getting late, Daddy," she said with a somber look on her face. "We'd better be moving toward home. It'll soon be dark, and, as you reminded me yesterday, a lot of *mean things can happen out there* after dark."

Walter guffawed. Delba grinned. Lawanna kept a straight face, and the three headed for the car.

TEA AT THE ROCKWELLS

"Lawanna, I've just found the perfect book for you to review next year," exclaimed long-time friend and house guest, Grady Nutt. "I've just finished reading *My Adventures As An Illustrator*, by Norman Rockwell, and it is a *must* on your list. Then he handed Lawanna a well-worn paperback edition of the autobiography.

"Read it and see for yourself," he added with a grin. Lawanna took the book and thanked Grady with a bear hug.

Professional book reviewing is a disciplined, demanding responsibility. It involves reading or browsing dozens of books, selecting the right autobiography or biography, working hundreds of hours condensing the contents of the book to one hour, memorizing the manuscript, and "crawling into the skin" of the author and presenting the material in first-person style. Lawanna had recently been introduced into the field. Resurrecting her background skills in speech and drama, she had picked up her "rusty tools" (as she put it) and moved into the competitive arena.

She soon discovered there are hundreds of civic and book clubs in the southwestern part of the United States. And she learned the hard way that a good reviewer will often speak four or five times a week before these various clubs. Lawanna was good.

"Grady, you are a God-send!" she exclaimed as she took the book from her friend. "You've helped me more than you can know. The hardest part of reviewing is finding the right book. If you say this is a must for me, I'll read it immediately."

Within three days she had finished the first reading, closed the book, and said with a sigh of relief, "Grady was right. I've found my book for next year."

ROCKWELL'S BOOK A HIT

Rockwell's book was read again and again in the coming weeks. It was marked, condensed, outlined, and committed to memory—just in time for the review season which began in September and lasted until May.

"There's just one thing lacking," she said to me one morning. "I really need a hard-bound copy of the book to display during the presentation. I've checked book stores all over Dallas and not one can be found. In fact," she continued, "there's only one copy for all of the public libraries in the city."

And, after checking with rare book dealers from the east to the west coast, she concluded that Rockwell collectors were not about to turn loose their copies.

"Why not go to the source?" I suggested. "Why not contact Norman Rockwell himself, tell him what you're doing, and see if he can help you?"

That's all it took. She sat down immediately and penned a note to him in Stockbridge, Massachusetts. She congratulated the illustrator on his eighty-second birthday (she'd read about it in the papers), wished him continuing health, and explained her dilemma.

To my surprise (but not hers) a handwritten reply came within a week. It seems that Rockwell was impressed that anyone would want to review his book—so impressed that he had personally searched for a good copy. He had found one—a first edition copy no less—in Melvin's Bookmark, located over a drugstore in Great Barrington. But Melvin wanted ten dollars for the book.

"Would ten dollars be too much?" Rockwell wrote.

Ten Dollars! Lawanna was excited enough to pay one hundred!

For the next several months she reviewed *My Adventures As An Illustrator*, by Norman Rockwell. She reminded her audiences that the artist had painted 318 covers for the *Saturday Evening Post*, each seen by an average of four million people. His works had appeared in or on every major magazine published in this land. His advertisements had sold air travel, bicycle tires, cough medicine, encyclopedias, fountain pens, insurance services, toothpaste, and scores of other products. In addition, he had illustrated the lives of Benjamin Franklin, Tom Sawyer, Huckleberry Finn, and an uncommon soldier named Willie Gillis.

Lawanna underscored in her reviews that Rockwell was, and is, "Americana at its best." His paintings illustrated everyday happenings in average America—the awkwardness of youth, family vacations, homecomings, visits to the family doctor, the comforts of old age, pride in country and heritage, and reverence for life. His portrayal of America with such affection brought him the title, "an interpreter of his nation's life."

The review season was almost over. Rockwell's book had been a smashing hit with audiences. Lawanna was already scheduled for several more years to continue sharing the illustrator's delightful story.

A PERSONAL NOTE

Then one day I came across Lawanna in her study . . . in a reflective mood. I could almost see the wheels turning in her mind as she sat there.

"Do you think . . . would it be presumptuous . . . do I dare . . .?" she mused to no one in particular.

"Why not!" she exclaimed as she reached for a pen and stationery.

"I am securing one of your "triple-self-portrait" prints," she wrote, "to frame for my personal memorabilia wall in our home. It would mean so much to me to have one of your worn, discarded paintbrushes—large or small—with or without bristles. I'd love to also frame it under your portrait."

Brilliant psychology! I thought. *Poor old Norman doesn't know what he's up against.*

A week later another note came from Rockwell. And along with the note was a carefully wrapped *autographed* paintbrush—with traces of paint still clinging to its well-worn bristles! This precious gift became all the more meaningful when it was announced a few days later that the elderly artist had painted his last picture and had laid down his brushes. Within a few months he was dead.

A short time later Lawanna visited with her friend, Sandra Gill, a member of our church and a collector of Rockwell memorabilia. She proudly shared the letters and the gift of the paintbrush.

"Why don't we make our own pilgrimage to Stockbridge?" Sandra suggested. "It'll give us the chance to see where he lived, feel the family atmosphere of the community, and maybe meet some 'locals' who knew him."

"That's a great idea" Lawanna replied excitedly. "One of my dreams has been to walk down Main Street, made famous in his 1967 *Christmas at Stockbridge* painting. Besides," she added, "it will give me the opportunity to visit with Kathie." Ironically, our oldest daughter, Kathie, with a couple of college degrees tucked away, was working at the time in Stockbridge as a piano accompanist and counselor for the "Beaupre Performing Arts" summer camp for young people.

"I'll make the reservations," Sandra offered. "We'll stay at the historic old Red Lion Inn." The hotel, built in 1773, was once a stagecoach stop and a pre-Revolutionary War meeting place. Several of Rockwell's original paintings graced the inn. It never occurred to Lawanna and Sandra that getting reservations at the hotel might be difficult. They were already packing their bags!

A few weeks later they checked into (you guessed it) the Red Lion Inn. Their third-story room overlooked (you guessed it, again) the quaint home of Norman and Molly Rockwell. The New England clapboard house, originally built in 1783, was surrounded by trees and a thick hedgerow. Rockwell's simple red-barn studio was immediately behind the house.

Lawanna, Sandra, and Kathie spent a week walking around the town center, visiting with locals who had modeled for the illustrator, browsing the picturesque shops depicted in the *Post* covers, touring the Town Hall, paying grateful homage at Rockwell's grave in the Stockbridge cemetery, visiting the small Old Cornerhouse Museum, and drinking coffee on the front porch of the inn.

Late one morning over a second cup of coffee, Lawanna mused half aloud, "Do you think . . . would it be presumptuous . . . do I dare?"

"What are you talking about, Mother?" Kathie asked.

"Kathie, go inside to the front desk and get me some hotel stationery and a pen," Lawanna responded with an all-knowing smile in her eyes.

Ten minutes later the note to Molly Rockwell had been written and sealed.

"WITH GRATITUDE . . ."

In it she expressed gratitude for the illustrator's help in securing the first edition, hardcover copy of his book and for the priceless gift of the paintbrush. She shared briefly with Molly the warm response of people to her husband's story through the book reviews, reflecting their continuing appreciation for "America's favorite painter." She closed with a word about the pilgrimage that she and Sandra were making and wished Molly the best.

The note was finished, but the problem had just begun.

"Let's walk across the street and put this in her mailbox," Lawanna said to Sandra and Kathie.

Good idea. But when they crossed the street they discovered there was no mailbox. Lawanna then remembered from her book reviews that the Rockwells *had* no mailbox. Instead, Norman's practice each day had been to paint during the morning hours, break for lunch, rest for an hour, and then ride his bicycle down Main Street to the post office to collect the mail. The exercise was good for him; so were the informal chats with the locals along the way.

On the other side of the street Lawanna surveyed the situation. The only thing separating her from the screen door of the house was a clump of thick trees and a hedgerow.

"I think . . . I think I can make it around the trees," she pondered, "and maybe . . . under the hedge."

"Mother, you wouldn't!" Kathie exclaimed.

But she would—and she did. On hands and knees she crawled under the hedge, slithered around the trees, and slipped the note under the screen door, listening to the stifled giggles of Sandra and Kathie in the background. Only as she struggled through the hedge again on her return did she realize she had been at the *back* of the house, not the front!

But, in spite of the misdirection, it was worth the effort for later that afternoon a handwritten note addressed to her was delivered to the hotel desk. Molly Rockwell had invited the three to coffee the next morning!

After an exciting sleepless night, they found the proper gate and walked up to the *front* door with all the dignity and poise they could muster. A lovely, gracious, white-haired Molly opened the door, invited them in, and thoroughly thrilled Lawanna by inviting her to sit in Rockwell's own easy chair. Over coffee for the next hour she talked about "her Norman," his work schedule, their children, and the "simple things" of life that meant so much to him. When the visit was over she graciously posed for pictures with Lawanna and thanked them for coming.

As they circled the house and passed by the thick hedgerow, Sandra reckoned out loud, "Wouldn't Norman have enjoyed painting you on your hands and knees, crawling under that hedge?"

"Yep," Lawanna giggled, "rear end and all!"

From what the curator of the magnificent new Norman Rockwell Museum told her on a later pilgrimage to Stockbridge, Lawanna is probably the only person who has a signed paintbrush from the artist.

And as far as we know, she is the *only* person who ever crawled under his hedge to get to his back door!

POSTSCRIPT:

Thirty-five years after marrying Lawanna, I can pray with all honesty, "Thank You, Lord, that in life some things do *not* work out. But, Lord, thank You that some things *do*."

A famous line from one of Robert Browning's most elegant poems goes like this:

> Grow old along with me!
> The best is yet to be,

The last of life, for which the first was made.
Our times are in his hand.[1]

That's how it is—how it's always been with Lawanna. Dad, she's a gift from the Lord . . . worth waiting for.

---

[1] *Bartlett's Familiar Quotations*, ed., Emily Morison Beck (Boston, MA: Little Brown and Company), p. 544.

Just Bark off the Old Family Tree

My brother, affectionately called "Sip" by family and friends, died suddenly a few years ago. I immediately caught a plane and flew home to North Carolina to help my sister and others make plans for the memorial services. These plans, as most families learn sooner or later, included setting the time and place for the service, purchasing the casket and other equipment necessary, writing an appropriate "obit" for the weekly paper (double-checking to be sure no name was left out and all names were spelled correctly), and selecting flowers, music, and the preacher.

And setting the time for "visitation."

As we worked through the details step by step, I discovered all over again that the visitation hour (actually two hours) is most important and could not be avoided. It's usually scheduled at the mortuary, or funeral home, the night before the memorial service to provide an opportunity for people in the community to do what the word suggests—visit. Family members, near and distant cousins, neighbors, old classmates, business associates, and a few who are just plain curious gather to express their feelings and share their sympathies. It's as much a part of the memorial process as any message by any preacher. It's woven into the fabric of social cultures.

So we scheduled it and promptly at seven o'clock the guests began arriving to pay their respects to "Sip" and to share prayerful concerns for the family. The open casket in the "viewing room" was banked with flowers, some of them bearing personal notes. Friends and relatives came from the hills and valleys, from creek banks and wooded areas, from neighboring villages and crossroads, and from the two-block-long main street in my home town.

It was really quite impressive—and moving. Obviously I had experienced some of this in my thirty-year pastorate in a growing church in the metroplex of Dallas, but not on this scale.

I was back home and fatigued as I was, I was grateful for the simple outpouring of kindness and love.

By 7:30 P.M. the funeral chapel was crowded with scores of good people, each voicing his own feelings and recalling his own special memories. That was the problem.

It's difficult for more than a hundred people to voice concerns and swap stories without raising their voices. The noise and din increased minute-by-minute, decible-by-decible until it was almost impossible to carry on any kind of conversation. This had nothing to do with lack of respect; it was just a matter of verbal survival. Before long it grew into a modified kind of "Baptist-Irish wake"—without the hard stuff.

A CAPACITY CROWD TURNS OUT FOR "SIP"

By eight o'clock the place was packed to capacity and I felt absolutely exhausted. It had been less than six months since my second open-heart surgery and I was drained, both physically and emotionally. Depleted. In desperation I looked around the room for some means of escape, but everywhere I turned I bumped into more people.

I paused, tried to collect my wits, and remembered what I had been taught in my recent post-operative therapy: "Create your own space . . . take a deep breath . . . relax . . . close your eyes . . . breathe . . . slowly and deeply. Now, find the rhythm. Good. Inhale . . . exhale; inhale . . . exhale; inhale . . . ex . . ."

On my third "exhale," with eyes tightly closed and hoping no one was watching, I had a strange feeling that someone had invaded my space. I opened one eye ever so slowly to check things out, and, sure enough, there he was—standing immediately before me . . . grinning.

"Remember me?" he asked with a chuckle.

Frankly, I've never known how to answer that question, especially if I don't remember the person. I've never been brazen enough to respond with a "Why should I?" or "I don't have the faintest idea." Neither have I had the courage to do what my friend, Ross Coggins, did at a national convention. He printed in tiny letters on his lapel identification badge, "I can't remember *yours* either."

But in this case, in the middle of the viewing room, I really didn't have a clue, so I just stood there with a blank look on my face and a sinking feeling deep down inside as this stranger just kept grinning back at me.

His closely cropped thin hair accentuated his round, ruddy face. His tight-fitting, multicolored sports coat with wide lapels, vintage seventies, made him look even larger than he was. His narrow black tie, vintage sixties, was obviously worn only on "special occasions." And Sip's death certainly qualified as one of those.

"Oh, c'mon," he urged. "You remember me. *Sure you do!* Try hard."

LEROY WHO?

"Well . . . ah . . . golly . . . I'm trying," I stammered.

"Me and you used to play together down on the farm when we was little boys," he persisted.

I had no idea what farm, but I did some quick calculations and figured that "little boys" meant at least sixty years ago. And I had lived in Texas nearly fifty of those!

"I'm trying," I struggled, "I'm still trying."

"Sure you remember," he teased with kind eyes, "I lived a few miles down the road from you."

That information didn't help a bit.

"I'm sorry," I pleaded. "You'll have to forgive me. I've had a lot on my mind today, and it has been a long time since . . ."

"Shucks," he said as he jabbed me good-naturedly on the shoulder. "Don't worry none about it. Name's Leroy."

Leroy? I thought. *Leroy who? I know a dozen people named Leroy, but they're all in Texas.*

I struggled to play it cool, took another deep breath (just like the therapist had taught me), shook hands with him, and said as positively as possible, "Oh, Leroy, so good to see you. Thank you for coming."

He didn't let go of my hand. Instead, he held on, looked me straight in the eyes, and studied me carefully.

"Yep," he added, "you and me and Sip all three used to play together on the farm. Always did like you brothers."

His voice trailed off then as he looked over at the open casket six feet from where we stood.

"You and Sip," he mumbled half to himself. "Bruce and Sip. Sip and Bruce."

By now it was obvious that Leroy was confused. He released my hand, took a step backwards, and sized me up again. He put his hand on his chin and turned a second time toward the casket in perplexed silence.

WHO'S WHO?

Then after what seemed like half an eternity, he took a deep breath, turned back to me and asked quizzically, "Let's see, are you him? Or is that *you* over there in the casket?"

I strangled, swallowed hard, stifled my feelings, and motioned to Lawanna who was standing in the middle of the crowd a few feet away. I turned my head away from Leroy and mouthed the unspoken words, "Get me out of here—NOW!"

Poor Lawanna read my lips and panicked. She thought my heart was acting up (it was!), pushed around people, grabbed my arm, and escorted—or dragged—me out of the room.

"Helen," she called, "open your office door immediately! Something's happened to Bruce!"

Helen Buckner, a favorite cousin, was the owner of the funeral home. She quickly opened the door, grabbed me by one arm while Lawanna held the other, and ushered me to her own office chair behind the desk.

"Quick!" Lawanna blurted. "Call a doctor."

"Don't bother," I strangled hysterically as I collapsed across the desk. I'm OK. At least, I think I am."

"But please close the door," I pleaded, "and keep everybody out—especially a guy named 'Leroy.'"

I then told them what had happened.

"One other thing," I added, wiping tears of laughter from my eyes, "Go out there and take another look at Sip. *Then let me know if I'm him, or if he's me!*"

Postscript: "visitations" are a part of life—and death. I wouldn't try to change that. Leroy meant well. I survived. And I know Sip would have loved this story.

TRAVELING . . . TOGETHER?

Speaking of my brother, "Sip". . .

For many years he owned a monument company in North Carolina.

It was a "full-service" kind of operation. A customer could choose a marble or granite stone from the display lot, order it cut to the proper size, select designs and inscriptions to be engraved on the stone and determine the date when it would be placed, or "set," in the cemetery. It was a good business for my brother, but it was also a helpful ministry to families.

On one of my infrequent trips back home I enjoyed browsing through the display lots, reading the inscriptions engraved on purchased headstones. They varied from marker to marker, often reflecting more sentiment than theology: "Asleep," "Angel," "Now Singing in the Angelic Choir," "Waiting for the Sunrise," and "Peace," or "At Rest."

One day I stumbled across a huge double headstone that grabbed my attention. It was cut out of some of the most beautiful granite to be found anywhere, and neatly engraved across the center in large letters was the family name. Then, on the left side of the marker was the name of a man and the dates of his birth and death. A casual glance told me that he had recently died. That same glance told me that somebody had spent a lot of money—big bucks—on the marker.

What intrigued me most, however, was the carving just above the family name. It was not an angel or a harp or a sunset. It was a perfectly proportioned engraving of a Winnebago motor coach. Just beneath the Winnebago were the words, "Traveling Together Through Life."

I turned in bewilderment and asked Sip, "What in the world does this mean? There's bound to be a story here somewhere."

"Well, there is," he replied. "This couple lived in a town not too far from here, and when they retired they bought this motor home. It was a dream come true for them and for two years they traveled happily across the nation together in their new 'home.' She said they had some of the best times ever on these trips. Then the man became ill and died suddenly. The grieving widow came in a few days later and picked out this stone—one of the nicest on the lot. When the purchase was completed she made an unusual request. She asked if we could engrave a replica of their motor home on the stone. And," Sip continued, "she said she wanted 'Traveling Together Through Life' under the engraving."

ETCHED IN STONE

Sip told me that he had secured a picture of the motor home and he and his crew made the appropriate line drawings on the stone. The sandblasting began and within hours the family name, picture, and words were permanently etched—a testament to family devotion, enjoyment, and togetherness.

It was a sweet story. I was almost moved to tears—and I didn't even know the people.

A year later I was back home, once again browsing through the monuments on display. I came upon one and did a double-take.

"Hey, Sip," I called. "Here's this Winnebago. You engraved this stone a year ago. Why is it still here on your lot instead of in the cemetery? What happened?"

"I really don't know the whole story," he replied. "But the widow came by and paid me what she owed. She told me that she had married another man, canceled the order, and then she and her new husband took off in the Winnebago, waving and smiling as they drove away."

The last time I visited the monument display lot, a few months before Sip died, I checked and the "Traveling Together Through Life" stone was still there.

But there was no sign of the Winnebago.

GRAMPA MOODY AND THE MAYO BOYS

I dialed my mother's telephone number and waited nervously for her to answer. The variety of strange tones—bleeps, hums, buzzes, and muffled bells—reassured me that the communication system was straining to make the journey all the way from Texas to North Carolina. I was grateful. And I was also grateful that new technology had replaced "operators" who had usually asked, "City, please?"

"Siler City," I would reply proudly.

"How do you spell it?"

"S-i-l-e-r C-i-t-y," I spelled slowly with mild irritation. I couldn't imagine that anyone didn't know where my hometown was. Even Andy Griffith talked about it frequently on his television series. Why, there isn't a "Mayberry" in the whole state of

North Carolina, but there's certainly a Siler City, and everybody ought to know how to spell it. Or so I thought.

"And what is that town close to?"

"Greensboro," I would answer with growing impatience.

After a lengthy pause, while I wondered if the telephone company's meter was ticking and if I would be charged for all this research, the operator would finally say, "Thank you. I've found it."

And then the inevitable question: "Now, what is the number you wish to call in Siler City?"

"Eight-F" I would respond meekly.

"Yes?" Hesitation. "And the other numbers?"

"Eight-F! There aren't any more numbers. Just plain 8-F!"

"Oh, I see. Just a minute, sir." Another pause.

Finally, "Here it is. Stand by and I'll ring. That's two shorts and a long."

The whole process was downright humiliating. I was proud of my hometown, my roots, and my friends. But "8-F" for a telephone number? Two shorts and a long? Frankly, I was grateful for a new day when weird digital sounds replaced the southern drawls of inquiring operators.

My recollections, punctuated with a hint of a smile, were interrupted by Mother's voice:

"HELLO—HELLO. ANYBODY THERE? HELLO."

Mother, like most of her brothers and sisters, had experienced hearing difficulties in the aging process of life. Just trying to communicate by telephone was a difficult, draining experience—for both of us.

"Mother," I spoke loudly into the mouthpiece, "I've got some great news. It looks like my hip can be fixed."

"Your WHAT can be fixed?"

GOOD NEWS FOR AN OLD MALADY

"My HIP, Mother. There's a new procedure that's been developed—a new operation—and the doctors out here seem to think that it might work in my case."

I was thrilled to be able to share the news with her. For forty-one years I had limped through life with a medically fused hip. My problems had begun with osteomyelitis, a bone disease that settled in the hip joint when I was a boy of nine—several years before the availability of penicillin and other "miracle drugs." Three major surgeries, months of hospitalization, numerous blood transfusions, daily doses of horrible-tasting cod liver oil, and a body cast that eliminated all motion in the hip until the joint became solid bone got me through the worst of the crisis—and through the next four decades.

Now there was hope that the long-term fusion could be reversed. A new hip joint seemed possible. Obviously it was too late for me to participate in sports activities, but just the thought of bending, twisting, and stooping like other people elated me. I wanted to share this with Mother, but I didn't want to cause her any worry about another operation. We'd been through enough of those.

"Mother," I continued, "my doctors in Dallas think the surgery can be done, but they want me to go to the Mayo Clinic for further evaluation."

"That's wonderful, Son," she replied. "The Mayo Clinic is a fine place to go for help. I know all about it."

I was confused by her answer. I knew that Mother knew about the Chatham Hospital, a small hospital located in our hometown; and, of course, she knew about Duke Medical Center where I had been a patient as a boy; and there was the Matheson Clinic fifteen miles down the road at Pittsboro. But the Mayo Clinic?

"No, Mother," I replied firmly, but politely, "I'm talking about another clinic. It's one of the best in the world; it's located in Rochester, Minnesota. It's a diagnostic clinic that specializes in unusual and difficult cases."

MOTHER KNEW ALL ABOUT THOSE MAYO BOYS

"I know all about that clinic," she interrupted with uncharacteristic impatience. "I know what they do there, and I know all about the Mayo brothers, Charles and Will. Those boys operated on Pa."

I couldn't believe what I had just heard. Mother—bless her heart—must have had difficulty hearing me, or understanding me. *After all,* I reasoned, *it's a long way from Rochester to the rural area of North Carolina. And the Mayo brothers operating on my Grandpa, Jasper Moody? No way.* I smiled to myself and ended the conversation by telling Mother that I loved her and that I hoped to visit with her soon. Meanwhile, I filed "Grandpa's surgery" and the Mayo brothers in the back of my mind.

But it wasn't in the back of Mother's mind. It was the first thing she wanted to talk about on my next visit home. The truth is, I think she was a little vexed with me because I questioned her in our telephone conversation. She insisted that I pull up a chair and listen. Like an obedient child I did, and I heard the full story for the first time.

The year was 1914. Mother, then an older teenager, was staying temporarily at home with her parents between teaching responsibilities in neighboring communities. "Ma" and "Pa," as she called them, lived on a farm in Chatham County. They were poor but they had been able to grub out enough from the raw land to feed and clothe ten children and see most of them move on to other places and other responsibilities. Their farmhouse was a mile from the Rives Chapel Church, located on Tick Creek—five miles from Bonlee, six miles from Ore Hill, and seven miles out in the country from Siler City.

But most of these towns and crossroads might as well have been a hundred miles away, for hard work and poor roads made travel anywhere difficult. So like most everyone else, they lived of necessity in their own world—struggling with the soil, harvesting the meager crops, helping neighbors who were in trouble, gathering at the church house on Sundays, and sharing stories and laughter after an evening's meal. Telling stories—and embellishing them—was at times the only entertainment they could afford. And they were good at it.

One day, according to Mother, Pa had the stomach ache. Ma put him to bed and treated him with all the home remedies available. Throughout the day and into the next his condition worsened. Finally, one of the boys got on a horse and rode to Ore

Hill to get Dr. Stroud, an old country doctor who for years had been the only physician in the area. The kind man listened to the need, hitched his best horse to a buggy, picked up his medical satchel, and two hours later arrived at the Moody farmhouse.

"He examined Pa for several minutes," Mother said, "while all of us children stood on the porch wondering what he would say. We knew that Pa was a mighty sick man."

"Then," she said, "Dr. Stroud left the room, walked past us, and motioned for Lee to come with him." Lee was one of the older boys in the family.

A FASCINATING DRAMA

"The two of them walked slowly down to the corn crib and spoke in hushed tones. I can still see them down behind that crib," Mother added with a faraway look in her eyes, "talking seriously and quietly to each other. I kept watching them and wondering what they were saying. I had a feeling it was bad. Finally, they headed back toward the house and when they reached the old well, Ma and the rest of us met them.

"We listened without saying a word as the doctor spoke. 'Mrs. Moody,' he said softly, 'your husband is a very sick man. He seems to have a growth either in his stomach or intestines. It's so big I can feel it. But I'm afraid I can't help him. There just doesn't seem to be anything that can be done. It's a matter of time. I'm so sorry.' Then, with a long look on his face, he climbed into his buggy and drove off."

By now Mother was re-living the story, re-creating the experience as she told me the story. The tale had come to life. I listened in rapt fascination. I was a child again . . . at my mother's feet.

"We all stood around the well in disbelief," Mother continued. "We were stunned . . . overwhelmed . . . too shocked to cry."

"Then one of the boys said, 'We're not just gonna stand around and do nothing and let Pa die. Not 'til we've done everything we can. I heard there's a new doctor in Siler City—a Dr. Wren. Let's go get him. He might see something different.'"

Courage. Dogged determination. Those were trademarks of the family, and they started with Pa and rubbed off on the children. Jasper Moody had seen his own father stumble home from the Civil War, crippled for the rest of his life; he had lost two brothers and a sister—all three at the same time—with typhoid fever; he and Ma Moody had built their first farmhouse, only to see it go up in smoke and flames a few hours after he made the final payment on the money borrowed to build the house; and he had watched crops devastated by droughts and by rains.

Through it all he had been a survivor. Now the family decided that it was time to try to keep on surviving.

So another horse was saddled, and one of the boys galloped off to Siler City to try to locate Dr. Wren. Several hours later the young doctor arrived and, once again, the children gathered around the old well in the yard while Pa was examined again.

"He's a very sick man, Mrs. Moody," the doctor said when he closed the door and walked out of the house. "There's not much hope for his recovery . . . unless we can get him to Greensboro and to the hospital there."

TO GREENSBORO, ABOARD THE "SHOO-FLY"

Greensboro? Why, Greensboro was nearly forty miles away, and Pa was dying. "But," my mother continued with a smile, "we didn't give up. I helped put a feather bed in the back of a wagon, the boys hitched up two horses, and several of us lifted Pa into the wagon. My older brother, Lee, and Dr. Wren then climbed up on the wagon and they headed for Ore Hill to catch the 'Shoo-fly.'"

"Shoo-fly?" I interrupted.

"Yes, the 'Shoo-fly.'" Mother said. "The 'Shoo-fly' was a little train that made a daily round trip between Greensboro and Sanford." I listened, and quickly calculated that the round trip distance would be about 150 miles.

"They knew that the train would be passing through Ore Hill late in the afternoon on its return trip to Greensboro, and they were determined to try to catch it," Mother added.

"When the train arrived they lifted "Pa" off the wagon and laid him down on the feather bed in the aisle of the train."

She paused and observed with gratitude, "That young doctor went with Lee and Pa all the way to Greensboro."

"What about Grandma?" I asked. "Didn't she make the trip?"

"Why, Son, there was no way Ma could go. Somebody had to run the farm and look after the children."

I continued to listen in silence, trying to comprehend the emotional impact of all this on a family as Mother kept talking. "The train pulled into the station at Greensboro and they unloaded Pa. Somehow—I really don't know how—they got him to St. Leo's Hospital. The doctors immediately examined him and confirmed what Dr. Stroud and Dr. Wren had said. Pa did have a growth, and they said that exploratory surgery needed to be performed without delay."

I was hanging onto every word as Mother spoke. I felt that I had been riding on that wagon, chugging along on the "Shoo-Fly," and standing in the corridor of the hospital with my Uncle Lee and Dr. Wren while waiting for a verdict from the examining physicians.

THE BIG-CITY OPERATION

Mother took a deep breath and then continued the story. "The doctors in the hospital said the operation would be critical, but then one of them added, 'In a way, we are very fortunate. We have two outstanding young physicians visiting with us and they are teaching new techniques in surgery. They're from out west . . . Minnesota, I believe. They're brothers—Will and Charlie Mayo.'"

"Well," she said with a lilt in her voice, "before that day was over those two boys had operated on Pa. Just as everyone expected, they found a tumor the size of a grapefruit. They bypassed the tumor, sewed Pa up, waited two weeks, and then performed a second operation and removed it."

I sat at Mother's feet in stunned silence. Disbelief.

Mother then leaned her head back, closed her eyes, and pondered for a moment.

"Now, let's see," she said, "That was 1914. Pa died in '34. That means he lived another twenty years."

A VOTE OF CONFIDENCE

Slowly, trying to comprehend what I had just heard, I looked up into my Mother's face. It was a face of courage and strength. For a brief moment, I saw that family conference by an old well, a galloping horse, a bumping wagon and a feather bed, and a train called the "Shoo-fly." And, I think I heard someone out of the past say, "We're not just gonna stand around and do nothing. . . ."

"Son," Mother said quietly with a knowing smile, "You make your plans to go to the Mayo Clinic. There's some mighty good people there."

And I believed her.

Then her voice trailed off as she added again, "Those boys operated on your Grandpa."

6

"But It Hurts Too Much to Laugh!"

I leaned back in my recliner chair, gently nursed a now-tepid cup of coffee, and stared blankly through the window into the pre-dawn darkness. The rest of the family was still asleep but the agonizing hours of tossing and turning were over for me. "Lord, be patient with me," I mumbled half aloud, "I'm trying to understand, but things just don't make sense."

In the middle of my pitiful (and self-pitying) whimper the telephone rang. *That figures*, I reasoned with half a smile, for I had learned as a pastor that Alexander Graham Bell's "gadget" had no respect for persons or privacy. It had the unique ability of intruding at the most inopportune moments—day or night. Or at six-thirty in the morning. I wasn't sure what heaven would be like, but I was confident of one thing: there would be no telephones. A compassionate God would simply not allow them there!

"Hi, Bruce," a bouncy, cheerful voice greeted me, "this is Bill."

The introduction was not necessary for I recognized the voice immediately. Bill O'Brien, a close friend, once served as Minister of Music at Wilshire. While on our church staff he and his wife, Dellanna, made commitments to serve as missionaries in Indonesia. And while on our staff he introduced me to Lawanna and later sang at our wedding. So the ties with Bill were deep and personal. I was glad he and his family were home on furlough after a four-year tour of service abroad. I was also glad they were living nearby in Fort Worth and we had opportunities to visit with them.

But I was not glad that he called this morning. I just wasn't in the mood to talk to anyone, not even a friend.

"How are you, Bill?" I asked, forcing the question.

"Oh, I'm great," he replied. "And you?"

There was an awkward silence, a silence that probed hidden thoughts and invaded realms reserved only for trusted friends.

"You haven't heard what's happening in my life?" I asked hesitantly.

"I don't know a thing."

"Then why did you call?" I asked innocently.

"I don't know," he replied, "I really don't know."

Bill didn't know. Few people did. Lawanna and I were still in shock and trying to absorb the jolting diagnosis. We were busy asking our own questions, nursing our own wounds, and wondering about the future. There just wasn't enough energy left to call others and try to fill them in.

So in that early morning hour, over cold coffee, I verbalized for the first time what had happened. I shared with Bill results of recent heart stress tests, follow-up visits with my internist and cardiologist, an overnight hospitalization for further tests, and the verdict of all involved: heart surgery immediately.

I also told Bill that I had resisted every test and denied every result recorded. I found some release of tension as we laughed together over my stubbornness and my "mule-headedness." And in a more subdued tone, I shared the news that the surgery would be scheduled immediately.

AN ENCOURAGING WORD

"Then this is why I called," Bill stated positively. "Listen carefully," he continued, "I got up early this morning to read my Bible before a seven o'clock graduate class I'm taking in the seminary. I read the sixth chapter of Judges, and for some reason I was impressed to write your name beside three verses—12, 14, and 16." I want you to get a copy of *The Living Bible*," Bill added hurriedly, "and read for yourself those verses. Sorry, but I gotta run. Nearly late for that class. I'll talk with you later today."

I hung up the phone, poured out the cold coffee, replenished it with a fresh cup, and mused over the conversation with my friend. *Strange conversation*, I thought. *Not like Bill at all . . . too early in the morning . . . devotional Bible reading in Judges (of all places!) . . . handing out verses of scripture to a person steeped in the mire of life . . . No, not like Bill at all.*

But out of curiosity I found The *Living Bible* and checked the verses.

". . . Mighty soldier, the Lord is with you" (v. 12).

". . . I will make you strong. . ." (v. 14) *Lord, I sure could use some strength!*

". . . But I, Jehovah, will be with you!" (v. 16).

I laid the Bible aside and slowly sipped the coffee. Nothing registered, except that I surely didn't feel like a "mighty soldier;" neither did I feel strong.

The sun came up. So did the rest of the family. The girls left for school and Lawanna made telephone calls to family members and friends, bringing them up to date on the test results and the anticipated surgery. Meanwhile, I sat and pondered. Life for me was on "hold."

About four o'clock in the afternoon, after a restless day, I paced through the den and saw a copy of a *New English Bible* on the end table next to the sofa. It had been a gift from Lawanna on Father's Day. I enjoyed the translation and used it occasionally in Bible studies and worship services at the church. It had a brown leather cover, excellent print, and a gold ribbon to mark special places. I casually picked up the Book and gently lifted the index ribbon and watched the Book open to . . .

Judges, chapter six.

Slowly, ever so slowly, I remembered.

The previous Wednesday evening, just before the heart test at the hospital, I had prepared to speak briefly at a prayer service at Wilshire. I had planned to talk about Gideon, a farmer and an ordinary man who was challenged to be a leader for God's people. But a children's choir had sung in that service and some special recognitions had been made. Time had run out. Before the benediction I had held up my Bible—this same brown Bible with the gold ribbon—and said with a smile to the people, " I came with a prepared message, but the time is up. The message can wait."

As I quietly stood in the den that afternoon and looked at the Gideon passage, I couldn't help but notice that verses 12, 14, and 16 had been clearly underlined for emphasis—the same three verses that Bill O'Brien had put my name beside.

Looking back . . .

The Lord must have said, "Bill, I've got a special job for you. Bruce prepared a Bible study last week and I tried to guide him in it . . . even impressed him to underline some verses that would have special meaning to him. But he's caught up in a lot of trauma today, and he's having a hard time remembering or believing anything. I need you to help me remind him. . . ."

Far-fetched?

I think not.

And I remember.

PAINFUL IN MILWAUKEE

"Mr. McIver. Mr. McIver!"

Somewhere in the distance a voice called, "Time to wake up."

I moaned, opened one eye in groggy confusion, and struggled to see. Where was I? What was going on? Who was calling? And was my name really "McIver?" After twelve hours of heart surgery, three full days—and nights—in Intensive Care, five days in a private room with endless comings and goings of medical teams and personnel, my body and I had finally collapsed in exhaustion. My last conscious thought had been, "Lord, please—just ten minutes of uninterrupted sleep . . . and I'll never ask for anything else!"

Gratefully, my prayer was answered, but I was given only *eight* minutes, not ten.

"Mr. McIver," a woman's voice called again, "time to wake up. We've got a lot of work to do this afternoon."

Work? My thoughts raced because I was too weak to talk. *She's got be to kidding. What kind of work?* My chest had been cut open and wired back together, my legs were throbbing from my heels to my thighs because of "scavenger searches" for veins healthy enough to be used in artery by-passes, my arms ached from IV tubes, and my throat was so dry that I could hardly swallow. Now, some ghostly voice had awakened me from the only sleep that I had had in days to tell me that we had "work" to do! And another thing—what was this "we" stuff? I was the only person whose name was on the door, and to my knowledge I was the only patient in the room.

My brain felt well enough to complain.

"Just a minute; I'll help you sit up." Then I heard the whir of the electric motor and felt the head of the bed begin to rise slowly. I blinked hard to focus my eyes on a figure in a white uniform, now standing next to me, who reached out and gently lifted me to a half-sitting position. For the first time I realized it was Nancy, my nurse from the day shift. She was my favorite of all the nurses—until that moment.

"Nancy," I mumbled. "You startled me . . . couldn't figure out what was happening . . . didn't know where I was. . . ." My words were slurred.

WHAT'S ALL THIS "WE" STUFF?

"You're fine, Mr. McIver," she said in a soft, reassuring tone. "You're in St. Mary's Hospital in Milwaukee, and you're doing great. Just a little sleepy right now, but you'll be good and awake before long. And then we'll get to work.

I didn't have the foggiest idea what she meant by "work."

"Here," she said as she handed me faded blue hospital pajama bottoms—the "one-size-fits-all" kind. Then she added, "I want you to put these on."

This was a new experience. For ten days I had worn a typical surgical gown that was designed to tie in the back. But since no one ever bothered to tie it, and since I couldn't reach around to tie the ends of the worn strings myself, the gown usually fell loosely over the front of my body. I had learned quickly how modesty was the last thing patients cared about following surgery.

"Please put the pajama bottoms on now," Nancy said as she moved toward the door. "I have to check on another patient but I'll be back in a minute."

I sat alone in the room. It was the first moment of privacy I had experienced in more than a week. Then, slowly and painfully, I reached down to try to put one foot, and then the other, into the appropriate leg holes of the pajama bottoms. Panting for breath and wobbling to keep my balance, I tugged and tried to pull them up. When they were just above my knees I stopped to catch my breath and looked down. I forgot all about Nancy, and our "work;" I even forgot about the soreness of my body as I slumped backwards on the side of the bed. Weak with fatigue, I gasped for strength and energy . . . . and then . . . something happened.

I laughed.

It hurt, but it was worth it. A ridiculous thought flashed through my mind. It came from a childhood memory back in my home state of North Carolina.

I remembered the changing colors of the leaves on trees in the fall, cold days and heavier clothing, long underwear and shoes that rubbed blisters on the heels. . . . and hog-killing time. . . .

Every November our family and most of the families around us went through the same ritual. The hogs that had been "slopped" and fattened for months were killed for bacon and ham and fatback.

And just as surely as November came, so did Johnnie Alston—a large, rotund, gregarious black man. I didn't understand it then, but Johnnie was essential to hog-killing season. Like the first frost and the falling of the first leaves, Johnnie arrived right on schedule. The old *Farmer's Almanac* was every family's guide and could have included under the prediction, "first freeze," the words, "Johnnie arrives." No one ever told me he was coming; I just knew.

HOG KILLING SEASON

Johnnie Alston would steer his 1931 Model A Ford pickup into the dirt driveway to our house, and chug across the backyard and through the open gate (we knew he would come), and into the small pasture where we kept our one milk cow. Johnnie would park his truck at the pigpen next to the small barn. The already limp, dead hog that had just been shot by my father would be loaded into the back of the truck and Johnnie would drive off and disappear.

It never occurred to me as a boy to ask where he was going, or why. Four or five hours later he would return in the same pickup with the lifeless hog bouncing in the back of the truck when Johnnie hit a bump—minus all hair and bristles. And minus also a few other parts that Johnnie got as payment for scrubbing and cleaning the hog. No one at our house ever complained about his price.

Johnnie fascinated me. I marveled that this loyal man could take a muddy pig that I had fed twice a day for months, load it in the back of his truck, drive away for a few hours, and then return it clean, slick, and almost white—ready to be carved up into hams and shoulders and tenderloins. Because of Johnnie, hog-killing was not work; it was an event.

Back in the hospital room, sitting on the side of the bed, I looked down at my own clean, white body that had been carefully washed and scrubbed and (heaven forbid!) thoroughly shaved for surgery a few days earlier. I smiled at the sight and chuckled softly. "Johnnie would be proud. And he would be especially proud of whoever 'prepped' me for surgery."

Thoughts of cold weather, falling leaves, and hog-killing times were interrupted when Nancy re-entered the room.

"Mr. McIver," she said in mild reprimand, "you haven't even tied your pajama bottoms. What have you been doing while I've been gone?"

"I'd tell you, but I doubt you'd understand," I whispered.

She wasn't curious because she was in a hurry. "Get those bottoms tied so we can get out of bed. We have a lot to do and we're already behind schedule."

Nancy's back into that "we" stuff, I thought.

Suddenly, the door burst open and Tonya, a hefty, no-nonsense hospital aide, marched in as if she owned the place.

Oh, no, not Tonya! I thought, but dared not say it out loud. Everyone, including the medical staff gave this woman plenty of room. She enforced rules and regulations, drove out visitors, made patients sit up and cough, adjusted and re-adjusted IVs, and pretended not to hear when patients cried out for mercy. Tonya "took no prisoners" on her wing of the hospital.

"All right!" she barked, "Everybody up. We're going for a walk."

I didn't have the strength or the courage to argue. I knew "everybody" meant me. I did believe, however, that someone should try to inject some sanity into this situation. So barely above a whimper, I muttered, "I'm not sure I can take a walk. Both legs are hurting badly this morning, and the sternum and ribs are sore, and . . ."

"Just move it, Buster," Tonya raised her voice. I trembled, and suspected that she was well experienced in situations like this. Golly, maybe she really *did* own the hospital!

"Yes Ma'am," I replied politely. Here I was, sixty-two years of age and just about as intimidated as I had ever been in my life. I felt like a little boy answering to his mother. Tonya meant business; so did Nancy.

PLENTY OF GOOD EXCUSES

"But I still have oxygen tubes in my nose," I pointed out hesitantly, "and the tubes are connected to a valve in the wall behind my bed. I can't leave the room without oxygen. Besides," I added hopefully, "I still have a large IV in my left arm."

"No trouble at all," Toyna clipped as she dragged a hideously green oxygen tank across the room and over to the side of my bed. She quickly switched the connections in one smooth, efficient motion. She then hurried to the other side of the room, grabbed a tall, skinny metal contraption, and wheeled it to the left side of my bed. Again, with precision she lifted the bag of intravenous fluid from the ceiling hook over my bed and hung it over the portable stand. She stepped back, surveyed the situation, and declared, "Now, on your feet; we're going to physical therapy."

Could this be real? Physical therapy? Was this really happening? I was too weary and weak to battle with words any longer. So I climbed awkwardly out of bed, stood shakily on my feet while Nancy took me by one arm, and Tonya the other. We shuffled toward the door that led out to the hallway. With their free hands, Tonya dragged the green tank of oxygen and Nancy pulled the clumsy IV stand.

Other patients and visitors watched the unlikely trio wobble down the hall. They gave us plenty of room. I had the feeling that no one wanted to get entangled with this procession.

We managed to get to the end of the hall, made a left turn, and unexpectedly bumped into Lawanna and Dr. Bettye Whiteaker, a friend from Dallas.

Bettye is a dentist specializing in periodontics and the wife of my former associate pastor, Kermit Whiteaker. She is a loving, caring, sensitive person. In a beautiful expression of friendship she had taken time off from her practice to be with Lawanna during my heart surgery. On this particular morning both women knew that I was trying to sleep, so they took a leisurely walk and enjoyed a late breakfast.

We hugged briefly—and very carefully—as we met in the hall. Nancy invited them to meet us in the rehabilitation room. That sounded like a good idea since there was no way five persons, a tank of oxygen, and a rickety IV stand could travel down the hall together. Lawanna and Bettye smiled at me and moved on ahead. Nancy, Tonya, and I struggled along until we reached the next wing. We reduced "speed," made a right turn, and headed for the third door on the right. With much maneuvering of the twisted, tangled tubing, we finally made it through the door.

WHAT A PICTURE!

The sight in the room held the potential of becoming the next "Norman Rockwell original" and could easily have graced the cover of any magazine. Before me sat fifteen other patients with their own "Nancy's" and "Tonya's," oxygen tanks, and makeshift portable IV stands. Spiderlike tubes connected to tanks and stands were everywhere. All fifteen patients were gasping for breath and looked as slick and pale as Johnnie Alston's hog. We resembled relics of a Civil War battlefield. The heads of at least half of those in the room slumped forward or to one side. They were sound asleep. Two or three snored. Most of the others managed to hold their heads up and their puffed eyes open, but their blank stares were hollow and haunting.

The physical therapist stood at the front of the room to welcome all the patients with a rehearsed speech. She congratulated us on making it through surgery, told us how great we looked, and assured us that our best days were ahead. She also told us that we were all going to have a "good time" for the next few minutes. Those of us who were awake doubted her words. The others couldn't have cared less. I looked around the room and envied those who slept through the welcoming address.

Then came the good news—or, so we were told. We had a choice to make. *This is great,* I thought. *This is the first time since I've been in this hospital that I've been able to make a choice. . . . about anything.*

"You can choose your own exercise," the physical therapist said sweetly. "You can either ride the exercycle for fifteen minutes, or you can walk on the treadmill for fifteen minutes."

The poor girl was hallucinating. In my condition I couldn't even climb *up* on an exercycle, let alone do fifteen minutes on one; I couldn't even take six steps on a treadmill, much less walk on one for fifteen minutes. No way!

"Which do ya' want?" Tonya commanded. Her tone ruled out any alternative options.

"I'm not sure. . . ."

"Jest make up your mind. Exercycle or treadmill?"

I sighed, "Well, I do have a treadmill at home. Maybe I can manage it a little better. But what about the oxygen tank? And I'll have to have the IV stand . . . and I'll need some help in stepping up on the treadmill."

I was building my case, certain that the obstacles I mentioned were greater than the challenge. Tonya disagreed.

"Here's the tank," she announced as she clattered it across half the room. "And here's the IV stand next to your left arm. Now, up we go on the treadmill," she added as she pushed the buttons and I was forced to start walking.

Fifteen minutes later I was more than exhausted; I was depleted.

Trembling. Tearful.

But at least I was aware and conscious. Some of my fellow patients had closed their eyes and fallen asleep again. One old lady slouched in a chair. Her mouth was open and drooling. She was breathing laboriously . . . snoring . . . wearing a loose fitting gown . . . legs spread wide apart . . . and totally unconcerned about her propriety and decency—or lack thereof. No one else in the room cared either.

ON THE ROAD TO RECOVERY

We had enjoyed five minutes of break time when a young, petite, attractive blonde skipped through the door and took charge of the session. She had all the marks of a fresh graduate out of training school and on her first job. She introduced herself to us as a nutritionist, and said her goal was to give advice concerning the right foods to eat and how to prepare them. I was glad Lawanna and Bettye were in the back of the room for this part of the session. I knew that Lawanna would take careful notes on everything.

The young nutritionist talked about food groups and their importance to the health of the heart. She discussed calories, fats, and cholesterol. She didn't miss a page in her textbook. The session was almost over. So was I.

She closed her notebook and made one last observation. "Now, many people ask about having sex following heart surgery. They wonder if there is any danger?"

I couldn't help but notice that those who had fallen asleep woke up instantly. Others managed to blink their eyes in bewilderment. Everyone was listening—for the first time—except the old lady in the loose gown with her legs apart.

"We've done extensive research on this," she continued demurely, "and our studies show there is no danger to the heart when having sex relations following surgery." She paused with a smile, "So when you get home and you have the urge, go right ahead and have sex with your husband or wife."

There was silence. Blank stares. The only sound in the room was the old lady snoring. Two others slumped forward in disbelief and went back to sleep.

Mustering all the strength I had left, I managed to raise my right arm.

"Yes sir, do you have a question?" she chirped with youthful enthusiasm.

"Yes ma'am," I panted for breath, while those patients who were awake perked up to listen. I mustered all the strength possible and asked in a weary, wispy voice, "Do we . . . do we *have* to?"

The therapy room instantly filled with half grunts, suppressed chuckles, and controlled "heh, heh's . . . heh, heh's." It was too painful to laugh. The nutritionist blushed slightly and looked away from the audience. Lawanna and Bettye ducked out the back door, doubled over in laughter. Nancy quickly reached for my arm, helped me out of the chair, and balanced the IV stand. Tonya pointed me toward the exit, grabbed the oxygen tank, tugged me through the door. . . .

And giggled.

THANKS, MRS. MALAPROP!

In 1775 Richard Brinsley Sheridan, an Irish-born English dramatist, wrote a play called *The Rivals*. One of the characters in the drama was a "Mrs. Malaprop" who was forever blundering in her use of words. From her comes the term "malapropism," found in the dictionary and meaning "the habit of ridiculously misusing words."

Mrs. Malaprop is alive and well today, roaming the corridors of every hospital in town. I know; I have encountered her!

"Pastor, I'm doing fine, 'cept my kidneys won't work and they had to put in this *casper.*"

"My *prostrate* is bothering me today."

"My throat is giving me trouble and the doctor says he's going to have to remove my *learnex.*"

"When we knew we were coming to the hospital we had to take care of some legal matters quickly. We didn't have time to wait, so a friend who is a judge gave us one of those *Alfred Davids.*"

"See, right there. That's where they cut the *unbiblical* cord on my baby."

"I've met some wonderful people here in the hospital—Baptists, Methodists, Episcopalians, and Catholics. But there's one group I don't understand. Would you explain the *Seventh Day Advantages* to me?"

"My heart is giving me some trouble. They're going to *cauterize* me tomorrow and put dye in my arteries."

"I'm feeling better, except for this *inner-gestion.*"

"My *hyena hernia* is acting up today."

And, then there was this little lady in deep East Texas who asked for prayer for her son during the mid-week prayer meeting. "You'all please pray for my boy," she pleaded. "You know he's a farmer. Yesterday he had an accident! He fell off his *concubine*!"

Thanks, Mrs. Malaprop. You make hospital visiting *so much more enjoyable!*

7

Growing Children

Uncle June was Mother's youngest brother and like Mother, he was born in North Carolina in a farmhouse seven miles from Siler City, five miles from Bonlee, and four miles from Bear Creek. Like all of the other Moody children, he was born at home. By the time June came along his ma and pa had almost run out of names so they asked the siblings to help. Aunt Minnie, affectionately called "Punk" by nieces and nephews in later years, gave him the name "June." It was perfectly logical, she insisted, since he was born in the month of June. So the name stuck, and "June" it was for all of his seventy-six years.

The land was poor and life was hard. From sunrise to sunset they planted, plowed, reaped, and harvested. They milked cows, raised chickens, hunted rabbits, squirrels and 'possums for food. They were poor, very poor, but so was everybody else after the turn of the century, so they didn't realize it.

June used to tell me that he and "the old mule would work all summer so the old mule could eat in the winter." He also said that Pa would buy an old sow (a mother pig, to you city people!) and raise a litter of piglets. He'd fatten them up and take them to Bonlee to sell them. While he was gone the ten children would stand around talking about what surprises Pa might bring home to them from the sale of the pigs. They fantasized chocolate drops, peppermint candy canes, oranges, and maybe—just maybe—a new pair of shoes. Late in the afternoon when they heard the clatter of the horse-drawn wagon cross the nearest bridge, they would run down the dirt road to see what he had brought them. The "oinks" from the back of the wagon told the story and shattered their hopes. Pa had sold the pigs and used the money to buy another old sow!

It was called "survival."

Like everyone else who struggled for survival along Tick Creek, under the shadow of Hickory Mountain, the Moodys had no money for entertainment. So to their credit, they entertained themselves—by telling stories.

The boys would lie on the long porch late in the afternoon after a hard day in the fields and swap yarns. They would laugh until they almost rolled off the porch. Later, they would pull up ten or twelve chairs around the dying embers of a fire and continue to tell stories.

THE RARE GIFT OF HUMOR

As a growing boy I listened and laughed. I didn't realize it then but this was humor in its purest form. It was not caustic, racist, offensive, or embarrassing. Neither was it comedy nor showmanship. Instead, it was the ability to look at the simple things of life and find in them a reason to smile, a cause to chuckle. And more important, it was the ability to laugh at oneself.

The Moody clan survived well on a "poor dirt" farm. The overworked soil never produced bountiful crops, and poverty and riches were still measured by sows and piglets.

But they laughed and lived and loved. And they kept telling their stories until the last Moody—my mother—died at the age of ninety-four.

Uncle June became a policeman in my home town, Siler City, and a few years later he was made police chief. Respectfully, I'm sure there must have been some who knew more about the technicalities of the legal system, but no policeman knew more about people and life than June Moody.

I believe this is called "wisdom."

Several years ago Uncle June moved into a new house in a wooded area of my home town. Aunt "Bea" of "Mayberry RFD" lived two or three houses up the street from him. June, a man of the earth, worked hard putting in his new lawn. He cultivated the ground and sowed seeds for grass. The grass would peep through the soil and then be trampled down by neighborhood kids, ages five or six, who played baseball in his yard. To their delight the Chief of Police loved them, encouraged them, and played with them. Before long the children were ringing his doorbell, asking if "Chief" could come out and play with them. A few weeks later "Chief" became their coach.

Almost every afternoon the gang would gather for batting practice, or to learn how to slide into second base or to chase fly balls hit to them by "Chief," who was now their "coach."

When baseball season was over the cycle would begin again. June would seed the lawn, green grass would peep through the rich soil, only to be trampled down in the coming weeks of play.

An impatient neighbor watched this cycle for two or three years. Finally in exasperation, she exclaimed, "Mr. Moody, don't you know you can't grow grass with all those children playing in your yard?"

Uncle June thought for a moment, then answered: "Lady, we can grow grass anytime; *right now we're growing children.*"

"SIC 'EM, BEARS!"

So much is involved in "growing children," as Uncle June put it. Just like "big boys and girls," they nurse their hurts and aches and they bandage their cuts and bruises (granddaughter Emily calls them "owies;" granddaughter Ali calls them "boo-boos").

And they struggle with their own disappointments and rejections. Their little bodies have a thousand (no, ten thousand!) receptacles picking up everything they see and hear and sense. These "messages received" are often returned in spontaneous, uninhibited, and sometimes unlikely ways.

For instance, Emily's parents Shannon and George are graduates of Baylor University. Like most Baylor grads they are avid, sometimes fanatical, supporters of the "Baylor Bears." Emily has attended Baylor University football games since she was a toddler. Happily, she's been so absorbed in the theatrics—marching bands, cheerleaders, and live bears—she hasn't known or worried about the scores. May her childhood innocence continue!

When she was three years old, she came home one day from Sunday school, sat down in her high chair to eat her lunch, and volunteered to sing her "new song:"

> Zacchaeus was a wee little man,
> A wee little man was he;
> He climbed up in a sycamore tree
> The Savior for to see.
> And when the Savior came that way
> He looked up in the tree and said . . .
> Sic 'em, Bears!

We think she learned most of the song in Sunday school. However, we have no idea where she learned her theology!

OUT OF THE MOUTHS OF BABES

Paul Cox, then five years of age, wondered about his pastor's theology one Sunday morning. He was seated near the front with his parents, Carolyn and Byron. I was "preaching away," as they sometimes say, exhorting people to a deeper understanding of God and to a stronger commitment to Him and to His church. In an attempt to sound profound, I paused, leaned forward over the pulpit, and raised a rhetorical question: "And God—who is God?"

In the hush of that moment Paul looked up at Byron and asked loudly enough to be heard by half the congregation, "GREAT DAY, DAD, DOESN'T *HE* KNOW?

CONFERENCE WITH A SIX-YEAR-OLD

Blair Miles was my six-year old little friend who talked like an adult.

"Bruce," he asked after church one Sunday, "could I have a conference with you?"

Blair, like most of the children in our church, called me by my first name. This wasn't something that I tried to "program;" it just happened, and it stuck. Of course, uneasy parents at first corrected the children and tried to steer them toward "Dr. McIver" (does he give shots?), or "Reverend McIver" (there were times when I didn't feel like a "reverend"), or "Brother McIver" (does that make Lawanna "Sister McIver"?). Interestingly, the parents would reprimand their child for not "showing proper respect," but before long both the parents and the child would be back to calling me "Bruce." I took this as a compliment, a special kind of bonding.

"Of course, Blair," I replied, "I'd be happy to visit with you anytime."

"First let me talk to my parents and see when they can bring me to your office," he suggested. "I'll give you a call. Thanks."

The six-year-old then shook hands with me and walked away with the demeanor of a bank president who had just closed a deal. I smiled and wondered, *What's on his mind? Maybe he wants to see my cane collection—canes from all over the world. Or, maybe he wants a closer look at the framed photograph of the Middle East taken on one of the first space flights. On the other hand, maybe he just wants to see where I sit and work.*

Three days later Blair sat in my office. He came straight to the point.

"I have a question to ask you," he began.

"Fine, Blair, what's your question?"

"How did that hole get in the sky?"

"I beg your pardon," I stammered in uncertainty.

"Well, Bruce, you remember it says in the Bible when Jesus was baptized "the heavens opened."

I gulped.

He continued, "What I want to know is how did that hole get there?"

SPEECHLESS—AGAIN!

My silence was deafening. I had read this passage in Matthew's Gospel hundreds of times through the years. I had preached on it. I had read commentaries about it and had listened to professors in the seminary discuss it. But I had never dealt with how the hole in the sky got there; neither had anyone else that I knew!

Blair waited patiently for my answer. There wasn't a hint of his trying to be cute, or "uppity," as they used to say when I was a boy in North Carolina. Blair's question was genuine. Thankfully, even though I had no definitive answer at the moment, I did have enough sense to refrain from a pat on the head and a "there, there, son, that's a big question for a little boy."

Whatever I did manage to say seemed to satisfy Blair for the moment. Then I made my big mistake.

"Now, Blair, do you have any other questions you want to ask me?"

Dumb. Big-time dumb.

"Yes, Bruce, how did Jesus walk on water?"

Gulp again.

I squirmed and coughed, wondering how I could give an answer to a perceptive child, or to an adult for that matter, without using theological jargon or pious verbiage.

Blair sensed my discomfort. "That's OK, Bruce; I guess if He could *make* the water He could walk on it."

In that moment a child became my teacher.

By the way, didn't Jesus say, "Unless you change and become like little children, you will never enter the kingdom of heaven" (Matt. 18:3 NIV)?

ANDREW'S AMAZING UNDER-THE-PEW INVESTIGATION

One Sunday morning in my sermon I pleaded with the congregation to use their minds as well as their hearts in Christian living (my visit with Blair Miles probably inspired this message). "Think!" I exhorted enthusiastically, "the Bible tells us, 'Love the Lord your God with all your heart and with all your soul and with all your mind'" (Matt. 22:37 NIV).

Throughout the congregation I saw individuals nodding. Admittedly, a simple "reality check" would have probably indicated that some of these were nodding sleepily, but most preachers who are struggling to communicate will take any kind of a nod! I did, and railed on.

"Ladies and Gentlemen," I exclaimed loudly, "you don't come into a worship service, sit down on a plush cushion, unscrew your head, and place it under the pew!"

When the service was over a concerned mother waited to speak to me in the foyer of the sanctuary. Clinging to her hand and leaning against her body was five-year-old Andrew, obviously tired and worn out.

"Pastor, I do hope my child didn't disturb you while you were preaching today."

"No," I replied warmly, "I wasn't aware of any distraction."

"You probably couldn't see it," she continued, "since we were near the back of the sanctuary."

"What happened?" I asked quietly.

"Well, after you talked about "unscrewing heads and putting them under the pews," Andrew became very fidgety. He just wouldn't sit still. I tried hard to concentrate on your message and to do what you asked us to do—think. But while I was thinking," she continued, "Andrew somehow got off the pew and began crawling around under it."

"Don't worry about that," I reassured her with a smile. "Children often get restless in a worship service."

"But he wasn't restless," she said with a wry smile.

"What was he doing?" I asked.

"Pastor, that's exactly what I leaned over and asked him."

"And?"

"And he said, "*I'm looking for heads!*""

POSTSCRIPT

You're right, Uncle June.

"We can grow grass any time; right now we're growing children."

And they're "growing" us!

A Profile in Courage?

Pastor, this is Alfred. I realize it's late but could you come to our house right now? Please?"

I recognized the high-pitched voice even though I had known Alfred for only a few weeks. The voice was one of Alfred's distinctive physical characteristics, along with a tall, lanky body and nervous eyes that darted in unpredictable patterns when he talked with you. This time the voice bounced between the obvious note of anxiety and the more subtle whine of "poor me."

"It's Ernestine," he rattled on. "I can't do a thing with her. The police have been out once tonight and I thought we had her calmed down, but—'scuse me for a minute, Pastor."

There was a pause, followed by loud crashing sounds.

"You gotta come quick," Alfred shouted, "she's throwing all the furniture out the windows and out the back door. Hurry! Please!"

On the drive across the city to their house, I shook my head as I recalled a recent conversation with a layman who had no idea what a minister did.

"It's a real world out there," he had insisted. "It's a tough world, Pastor. You'd be surprised at some of the things you'd find out there."

As I continued the drive, I glanced at my watch and saw that it was two o'clock in the morning. In a strange, twisted way I wished for the layman who tried to tell me about a "real world out there."

Then I chuckled and said out loud, "Lord, if it gets any more *real* than this, deal me out." I drove on, confident that the Lord understood my feelings.

I pulled into the driveway at Alfred's house, got out of the car, and stumbled over broken chairs and tables. The entire backyard looked like it had been hit by a Texas tornado. Shattered stuff was everywhere.

"I told you, Pastor," Alfred whimpered as he tried to clear a path for me, "I told you she was tearing everything up."

"Where is she?" I asked.

CHECK ALL GUNS AT THE DOOR

"She's upstairs with the door closed and I think," he added with a whisper, "she's got a gun."

"This is serious," I observed, followed by a haunting feeling that I had just uttered quite an understatement.

"Now, Pastor, I want you to go talk to her," Alfred begged.

"Why don't *you* go talk to her?" I asked hopefully.

"Because she might shoot me but she won't shoot you; you're a 'man of God.'"

Alfred's theological interpretation of the situation was no comfort to me—none at all. I didn't feel much like a 'man of God' as I crept hesitantly up the steps, calling gently, "*Ernestine, Ernestine.*" On the contrary, I felt very vulnerable, very fragile.

After what seemed like half an eternity she finally opened the door and walked slowly down the steps toward me. I breathed for the first time in two minutes when I saw that she didn't have the gun.

The "drama" was over for the moment, and we sat down among the debris and talked and prayed. Then we picked up broken pieces of furniture.

A week later I received another call from Alfred. "Pastor, I need you to come to our house this evening. . . ."

"Are you still having problems, Alfred?"

"No, its not that. Things are much better and . . . well, Pastor . . . we'd like to join your church."

"You want to do *what?*" I asked incredulously.

"You see, Pastor, I've been calling you 'pastor' for several weeks and we're not even members of your church. Ernestine and I have been talking about it and we want to be baptized. Can you visit with us?"

Normally a call like this would excite any minister, but I had a sinking feeling the minute I hung up the phone. I just wasn't sure about my new "converts."

Later that evening I met with them and did everything I knew to help them re-think their decision. I suggested that it might be good for them to visit other churches and get to know other ministers. I stressed the long-range significance of the commitment they were considering and reminded them that it should not be taken lightly. I played for time.

"Don't rush into this," I said in what I hoped was a calm, caring voice. "You may feel differently in the weeks to come. Besides," I continued, "you can make your own commitment in your heart, just between you and God, and you can think about baptism later."

I realized this was "evangelism-in-reverse," but I left their house that evening feeling, almost thankfully, that I had talked them out of making a public decision—at least, for now.

BUT I COULDN'T TALK THEM OUT OF IT . . .

I discovered my tactics had failed when the following Sunday morning they came down the aisle during the singing of the closing hymn and requested membership.

The congregation rejoiced; I whimpered.

In the ensuing weeks I visited with them, talked with them, prayed with them, and read the Bible with them. I did everything I knew to make sure they were prepared for baptism.

"We're ready, Pastor!" Alfred exclaimed one day after an extended visit. "We're ready to be baptized." Ernestine nodded in agreement.

I left their house that night, sighed gratefully, and thought, "Maybe . . . just maybe . . . I've seen another miracle out there in the 'real world.'"

The physical preparations were made. The baptistery was filled with water, the instructions were given, and those assisting in the baptismal service were in place. The organ music played softly and the lights dimmed. A reverent hush settled over the entire congregation.

I baptized Ernestine first. There was an angelic look on her face as she came down into the water dressed in a white robe. My heart skipped a beat. Miracles really do happen! In my most serious ministerial tone I quoted from Romans, "Buried with Christ by baptism into death," and then lowered her briefly under the water. "Raised to walk in newness of life!" I proclaimed as I lifted her out of the water.

It was a beautiful moment—one that makes the work of the ministry worthwhile.

Ernestine moved up the steps on her way to the women's dressing room. I turned in the opposite direction, smiled at Alfred, and nodded for him to enter the water. By now I was not only feeling good about the baptisms; I was delighted.

Alfred reached the center of the pool, turned around (just as I had instructed), folded his hands over his chest (as I had instructed), and closed his eyes in prayerful contemplation. I raised my right hand high (as I had been instructed as a young student in seminary) and paused for effect.

What a beautiful, moving picture for the congregation! Dimmed lights and soft organ music, white robes and gentle stirrings of the waters, personal commitments and public affirmations—all symbolizing "newness of life."

By now Ernestine had reached the top step and was out of view of the congregation. She was met there by a gracious lady, a faithful member of our church who had volunteered to assist in the service. The lady smiled warmly, handed her a dry towel, and suggested in a soft voice, "Perhaps you'd like to stand here for a moment and watch your husband be baptized."

As the organ played softly, as Alfred closed his eyes and prepared to go under the water, and as I held my right hand high toward heaven, a voice from the top step on the women's side shrilled loudly . . .

"I HOPE HE DROWNS!"

CHARIOTS OF FIRE

It was our last night in London before catching an early morning flight back to the States. I wanted it to be special—a memorable climax to a perfect "holiday," as our British friends would say. I also wanted it to be a time when we could say a special thanks to our hostess for the visit, Beryl Goodland.

"Beryl, you've been wonderful to all of us," I remarked as we stood in Trafalgar Square in the heart of London. "This is your night. We'll eat anywhere you wish; and we'll do our best, even at this late hour, to find tickets to any play you want to see in the theater tonight."

Lawanna nodded her head in agreement; so did Wendell and Margaret Cook. Wendell, a petroleum engineer consultant, was chairman of the deacon fellowship back in Dallas and Margaret was a leader in the many mission activities sponsored through our church. The three of us, plus twenty others, had spent several days in Gorsley where Beryl's husband, Pat, served as pastor. Gorsley is a quaint village in the rural part of England, located eighty miles west of London and ten miles from the border of Wales. It has a school, a pub, and a church. Lawanna and I had discovered on previous visits that some of the most wonderful people in the world live there. Pat and Beryl, our good friends for years, had also found wonderful people in Dallas on their visits with us. This interchange of friendships led to the idea of a "link up," as Pat described it, between our two churches.

While in Gorsley we lived in the homes of the people. There were no hotels, but 400-year-old houses proved to be better than the most luxurious inns anywhere. We strolled down narrow lanes with our new friends, exchanged ideas and shared experiences, and drank a barrel of tea and ate a bushel of scones around their tables. We sang and worshipped in their church and in their homes. Walls of inhibition came tumbling down and to everybody's surprise, we laughed together. Perceptions of Texans garnered from television's *Dallas* died a natural death with our new friends. They expressed delight that we were not all like the disdainful "J. R.," and were surprised that some of our group had never been to "Southfork." And, our impressions about proper and staid Britons were soon forgotten in warm hospitality and hugs of friendship.

After our visit in Gorsley, Beryl graciously escorted our group on a coach tour through Wales, the Lake District of England, and the Highlands of Scotland. When we reluctantly returned to the snarled traffic and din of London, most of the people from Dallas scattered for a free evening on their own. Lawanna and I welcomed the opportunity of a last visit with Beryl before leaving the next morning. Happily, Margaret and Wendell had also joined us. The four of us wanted to express added thanks to Beryl for the tour that she had arranged and for her special "touches" as the tour guide.

So . . .

AN UNEXPECTED PLEASURE

"Beryl, this last night is yours," I said. "Name your favorite restaurant and the theater you'd like to attend."

She hesitated for a moment and then said, "There's a good Chinese restaurant just around the corner in Picadilly Circus. It's not far from here."

"Great!" I replied. "We'll eat there."

"And," she added after another pause, "there's a new movie that's been made about a friend of mine—a missionary who was in China when my family and I were there. I hear the film is rather good," she continued in her distinct British accent. "I think I would like to see it if we can still get tickets."

"That's fine, Beryl," I responded with a forced lilt in my voice, hoping to disguise the disappointment I felt.

For heaven's sake, I thought. *Our last night in London and we end up going to see some low-budget, second-rate religious movie about a missionary who served in China forty years ago!* But I had given my word to my friend and I intended to keep it, painful as the experience might be. What did she mean, "if we can still get tickets?" *Surely*, I almost laughed to myself, *anyone in London can get tickets to some unheard of movie about missionaries in China.*

As we finished our dinner Wendell looked at his watch and volunteered, "I'll go now and pick up the tickets so you folks won't have to wait in line."

Line? I thought. *What line?*

We thanked him, and he was on his way. Lawanna, Beryl, Margaret, and I had another cup of tea and waited . . . and waited. During the wait Beryl talked softly, remembering her friend about whom the movie had been made.

"He was a great runner," she said, "and one of our greatest heroes. He was from Scotland where I lived as a child with my family before my parents went to China as missionaries. In the 1924 Olympic Games he was Britain's hope for the 100 meter race, and our nation's only hope for its first gold medal. The trial heats were scheduled for Sunday and Eric had strong Christian convictions about racing on Sunday. So he withdrew from the race. It created quite a sensation, both in Paris where the Olympics were being held and back here in England. The Olympic Committee and some of the national leaders tried to get him to relent, but he stood by his convictions."

"Later," she continued, "he decided to enter the 400 meter race and to everyone's surprise, he won by five meters, setting a new world record and bringing home our nation's first gold medal ever." They called him 'The Flying Scotsman.' You may have heard of him."

I hadn't—but I was fascinated with the story. I was also deeply moved by the way Beryl talked about the athlete. I sensed that there was more here than winning races and bringing home medals. Much more.

"A year after he won the gold medal," she added, "he surprised everyone by announcing that he was going to the Shantung province of China as a missionary. Hundreds saw him off at Waverly station in London and he led them in singing, "Jesus Shall Reign Where'er The Sun."

"What did he do in China?" I asked.

"He taught science in a middle school and directed the athletic program. He did this for several years until . . ."

"Until what?" I asked.

"Until the Japanese invaded China and he was arrested. He was sent to the Weihsien Concentration Camp, one hundred miles inland, where my parents, my two brothers, my sister, and I were also imprisoned. There were 1,400 of us including 500 children, crowded into the camp. I was about twelve years of age."

"How long were you in the concentration camp?" I asked, oblivious to the time and to others around us.

"Three years," she replied. "But he . . . 'Uncle' Eric . . . made life better for us. He was always full of life, always smiling and laughing. He organized races and games for everyone, taught science, and tutored personally those who were lagging behind in their studies. He was kind and good."

I was ready with another question as Wendell walked through the door, smiling and holding up four tickets. "The last in the house for the late show," he beamed. "I had to stand in a line nearly a block long to get these."

Promptly at nine o'clock we crowded through the doors with hundreds of others as the theme song of *Chariots of Fire* reverberated throughout the theater. The lights dimmed and we watched the opening scene of a young athlete running on the beach. Lawanna was seated on my right; Beryl was on my left.

The music swelled and my heart pounded with every note. The young man on the screen threw back his head and ran faster and faster in unorthodox style. His arms were in perpetual motion, flapping by his side, and his knees were lifted higher with every stride. There was laughter on his face and he ran with reckless, joyful abandonment.

I turned to express my excitement with Beryl and noticed tears trickling down her face. Then she whispered above the music, "That's him! That's him! They've captured his personality on film!"

My own emotions ran the gamut the next two hours—joy, laughter, tears, and celebration. And gratitude, too, for sitting beside the one person in the theater who could understand and experience fully *Chariots of Fire*.

I limped out of the theater, emotionally and physically drained.

A week later I stood in the pulpit at Wilshire in Dallas and said, "I don't normally use this time to recommend movies. But, I saw one in London last week that was the most inspiring I've ever seen. Now, I doubt that it will ever make it to Dallas," I added, "but if it does, don't miss it."

I was wrong. It made it to Dallas, and to all of America. And six months after I had "experienced" it in London, *Chariots of Fire* won the Oscar for the best picture of the year.

THE REST OF THE STORY

In the ensuing years Beryl Goodland has pieced together other facets of the story. I never tire of hearing it.

After arriving in China, the "hero of Great Britain" met and married the daughter of other missionaries. Two daughters were born to the happy couple. As tensions increased between China and Japan, Eric Liddell sent his wife and girls to Canada, her native country, for safety. A third daughter was born soon after his wife arrived back home.

When Pearl Harbor was attacked on December 7, 1941, Eric was put under house arrest and later sent to the Weihsien Concentration Camp.

On February 21, 1945, the one who once made headlines around the world because of his convictions died in a crowded, bed-bug infested concentration camp—because of those same convictions. Forty-three years of age. Brain tumor.

He never held his third daughter or lived to see his family again.

Beryl Goodland, then fifteen years of age, served as a member of the honor guard as his body was removed from the camp. The next day she wrote in her diary:

> "Dear Uncle Eric died last night. It was so sudden. He wrote a letter to his wife just that day. Everyone was greatly impressed. I feel so sorry for her. Most people said he was the best man in the camp. What a loss! It snowed today. There was no coal."

POSTSCRIPT

Three months after returning from England I received a telephone call from Dan Vestal, then pastor of the First Baptist Church, Midland, Texas.

"Bruce," he said, "I have a friend in California who is interested in distributing a film in America. It's a good film—made in England—about an Olympic runner. My friend would like to have a private showing in Dallas to see how much interest there would be in the film. Would you help by telling some of your friends and contacts about the showing? By the way, I think they call it *Chariots of . . .*"

"Where are you now, Dan?" I interrupted.

"In my office."

"Standing or sitting?"

"Standing."

"Sit down, Dan; I want to tell you a story. . . ."

And I did.

Both Sides of the Coin

Alone. . . .

After fifteen years I am still unable to erase the picture of the young man from my mind. I first saw him as he stood silhouetted in the door of my study, obviously a shadow of what once was. The coat of his stylish conservative business suit draped loosely like a shroud over his shoulders. His perfectly matched tie and oversized shirt accentuated his thin, sunken face. His hands trembled slightly and his hollow eyes reflected fear. I did not know him nor to my knowledge had I ever seen him.

"Pastor, could I talk with you for a moment?" he asked hesitantly.

"Of course," I answered as reassuringly as possible. "Have a seat."

He walked across the study with some effort, steadying himself first on a conference table, then holding to the back of a chair. Everything about his presence indicated he had a serious medical problem.

"How can I help?" I asked, hoping the question itself would open a door of understanding.

"I just need a friend," he replied. "I'm a very sick person."

"Well, we'll get on that right away. I'm a trustee of one of the medical centers here in Dallas and we have one of the best facilities anywhere in the world. Many of the physicians on staff there are my friends; in fact, several are members right here at Wilshire. I'll get on the phone and make some calls immediately and . . ."

"No, Pastor, that won't work."

"What do you mean, it won't work? You need help and resources are available. We'll line up the best doctors . . ."

"No, Pastor," he interrupted again. "It just won't work."

"Well, if it's a matter of money," I suggested benevolently, "I'm sure something can be worked out. We have some limited funds here at the church for people in need and I'm sure the business office at the hospital will work with us. The important thing is to get you some help as soon as possible."

"It's too late," he said, shaking his head. "I've seen a dozen doctors elsewhere, and I've been through all the tests and several surgical procedures. There's no medical hope."

No hope, I thought. *In a city with one of the world's leading medical schools, several medical centers pioneering in areas of research, dozens of other excellent hospitals, and hundreds of physicians and medical support persons . . . no hope?*

NO OPTIONS—ONLY CHRIST

The young man read my thoughts and said again, "There's no hope. I have no more options."

By now I began to hear him and believe him, difficult as it was. Then searching for other means of support for him, I said, "Tell me about your family. How are they handling this?" "I moved to Dallas two years ago from West Texas," he offered. "My family knows about my illness but they have rejected me. We have no contact."

"What on earth do you mean?" I protested. "Are you telling me that they're not standing with you in this situation?"

He lowered his head and said with resignation, "I haven't heard from them in a year. They asked me not to call them again."

My emotions began to bounce from compassion to empathy, from concern to anger. He observed this non-professional display silently. Then he slowly and painfully rose from his seat, walked over to the window, stared outside for a long minute, and then quietly asked, "Do you think I could join this church? I'd like to get this one last thing settled before . . ."

We prayed together and embraced. He smiled and moved slowly out the door, leaving me to wrestle with my own confusion and bewilderment.

The following Sunday after my sermon we sang a "hymn of commitment," as was our custom. I encouraged any who wished to make a public affirmation of faith or join the church to meet me at the front as we sang. He struggled to walk down the aisle and greeted me as though he were "coming home." The congregation warmly greeted him.

Two weeks later I received word that he was in a hospital in a suburban area of the city. I planned to visit him the next day, then learned that he was no longer a patient there. He left no forwarding address.

Oh, well, I rationalized. *He's probably moved to a new apartment complex. Dallas is a big city and people are always moving around.* But I never could locate him and I never saw him in a worship service again.

Four years later I was in the office of a physician-friend. In the course of conversation we talked about a new disease that crippled the immune system and inevitably caused death. The physician then shared almost incidentally that two of his friends had been among the first doctors in Dallas to treat patients with this disease.

"In what hospital did they practice?" I inquired.

"Bradford Community," he replied. "I knew them and their work because soon after medical school I worked in the emergency room at Bradford at nights. It helped pay the bills."

I didn't respond and he looked at me with a puzzled expression, "Why do you ask?"

The wheels in my mind were turning and I spoke haltingly, "There was a young man . . . came to see me . . . joined our church . . . entered Bradford . . . said there was no hope . . ."

I then mentioned his name.

"I remember him," my physician-friend responded somberly. "I remember him well."

"How is he?" I asked eagerly. "Where is he?"

"He died that night. Never made it out of ER."

"What happened? What was wrong with him?"

"Acquired Immune Deficiency Syndrome."

AIDS.

When the shock subsided I managed to whisper the question, "Was anyone with him? His family?"

"No," the physician quietly said. "That's one reason I remember him. He died alone."

Alone.

FAMILY VALUES

The telephone rang before dawn one morning and I rolled over sleepily and grappled for the receiver. "Probably another crank call," I muttered to myself, or worse still, the "ex" of that fellow with a name similar to mine who had once lived in Dallas and who seemed to have gone underground. After taking "wrong numbers" for him all through the day and at weird hours during the night, I was convinced life would have been simpler for me if the other "Bruce" had lived in another city; or if he had just paid his bills and stayed home!

But the call early that morning was not for the phantom "Bruce," but for "Pastor."

I recognized the voice of the caller immediately—a young man who had attended graduate school in our city and had been a faithful member of our church in the process. It had been four years since his graduation and move to another state, but I remembered him fondly and gratefully.

"Joe, what on earth are you doing calling this early in the morning?" I asked with a teasing chuckle. And then I added, "You know I'm not a morning person. How are things in South Carolina? And how in the world are you?"

"I'm in Dallas, Pastor, and I'm sick—very sick."

"Sick? What happened? Where are you staying?"

In a weak, slurred speech he mumbled just above a whisper, "I came here yesterday for a conference, became ill last night, and was brought to the hospital by friends attending the conference . . . emergency . . . very weak . . . loss of body fluids."

He paused to catch his breath and continued, "I'm so sick . . . can't even get out of bed by myself. And I'm scared. They won't tell me much . . . just keep running tests on me."

"What can I do, Joe? Say the word and I'm on the way."

"I need you, Pastor," he pleaded. "And I need Lawanna. Could the two of you please come to the hospital now?"

Twenty minutes later we were on the way and forty minutes later we walked into his room. I was totally unprepared for what we found. His emaciated body, racked by pain, trembled as he reached out to take our hands. A tear trickled down his cheek as he labored and panted for strength to speak.

There are moments when words are unnecessary, when merely uttering them violates the significance of "presence." This was such a moment, so we simply held hands and cried with him.

When he gained enough composure to speak, he looked at us with pleading eyes and asked, "Would you please help me to the bathroom? Do you mind? I don't have enough strength."

Lawanna put her hands behind his back and gently lifted him off the pillow while I guided his thin legs toward the edge of the bed. We braced him while he sat in that position for a moment. Every movement, every action was a painful, exhausting struggle.

He paused to catch his breath and with a groan made an effort to stand on wobbly legs. He then draped an arm around the shoulders of each of us and shuffled in uncertainty, step by stumbling step, across the room.

The return trip was even more painful and exhausting and he collapsed in fatigue across the bed. Again, no one spoke for several minutes. Words were not needed, and they required more energy that any of us had.

He dozed while Lawanna and I looked at each other in concern. An eerie silence filled the room.

A TERRIBLE DIAGNOSIS

The brief respite was broken as two white-coated physicians opened the door and walked in and stood on either side of the bed. They nodded briefly to us and said to the sleepy young man, "Joe, the tests don't look good. We've been checking them all night and they just don't look good. Not at all."

"What are you trying to tell me?" Joe asked in confusion as Lawanna and I inched closer to the doctors.

"What's wrong? What do I have?" Joe pleaded.

"Your immune system has shut down and to further complicate matters, you have a severe case of pneumonia. Both lungs are involved and you have nothing left to fight the virus."

The other physician struck the final blow, "We're sorry, but it looks like you have . . . AIDS."

Stunned silence. Absolute silence.

"Where did I get this?" Joe whimpered.

"We don't know," one answered. "Your medical records indicate you had a vaccine in the Far East. Could have been a contaminated needle. Could have been something else," he added as his voice trailed off. "But our main concern now is to try to make you as comfortable as possible."

"Give it a few days," the other added as they moved from the bedside, "and you might be strong enough to return to South Carolina."

With that they slowly walked out and closed the door behind them. They were neither rude nor curt; there just wasn't anything else to say.

Lawanna, Joe, and I were left to ourselves in an empty room—a tomb. Prisoners to lab reports. Shattered. Isolated.

"My parents were called last night," Joe said. "They'll be arriving most any time. I can't tell them." He looked at me with a new kind of pain written across his face.

"I'll tell them," I offered.

"And someone needs to call Janice. Could you . . .?" he asked as he looked at Lawanna.

"I'll try," Lawanna replied, choking back the tears and wondering how she could break the news to Joe's lovely wife who was expecting their first child any day.

Two hours later the parents arrived and came to Joe's room for a brief visit. They were surprised, even shocked, to find him so sick, but they assured him of their love and told him not to worry about the finances or anything else. "We'll get you strong," the father said with a forced smile, "and we'll have you home in no time at all."

After a brief prayer they left to find a hotel room. I followed them out and asked them to walk with me to the "family room."

"It's private there," I volunteered, "and we can have a few minutes to visit without interruption." I tried to make the invitation sound as natural as possible, but I was trembling deep down inside.

When we reached the room we were joined unexpectedly by the primary physician on Joe's case. I welcomed his presence.

"Mr. and Mrs. Harris, I'm afraid I have some bad news for you," he said, getting straight to the point.

A look of shock registered on their faces. "What do you mean?" The father asked.

"Your son has AIDS."

"AIDS? Are you sure? Maybe there's been a mix-up in the lab studies. Not AIDS."

"AIDS, Mr. Harris. AIDS. I'm sorry."

SURROUNDED BY LOVE

"How long does he have?" the father asked in a broken voice.

"There's no way we can predict that. If we can get him over this pneumonia, maybe a year . . . maybe six months. But that's really out of our hands."

"I understand," the father replied with difficulty while the mother wept quietly.

After expressions of concern and offers to do all he possibly could, the physician slipped out of the room.

Once again—twice in one morning—an overwhelming sense of eerie silence. Before me sat two good, simple, God-fearing people from a rural village in a distant state. Their world had been shattered in less than two minutes. Life would never be the same again. They were dealing with an ominous disease that few people at the time, including the best researchers, knew anything about. But they were also dealing with a disease that many people, including preachers, had no hesitation talking about freely and pompously, amplifying all the stigmas involved.

In the eerie silence of that "family room" I pondered all this with anger, and compassion, and questions.

What would the parents do? How would they react? What would they tell their neighbors? Their fellow church members? Their pastor?

Finally, mustering all the courage I had at the moment, I asked, "How will you deal with this?" In some ways it was a dumb question; in other ways it struck at the very heart of their lives.

There was a pause, and then the father reached for his wife's hand. He stroked it gently and then held it in a spirit of divine togetherness.

In a clear, resolute voice he said, "We'll take him home with us, hug him tight, and love him until he dies."

They did.

A year later I stood by Joe's grave, joined hands with his family, and sang "Amazing Grace."

POSTSCRIPT

Two stories. Two lives touching my ministry. Two families. Two sets of "family values."

"Alone."

And, "We'll take him home, hug him tight, and love him until he dies."

10

All in the Family

After Dad died, Mother—affectionately called "Mommie Mac"—stubbornly insisted she could and would live her own life in her own house, relying on her own resources. Her fierce spirit of independence caused family members to smile in tolerance and wring hands in frustration. She would not move and she would not *be* moved!

"Thank you for your offers," she said repeatedly, "but I'd rather just live in my own house. Besides, I don't want to give up my things."

Her "things" included her own bed, a refrigerator and stove, some special pictures on the walls, a reading chair and large print Bible, and a few magazines and the daily newspaper (she always read the obituary column first), dresser drawers packed with family memorabilia, and a stray cat that hung around the back door. "Things" also included an eighteen-inch statue of "Rebekah at the Well" that had graced our parlor since I was a little boy. Mother had purchased the "gold-trimmed" figurine from a traveling salesman and had paid for it out of her egg money. As a child I had no idea who Rebekah was. I certainly didn't know that she had married the biblical Isaac, Abraham's son, but I got the idea early on that she was somebody very special and that the statue was not to be handled by children.

One of her "things" that made us all nervous was a step-stool in the kitchen.

Mommie Mac used it daily, either sitting on the padded top while drying dishes or climbing on it while searching for things in shelves high above the cabinets.

"Mother, please don't do that!" we pleaded. "Don't climb on the stool or on any other piece of furniture. You'll break your leg." She tuned us out.

Niece Susan even made a sign and taped it on the stool: "STAY OFF! THIS MEANS YOU, MOMMIE MAC!" She adored Susan, but she ignored the sign.

MOTHER'S INDEPENDENCE

Once on a trip back home, I walked into the kitchen and found her on the third step of the stool reaching for something on the top shelf, swaying back and forth while trying to maintain her balance. My heart skipped a beat and I gasped under my breath. Fearing that I might startle her, I swallowed hard, lowered my voice,and coaxed as calmly as possible, "Please, Mother, get down . . . slowly. I don't want you to fall." It was the same tone of voice I had used when I once called Renie, then about four years of age, to come "straight into the house and stop hugging that dog"—a strange Great Dane that had wandered into our front yard.

"He won't hurt me," Renie had responded as both her chubby arms encircled the neck of the huge dog, "he's my friend."

Mother's response was about the same as Renie's.

"Mother," I begged after her awkward, but successful, descent, "Don't ever do that again. I'm not going back to Texas until you promise me that you will never climb up on that stool again."

She reacted like a little child caught in the very act of something.

"I'm serious, Mother. I want you to promise me now, on your word, that you will stay off that stool. I'm asking this for your own good and for my peace of mind."

"Well, all right," she conceded while looking down at the floor. "All right, if you insist, I promise."

Then she looked up at me with a devilish twinkle in her eyes and added, "I promise I won't climb up there any more . . . unless . . .," she added with an impish grin, "unless there's something up there I really need."

I gave up. Thankfully, Mommie Mac survived step-stools. But watermelons and peaches did her in.

She could eat half a watermelon by herself, and often did. Then she'd stash the other half in the refrigerator and save it for the next day. She would do the same thing with fresh peaches. She'd buy a bushel, peel half of them for canning, and eat the rest. Her appetite was great; her nutritional balance was terrible. When her blood count dropped dangerously low, a hurried decision was made for her to move to Greensboro and live with my sister, Ella, a nurse and an administrator of a retirement center. It took a lot of talking on our part but Mother finally agreed and the doors to the white bungalow were locked. The forty-mile move was made in one day; the transition took in a lifetime.

"Annie," a fifteen-pound Boston Terrier with a pug nose and pleading black eyes, helped in the transition. Mother and Annie bonded. They ate together, walked together, and sometimes got into trouble together.

The telephone rang in Ella's office one day. Fay, the next-door neighbor, was on the line. "Now, Ella," she said, "I don't want to disturb you, but I think you should come home."

TROUBLE WITH "THE CHILDREN"

"What's the problem?" Ella asked anxiously, thinking that Mother had fallen or was ill.

"I don't know how it happened," Fay answered, "but your Mother and Annie are both locked in the dog lot in the backyard and can't get out."

Ella drove home with the key, unlocked the gate, and rescued her "children," as she called them.

One day a kind lady from my sister's church came to visit Mommie Mac. Her visit was part of a special ministry to elderly people who could not participate in the regular services of the church. As the visit concluded, the visitor suggested that the two of them might sing a hymn or a song and then have prayer together. The church visitor began singing "Jesus Loves Me" and Mother joined in. So did Annie. The three of them sang and howled through two verses, and Mother insisted proudly that Annie sang in "perfect pitch."

"I do wish I had paid more attention to Annie when she was little," Mother observed later that evening. "I do think I could have taught that dog to talk."

After a couple of broken hips it became necessary to find some help for Mommie Mac on a daily basis. This was more of a problem than anyone imagined.

Cora Mae, an oversized, elderly spinster, was the first one we tried. She made it OK for a few days—until she washed her underwear and hung it on limbs of the dogwood trees around the house, insisting "that's the reason God gave us sunshine." She achieved this by pulling the branches down with a garden rake, hooking the clothing on the branches, and then releasing the rake. Ingenious. So ingenious that neighbors stopped to stare. Blossoms look beautiful on dogwood trees in North Carolina; bloomers don't.

Janie worked as a "sitter" for about a month—until she began bringing her teenage daughter with her . . . and the two sat on the couch watching television all day while Mother cooked for them.

Others also came and went. One refused to give Mother raisins for her cereal each morning. No reason was given; she just refused. Another didn't like dogs so her days were numbered.

Then came Hilda Mae, a caring but somewhat overbearing black lay-preacher. Her presence effused piety—a piety oozing with scriptural admonitions and exhortations. One day when Mother was not feeling well, Hilda Mae urged her on.

"Now, Mommie Mac," she announced in a voice that could have filled a church house, "The Lord wants us to be HOLY; He jes' wants us to be HOLY!"

Mother ignored her for a moment as though she had not heard. It was obvious that she was in no mood for lofty exhortations and pious declarations.

"Hilda Mae," she finally said as she rolled over in the bed, "I'm not trying to be holy; I'm just trying to be *daily*."

Mommie Mac was *daily* until the day she died.

FIVE NICKELS AND A BEAR

Mommie Mac, ninety-four years of age, smiled as she opened the package that had just been delivered.

"It's just like the picture in the catalogue," she said proudly to Carol, her nurse, as she studied the silver-plated teddy bear bank. She had ordered the bank shortly after her granddaughter, Shannon, had told her that she would soon become a great-grandmother. This would be a "first" for Mommie Mac, and she was thrilled.

"Now, Carol, hand me those five new nickels we got at the bank yesterday—the ones with '1990' engraved on them."

Carol took the shiney coins from a bedside table and carefully placed them in the wrinkled and weathered hands. The elderly woman lovingly fingered a coin and hesitantly dropped it through the slot on the top of the bear's head. The "clink" of the coin signaled the completion of its journey from the head to the feet of the silver bear. It also signaled a rite of passage—the ending of one life and the beginning of another . . . a legacy from one generation to another.

Mommie Mac fondled the bear for a moment, handed it to her nurse, and observed softly, "There—those five nickles should be enough to get the baby off to a good start in life. Besides," she added with a grin, "we don't want to *spoil* the child."

Five nickels? How much is five nickels?

More than Mommie Mac ever had as a little girl at the turn of the century . . . more than the cost of an orange, an apple, and candy at Christmas . . . more than the price of a toy or a doll . . . more than the cost of twenty-five dippers of lemonade on the Fourth of July . . . or a pair of gloves . . . or a hat . . . or stockings . . . or a knife . . . or a teapot . . . or the vest-pocket edition of *Webster's Dictionary*.

Five shiney nickels—more than most any child living on a farm could imagine at the turn of the century.

"Now, Carol," she said, "I want you to take this bear and tie a nice pink ribbon around its neck."

"Do you think we should use pink?" Carol asked. "We're not sure if the baby will be a boy or a girl."

"It will be a girl," Mommie Mac announced with certainty. "No doubt about it, that baby will be a pretty little girl."

"Put the bear in a nice box and hide him away," she continued. "I won't be here when the baby is born, but I want you to make sure that my great-granddaughter gets this." And then she added with a smile of satisfaction and a characteristic twinkle in her eyes, "Don't tell anyone now; this will be our little secret."

MOMMIE MAC'S LEGACY

A month later Mommie Mac died—five months before little Emily was born. When we returned home from her funeral in North Carolina we brought with us the silver-plated bear bank containing the five new nickels. Shannon and her husband, George, placed it in their newly decorated nursery as a silent reminder of love . . . and legacy.

When Emily was two years of age, she and her "best friend," Troy, were playing in her room. Four little eyes spotted the silver bear and four little legs supporting two little bodies scurried up chairs and tables and desk tops to reach it. Shannon later found the bear toppled over, ribbon in disarray, lying on its side—empty. She picked it up and shook it. Not a single "clink" and not a single shiney nickel.

"Emily!" Shannon asked sternly, "Where are the nickels?"

"Troy . . . Troy . . ." Emily stammered with a quivering chin as she pointed toward the open door leading out of the house. Troy had made a fast exit.

"Did Troy take the nickels?"

She said as she shook her head from side to side and managed a mumbled, "No."

"Then how did he get them?" Shannon quizzed.

Emily looked at the floor and answered hesitantly as though she had done something terribly wrong, "I gave them to him."

That was several months ago. With Troy's help and with the help of his parents, three of the "1990 nickels" have been found, and they're still looking for the other two.

When I heard what had happened to the coins, I exclaimed, "Oh, no. Those nickels were picked out especially for Emily. That's a gift from a great-grandmother, no longer living, to her first great-grandchild. Why, that's a legacy . . . from one generation to another. That's the kind of gift you protect—on a very high shelf where little children can't reach it . . . or in a glass case . . . or in a dark closet."

The ensuing months and memories of my own childhood have soothed and softened my reactions.

Somewhere . . . somehow . . . I think I can hear Mommie Mac say, "Now you just hush, Son. I gave those nickels to that little girl. They're hers, not yours. If she wants to give all five of them away and if she wants to give away the bear bank also, she can do it. Now, stop fretting over something that's not yours."

The little boy in me listens . . . and answers . . . just as I was taught by benevolent parents in the hills of home, "Yes ma'am, Mother."

But Mother has not finished. "Don't you make that child feel bad about those nickels," she says. "She just wanted to be nice to her friend. You grown-ups leave those children alone."

"And, besides," she adds, "you only keep what you give away."

"Yes ma'am, Mother; yes ma'am."

LEAVING HOME

The long-awaited day had finally arrived. Renie, the youngest of our three daughters and the last one still at home, was leaving for college and I wasn't prepared for it.

Lawanna and I had watched Kathie, our oldest, drive off to Austin College; then on to Guilford College in North Carolina and finally to Greensboro College in the same state. But Kathie was the "big sister" who thrived on the academics, so her moving toward the university setting seemed the natural and appropriate thing to do. We had also watched Shannon travel a hundred miles south to enroll in Baylor University, but we knew that we would see her frequently and we also knew that one of the girls was still at home.

But that June morning of 1980 slipped up on me. I knew in my head this "rite of passage" in the McIver family was inevitable and it could lead to good, but my heart had difficulty getting the message. Was this really happening to us? Were all our children old enough to leave home? What would life be like for us with three empty bedrooms? And what would it be like for Renie? I pondered these questions as I surveyed the cluttered piles of clothing and furnishings yet to be loaded into the car. "There's not a room on the campus of Baylor University that can hold all this stuff," I chuckled out loud to no one in particular.

I pondered . . . and remembered another "leaving."

The year was 1942 . . . nearly forty years earlier. The place was Siler City, a small town located in the heart of North Carolina. I was sitting with my father at Buster Elder's Shell Service Station and Bus Stop . . . waiting . . . with a lump in my throat . . . trying to think of something to say.

"'Bout time for the bus for Asheville to come," Dad observed.

"Yep, I guess it is," I replied, swallowing hard.

"Take care of yourself, Son, and study hard."

"I will; I promise."

"Got your money?"

"Yes sir, all seventy-five dollars."

"That ought to get you started. Now if you need any more, let me know."

"Thanks, Dad."

The bus lurched around the corner and ground to a stop. We both knew, painfully, that time was up and the wait was over. I shook hands with my father and climbed on board, dragging up the steps behind me most of my worldly possessions in an old tin suitcase and a cardboard box. I placed them in the overhead luggage rack, found a seat, and waved a hesitant, awkward good-bye to Dad. Neither of us suspected as the bus slowly pulled away that the two-hundred mile trip through the Blue Ridge Mountains to Mars Hill College would two years later lead to a twelve-hundred-mile pilgrimage across the Red River and into Texas. And neither of us dreamed in that moment that the roots of my life and work would sink into the soil of another state and I would never return home again, except for all-too-brief-visits.

LETTING GO OF RENIE

But enough of this philosophizing, I thought, as I picked up one of Renie's boxes and headed toward the car in front of our house. Actually there were two cars, for there was no way that all her things could be packed into one automobile. Ingenuously, Renie had enlisted some of her friends to help her move from Dallas to Waco. She and Jana Jones had arranged to travel in Renie's faded-blue, second-hand Chevy Impala. Duncan Brooks and Doyle Knowles planned to follow them in Duncan's old Ford Mustang.

After two hours of constant work and careful juggling, both cars were crammed full of clothing and other belongings. "Leaving home" was about to become reality—if the drivers and the passengers could squeeze into the front seats.

"Just a minute!" I shouted with feigned excitement, "Let's get everyone together for a last picture."

"Great idea!" someone responded, "but we need to call Marcie and Laurie. They're swimming in the pool in the backyard." Marcie Murrell and Laurie Paschal, classmates and long-time friends of our girls, joined us in the front yard, dripping wet and dressed in skimpy bikinis. Other friends showed up out of nowhere to take part in the celebrative send-off.

Lawanna photographed the entire group and then took a picture of me writing a check and handing it to Renie. There were hugs and kisses, laughter and tears and final waves as they climbed into the cars. Lawanna and I turned and walked slowly back into our now-empty nest, pondering the adjustments before us. For more years than we had the energy to count we had been consumed by the girls' schedules: car pools, cheerleading practice, piano lessons and recitals, drill team practice, choir rehearsals, football games, retreats and camps, swim parties, and on and on. We had enjoyed these but I welcomed the adjustments.

As I closed the door and stepped into the den there was an eerie silence, as if the walls were asking, "What's happened?"

I smiled and said to Lawanna, "I'll miss all the girls but I'm looking forward to some peace and quiet around here."

Lawanna did not have time to respond. From the street came a piercing scream, "Mr. McIver! Mr. McIver!"

I dashed back out the door as someone shouted, "Duncan's car is on fire!" I looked and saw smoke billowing from under the hood of the Mustang.

WHERE THERE'S SMOKE, THERE'S FIRE

"Quick! Unload the car!" I yelled as I turned and ran back into the house.

"Lawanna, call the fire department! Duncan's car is on fire!"

"Are you sure?" she asked in bewilderment.

"Lawanna, *please* call the fire department!"

"Have you tried to smother it with . . .?"

"Now, Lawanna, NOW!"

Five minutes later the huge red fire engine careened around the corner, siren splitting the air, and stopped in the middle of the street in front of our house. Four helmeted firemen wearing yellow hip boots moved quickly and efficiently to Duncan's car, raised the hood, doused the flames and laid charred ignition wires on the ground. Their work was finished but they were gracious enough to linger to make sure that there were no other problems.

Or, they might have lingered to try to comprehend the sights before them. Clothing, lamps, books and albums, pillows, sheets, and graduation gifts littered the sidewalks and the four adjoining yards. A dozen high school students and graduates, some who had shown up to swim, wandered around in all kinds of dress, and undress on our own lawn. Neighbors came from houses up and down the block, took one look at the disarray, and shook their heads in disbelief. In the aftermath of the near-disaster, Laurie walked up to the driver of the fire engine and whispered something to him. He looked at her, scanned the crowd of students, shook his head and motioned to the other fireman that it was time to leave.

"Renie," I inquired quietly, "what did Laurie say to the fireman?"

"She asked him if he would take us all for a ride on the fire truck," she replied hesitantly.

I shook my head, looked at the scattered debris, and watched the fire engine as it chugged around the corner and said to Lawanna, "You know, Honey, I'm gonna miss all this excitement!"

POSTSCRIPT:

Thirteen years later the telephone rang. Renie, now the wife of John and the mother of Ali and "John-John," called from a distant state.

"Dad, we're all coming home for a week," she said excitedly.

"Wonderful," I responded, "what would you like to do while you're home?"

"Nothing, Dad; we just want to come home."

I thought of the hills of North Carolina . . . Buster Elder's Shell Station and Bus Stop . . . a tin suitcase . . . and a handshake. . . .

"I know what you mean," I replied softly, gratefully. "I know exactly what you mean."

NAPPINESS IS . . .

I opened the folder, removed the faded envelope, fingered it for a moment, and read the inscription: "Napoleon (Nappy) McIver, Ridge Spring Drive, Dallas, Texas."

Then I lifted the flap and studied the picture and the note inside:

> Dear Nappy:
>
> The doggie pictured on the card looks like one of my permanent resident orphans, Benny, who was one of your companions while you stayed with us. Hope you are doing well. Will be on vacation and out of town for about ten days, commencing the 19th. Give your folks my best wishes. I will get in touch with you when I return. Take care, stay out of trouble and out of the street. Your friend,
>
> Wes Porter

I laid the letter down and smiled . . . and remembered. . . .

Nappy—short for Napoleon Bonaparte—was a black miniature French poodle who thought he was a person. Over my protests he came to live with us shortly after my first open heart surgery. The girls and Lawanna insisted that I needed the companionship of a dog and that a dog "will help with the healing process," and "Dad, you need a male friend in this house filled with women." It was manipulation at its best, but what else can a person do when he's outnumbered four to one and he's about to be wheeled off to surgery?

"Okay," I relented in exasperation, "I hear you. We'll get the dog, but I'm not taking care of him; he's yours—and he's your responsibility."

"No problem at all, Dad," the girls responded in unison. "We'll do *everything* for him." Lawanna smiled her own affirmation.

When I returned home following surgery that tiny ball of fur with beady eyes greeted me with joyful barks. He circled my chair, stood on his wobbling hind legs, and whimpered until I lifted him up and let him sit in my lap. Later he found one of my shoes, dragged it up next to my chair, climbed into the shoe, and took a nap. It seems 8-medium was the perfect size for him too.

As Nappy grew, so did our problems.

"He can't stay in the house all the time," Lawanna observed. "And he doesn't like a leash," the girls added. So two thousand dollars later, a stockade fence was built around our backyard.

In spite of all we did, that tiny dog figured a way to sneak out the gate and vanish. He roamed the neighborhood at will, moving from yard to yard and house to house without any concern about city ordinances or animal control trucks. "Search and rescue" missions became a part of our daily schedule around the McIver household.

Nappy's nomadic spirit of adventure and his love of freedom often got him into trouble. From time to time he tangled with raccoons, opossums, squirrels, and some not-so-friendly dogs in the neighborhood. That's how he got into trouble with Tokey.

Tokey, a large German schnauzer with a wiry gray coat, spiked eyebrows, and a bristled beard, belonged to Ginny and Rusty Sutton, good neighbors who lived immediately behind us. Our fenced yards were separated only by an alley. The two dogs seldom saw each other, but the shadowy images they picked up while looking through knotholes set them off. They spent a part of each day barking angry messages across the alley from behind their respective fences. This was a workable situation, in spite of the constant noise, until the day Tokey and Nappy both escaped—on the loose at the same time!

TERRIBLE TIMING

I first suspected trouble when the barking in the backyards ceased and I heard high-pitched yelps of pain coming from the side of our house—just outside the kitchen window. Lawanna looked out, raced through the house, and shouted at me, "Tokey has Nappy by the throat and won't let go! He's killing him! Do something quick!"

I had just dressed for the morning worship services at our church—fresh shirt, coat, tie, everything. I dashed to the front door and yelled at the dogs as they rolled over and over across the lawn. Tokey's jaws were locked in a vise-like grip on Nappy's throat and neck. The yelps of the French poodle grew weaker as the larger German schnauzer clamped down harder.

"Do something!" Lawanna screamed.

"What am I supposed to do?" I shouted back.

"Just do something! Anything!"

Forgetting my bad hip and recent heart surgery, I ran out the front door and chased the dogs around the yard until I stumbled and fell on my face. As I went down, I managed to grab Tokey's hind leg. Refusing to let go, I slowly—and painfully—worked my way up his body until my left hand gripped his lower jaw. He looked at me out of the corner of one wild eye and clamped down even harder. Then quickly releasing his hind leg, I grabbed his upper jaw and pried with all the strength I had. Nothing happened. We were at a stalemate but I knew that I couldn't save Nappy if I turned loose. The unexpected happened as both dogs did a flip—in unison. I hung on for my life—and Nappy's—and flipped over with them. All three of us rolled and tumbled over the yard, creating a spectacle for neighbors who had heard the commotion and had gathered on their porches and in their yards to watch.

Finally Tokey, weary from the battle and confused by my intrusion, took a breath and relaxed long enough for me to yank Nappy free. The poodle's heart was racing as he cried softly and snuggled up close to me. There was a long, ugly gash on his throat and his black curls were matted with blood and saliva mingled together. Like the one for whom he was named, the "little Frenchman" had met his own Waterloo. I patted him gently, handed him to Lawanna, and limped back into the house. Neighbor Rusty raced across the alley from his house, surveyed the situation, and circled the yard twice before he cornered and caught Tokey. He apologized for his dog's behavior, disciplined him all the way back across the alley, and locked him up again in his own yard. We called the vet and made plans for Nappy's cuts to be sewn up. I took a quick shower (again), treated my own scratches and bruises, and put on clean clothes and hurried out the door for the morning worship services.

As I backed out of the driveway Lawanna exclaimed, "You won't need your next heart stress test!"

"Why not?" I asked.

"You've just had it. And after what you've been through these last fifteen minutes, there's no way any artery to your heart could be blocked!"

I smiled wearily and headed for the church—to preach on "peace" and "love."

SHORT-LIVED TRUCE

There was a canine truce in our neighborhood. It lasted for a few hours. The dogs were too tired to do anything but sleep. But by late afternoon—just like real people—they started barking again.

A few weeks later Nappy, with a short memory and a renewed thirst for freedom, sneaked out the gate again. He wandered north from street to street, meandered across yards and alleys, and ended up at the Wes Porter residence—or more specifically, the Porter "shelter." Wes, the president of the Humane Society, and his wife Nancy, loved animals and would do anything to protect them, nurture them, and get them back to their homes safely. They immediately checked Nappy's tag and called our house.

Lawanna, thrilled to hear that our dog was alive and well, arrived at the Porters' ten minutes later and greeted Nappy with excitement. He took one look at her, turned his head, and walked off to play with Benny and the other members of the shelter menagerie. When she persisted and picked him up, he snarled and growled and kicked all the way to the car. She put him in the backseat, closed the door, and drove off. He stood on his hind legs, looking out the back window, whimpering and whining all the way home. Needless to say that was not his last visit to see Wes and Nancy, Benny, and his other friends. In a "born free" attitude, he found freedom beyond the fence and friends outside the gate.

I folded the note, glanced again at the picture of Benny, and placed both of them back in the folder. The old file cabinet was once again closed and I was left with. . . .

Memories.

The Porters and Benny have moved; so have the Suttons and Tokey. Old age with accompanying arthritis, cataracts, and strokes finally caught up with Nappy. The weathered fence now leans in fatigue and the gate creaks and sags—a silent, two-thousand-dollar reminder of the inability to keep a dog (person) with a free spirit locked up.

But a word of wisdom from Nappy, who thought he was a person and sometimes acted like one:

"If you're determined to slip out the gate and wander across dangerous streets and through the strange yards of life, it's good to know someone like Wes Porter who's willing to take you in."

And to that Benny barks, "Amen!"

Chuckholes in the Road to Heaven

"Now, young people, you jest take it easy and tell us agin what the kidnappers looked like."

"I . . . that is . . . we're not sure they *were* kidnappers," I stammered. "We just don't know what happened. The car broke down at two o'clock this morning about twenty miles from here. Nip—it was his car—said we'd thrown a rod in the engine or something. We tried to flag someone down to help us, but there wasn't much traffic moving at that hour. Finally, about three o'clock a car stopped and . . ."

"Was it the kidnappers?"

"I'm really not sure who they were," I replied in mild irritation to the tall, lanky, grandfatherly-looking man who kept asking questions about the "kidnappers." But the badge that he wore on his khaki shirt read "Sheriff," so I figured I needed to be polite and answer anything he asked. Besides, I was too tired to argue. It had been nearly thirty-six hours since I'd had any sleep and fifteen hours since I'd eaten. And this was the first time I'd ever been in Crossville, Tennessee and the first time I'd ever needed the help of a sheriff.

"Now, son, we're here to help you so go back and start at the beginning and tell us what happened."

"Well, it all started yesterday," I began, "when four of us—all students at Southwestern Seminary in Fort Worth—left after lunch to drive home to North Carolina for the Christmas holidays."

"Now, let's see," the sheriff said as he lifted a small spiral notebook from his shirt pocket, "we need to get everyones' name."

"My name is Bruce McIver," I answered, "and this young lady is Richie Harris. She's also a student at the seminary."

"Now, what's the names of the boys who were kidnapped?" the officer asked as he shifted the plug of tobacco from one jaw to the other.

Figuring by now that it was useless to argue with the well-intentioned man wearing the badge, I responded, "Nip Anderson is one of them. He owns the car and he was driving. His home is Mars Hill—twenty miles north of Asheville. The other person is Al Crawford. He's an older student from a small town near Raleigh." The word "older" slipped out because Al was about fifteen years beyond the rest of us in age. I marvelled at him because he had entered the ministry "late in life," so I thought, and was determined that he would get some seminary training at any sacrifice. I was also intrigued by the fact he was a "fun" person, and "older" people could still be happy. I was glad he was riding home with us.

"You're doing fine," the sheriff observed as he touched the pencil end to his tongue. "Now tell me what happened after the other car stopped to help you."

"When the car pulled up beside us," I continued, "Nip walked up to the passenger side, told the two men in the car that we were in trouble, and asked for a ride into Crossville to get a tow truck or some other kind of help. Al whispered to us that he didn't like the looks of the men who had stopped and he was afraid for Nip to go by himself. So he got out of our car, told Richie . . . er, Miss

Harris and me not to worry. He said they would be back as soon as possible. Then the two of them got in the car with the strangers and rode off. That was fourteen hours ago and we haven't seen or heard from them since."

BROKE, STRANDED, AND SCARED

I tried not to let my own emotions surface as I talked with the sheriff. I didn't share with him my own fears and apprehension—the discomfort I felt about being left on the side of the road with a young woman . . . the long, seemingly endless black night . . . the painfully slow rising of the sun, and the lifting of our hopes . . . the hunger and thirst we both experienced . . . the heightened anticipation every time a car topped the hill . . . the disappointment as the car sped by and vanished around the curve . . . the guessing games . . . the "what if's?" . . . Al's suspicions and concerns about the men in the other car . . . our own hesitancy in leaving the car and our belongings to look for help elsewhere and maybe missing Al and Nip when they returned . . . and . . .

My silent, rambling emotions were put on "hold" when the Sheriff asked, "And how did the two of you get to Crossville?"

"After twelve hours of waiting," I answered, "we decided we had no other alternative but to try to flag down a car. About thirty minutes later a lady stopped, offered to help, and drove us into town. We went to the first garage we saw, hired a tow truck and went back out to bring the car and our belongings here."

"That's right," the slightly-built but feisty tow truck driver interrupted. "And they owe me nineteen dollars—a dollar for every mile—and they haven't paid me a dime!" It was obvious that he was more than mildly upset. He hadn't let us out of his sight since we got to town and had even trailed us to the sheriff's office. "Sheriff, I demand that you make them pay me. I want my money NOW!"

"I told him he would get his money," I explained to the officer. "He'll get every cent of it but I don't have it on me; neither does Miss Harris. We've pooled every penny we have and we're a little short. We just brought enough with us for meals and some gasoline. We hadn't counted on the breakdown and tow truck. But I'm going to wire my father for the money as soon as we finish this conversation and he'll send it immediately. Until then this man can keep the car and our belongings locked up in his garage as collateral."

The sheriff nodded in agreement, "Sounds like a fair deal to me."

The owner of the truck started to protest, then mumbled, "Okay, but I'll be at the Western Union office later this afternoon, and I'd better have my nineteen dollars by five o'clock, or else!" He turned abruptly and stalked off toward his garage.

"NOW, ABOUT THEM KIDNAPPERS . . ."

"Don't let him worry you none," the sheriff said as he looked at us with kindly eyes. "He's jest a mite testy. I can handle him and I'm sure the money will be sent to you. Now, if you'll 'scuse me, I want to get out an all-points bulletin about those kidnappers. We'll notify every law enforcement officer in this state and in the surrounding states to be lookin' out for 'em."

Richie and I thanked him, and walked off toward . . . nowhere. We had no place to go, and we didn't know a soul. And the sheriff had convinced us that our two traveling friends had actually been kidnapped.

"How much money do you have, Richie?" I asked hopefully as we walked away.

"Let's see," she said, opening her purse and counting, "three dollars and eighty-five cents. How much do you have?"

"Two dollars and thirty-eight cents," I replied dejectedly, emptying my pockets.

In the forties, this was more than enough to get each of us home under normal circumstances, but these were anything but normal circumstances. We were in a strange town where we knew no one; we were hungry and thirsty; we were nearly three hundred miles from our own homes across the Smokey Mountains; we had a tow truck driver watching our every move; and between the two of us we didn't have enough money to do much of anything except . . .

Send a telegram to my father:

"NIP AND AL KIDNAPPED STOP WIRE FIFTY DOLLARS STOP BRUCE"

After spending two dollars on the wire, we took stock of our resources and splurged on a couple of soft drinks and some crackers. We then sat down on the courthouse steps across the street from the telegraph office and waited. . . . and waited. . . . and watched for some signal from the operator that the fifty dollars had arrived. Ten minutes before closing time, we walked back to the Western Union office, hoping our presence might speed up the process. It didn't; neither did the presence of the tow truck driver who—true to his word—had come to collect his money. The minutes gave way to seconds as the clock on the wall ticked down. Promptly at five o'clock the operator removed his traditional eye shades, adjusted some papers on his desk, flipped the cardboard sign hanging by a string in the window to "Closed," and told us all good-night. He shut the door, turned the key, and walked away.

I watched him leave with envy, wishing I could also walk away. I couldn't. The tow truck driver was in my face, demanding his money.

Two hours later darkness had settled in on the small Tennessee town. The stores had closed and the people had gone to their homes. There was no sign the sheriff or any other officers were on the streets. Richie and I were in our place—sitting on the courthouse steps . . . thinking . . wondering . . . praying . . . hoping . . . facing a second night. . . .

Stranded.

NIP AND AL, TO THE RESCUE

"Look, Bruce!" Richie shouted. "Look what's coming up the street!"

I couldn't believe my eyes. Nip and Al in a larger, newer model car were slowly cruising the streets—obviously looking for us—towing behind them our car that had broken down. We were so thrilled to see them that we didn't vent our frustrations . . . until later.

"What happened to you guys?" I demanded. "You've been gone eighteen hours!"

"The men who picked us up at two in the morning were real nice to us," Nip responded. "We asked them to let us off in Crossville so we could call my parents but they told us there was a long-distance telephone strike and no calls could be made. They were driving to Knoxville—about seventy miles from here—and offered us a ride there. We knew that our chance of getting help there was better than here in a small town," he continued. "But by the time we got to Knoxville I figured I might as well catch the train over the mountains to Asheville, get my parents' car, and drive back and tow my car home."

"How did you find the car? I asked. "Richie and I had it towed in."

"I know," Nip answered. "When we didn't find it on the highway where it broke down we started asking around town. Most everybody we talked with knew about you, the 'kidnappers,' and the car. By the way," he added, "that tow truck driver has a mean temper. Don't mess with him. I paid him nineteen dollars and that seemed to calm him down some."

I breathed a sigh of relief, turned to Al and asked, "And where have you been for the last eighteen hours?"

"Oh," he replied with a weary groan, "I had to sit in the train station in Knoxville, waiting for Nip to come back through and pick me up."

"You mean you stayed in the train station in Knoxville and left us stranded by the side of the road? I can't believe it!" I exclaimed.

"Well, you don't think I enjoyed sitting on those hard benches all that time, do you?"

"I hope you got callouses on your behind! And besides," I whispered, remembering the most painful part of being stranded by the side of the road, "train stations do have rest rooms."

Al chuckled and Nip soothed any ruffled feelings by buying Richie and me a big steak dinner before we left Crossville and headed toward the Smokies and North Carolina. I never saw the mountains that night; I slept all the way across them.

When I arrived home I explained to my father what had happened. He had received the telegram at work and had raced out of the furniture factory to wire me the money. Obviously it did not reach me in time.

"But, Son," Dad said, "There's one thing I couldn't understand."

"What's that?" I asked.

"If Nip and Al had been kidnapped, why was the ransom only fifty dollars?"

"Dad, if you had been where I have been for the last two days, you'd think a fifty-dollar ransom was too much!"

POSTSCRIPT

Nip—now Dr. J. Harold Anderson—recently retired from his teaching position at Western Carolina University. He also pastored several churches in the mountains. Richie Harris-Whaley retired after thirty years of ministry with the Baptist Sunday School Board in Nashville. We've lost contact with Al. I wish him well but confess there are days when I hope he's on the side of some lonely road. . . .

Stranded.

DISILLUSIONED!

"I'm disillusioned!" I blurted out as I stalked through the door to the private office and flopped down on the sofa. "I've never been so disillusioned in all my life!"

I was glad to find one room in the complex called "Wilshire" where I could let my hair down, be honest about my feelings, and bang out my frustrations on the table. I'm convinced preachers—especially preachers—need such a place and frankly, if more had it, there might be less banging on the pulpits on Sunday mornings!

I was also thankful to have a friend who gave me the freedom to raise my voice and vent my feelings. Roy Austin was that kind of friend. He had joined our church staff to head up our counseling ministry. With a Ph.D. in psychology, a caring heart and creative counseling skills he became a special minister in our church and in our city. And to me. I often marvelled at his patience, sitting hour by hour, day by day, listening to hurting people and keeping more confidences than any one person ought to have to carry in a lifetime. There was no question about it: this ministry was good for the church and it was good for me personally.

"I'm disillusioned!" I hissed again through clenched teeth, lowering my voice as I remembered for the first time my voice might be heard by others in the building.

"That's good," Roy answered calmly as he motioned me toward an empty chair.

Good? is that what the man said? Good? What's he trying to pull on me?

Why doesn't he say something? Did he really say, *Good?* Maybe he didn't hear me correctly."

"You didn't understand me, Roy. You have no idea the reversals and emotions I've experienced this week. I said I'm *disillusioned!*"

He sat in silence for a moment and then replied quietly, almost casually, "And I said, 'that's good.'"

That made me mad. I didn't like the relaxed way he just sat there and I didn't like the calm, unperturbed expression on his face.

ONE VACATION . . . DOWN THE DRAIN

Hasn't this man heard me? Doesn't he care about me? I thought he was my friend. All he does is sit there with his hands folded while I'm churning inside. If he's not going to bother to probe around to find out what's upset me, I'll just spit it out myself.

So I did.

I told him briefly about the vacation . . . the south Texas ranch owned by friends Tom and Jean Martin . . . Santa Gertrudis cattle, fluttering quail and graceful deer . . . rattlesnakes and wild hogs . . . sunsets and evening fires . . . quiet stirrings of the embers of friendship . . . eerie, still nights punctuated by the occasional howl of a coyote—just the kind of vacation I needed.

Then I told Roy about the telephone call—the shrill, piercing ringing of Bell's contraption that somehow found me on a fifty-section ranch.

The caller had said there was a "crisis" in the church. No, the buildings had not burned and the staff had not resigned; neither had the deacons met secretly to evaluate the pastor while he was out of town. No one was critically ill and no one had died.

But apparently someone had said something that had been misunderstood or misinterpreted. Then statements had been made, either out of context or out of ragged emotions, that were not true. Feelings had been hurt and relationships strained. Although the matter had not involved me personally, it *had* involved strategic people in the church—and that meant both the program and the fellowship of the church were threatened.

Finally the caller had said, "Now, Pastor, I know you're on vacation and I didn't want to disturb you but . . . but . . . I thought you should know . . . but please don't let this bother you too much. Tell Lawanna hello. Have a nice vacation."

Just like that. Dump the load on me, then say, "Don't let this bother you . . ." and "have a nice vacation."

I *tried*, but the whole thing had begun to "gnaw" on me. I was so keyed up, I was ready to howl in unison with the lonely coyotes in the still of the night. Finally I aborted my vacation, packed the car, and headed back to Dallas.

I told Roy Austin all this. And I told him some of the thoughts and prayers I had mumbled on the three hundred mile trip home.

"LORD, I'M TIRED!"

"Lord, I've about had it! I'm tired of being 'Daddy Rabbit' and playing 'rescuer' to people . . . tired of having to pick up pieces of broken relationships. . . . tired of a lot of 'plain old stuff'! 'Scuse me Lord but when I told You I'd preach the gospel, I thought that's what I'd be doing. I don't mind doing that, Lord, but I'm fed up having to deal with adults . . . grown-ups who sometimes act like children. And besides, Lord, after all I've done for them, they mess up my vacation. . . ."

There. I had said it. I had bared my soul. I had shared my emotions and my bruised, fragile feelings about people in general and my own ministry in particular. I had confessed anger, irritation, and doubt. I was no longer Reverend McIver or Doctor McIver or Pastor or Preacher or whatever.

I was just plain Bruce—battered, bruised, and tired. Very tired.

With a weary sigh and a helpless gesture, I said to Roy for the third time, "I'm disillusioned."

Silence.

And then with a soft, understanding hint of a smile, Roy Austin, psychologist, counselor and friend said quietly—also for the third time—"Good."

That was more than I could take. "Don't pull that 'psychology stuff' on me, Roy Austin! I know as much psychology as you do!"

Of course, I didn't. I knew it before I said it, and I knew it when I blurted out the words. But in the heat of an argument there is often the tendency to "over-kill," and that's exactly what I had done.

Roy refused to play word games with me. Instead, he did the worst thing possible as far as I was concerned: he ignored my outburst. Like a parent watching the foolishness of a child's temper tantrum, he just ignored me.

After an excruciating period of silence, he said softly but firmly, "Now that you're disillusioned, we can begin to work with reality."

NO MORE ILLUSIONS

Ouch!

In the pain of that moment there was a flicker of understanding, a crack in the door and a lifting of a burden. So much of my ministry—and my life—had been lived under illusions:

- Give your life to God and you won't ever have any problems.
- Everyone will listen to, and always understand, the words of a pastor.
- Adults will act like mature adults.
- Life can be lived without entanglements and conflicts.
- Everyone will appreciate everything done for them.

- Every vacation will go uninterrupted and no telephone will ring.
- You can get lost on a thirty-thousand acre ranch.
- Only coyotes howl at night.

These illusions and a hundred more set me up for major disillusionments in life. This was not pessimism; just reality. The kind of reality that had a cross in the center of it.

I rose to leave Roy's office. "Thanks, friend," I said as I shook his hand, "you've helped me more than you can ever know."

I walked out the door, hurried down the steps hoping no one else on the staff would see me. Officially, I was still on vacation. I slipped out of the building and walked quickly to my car on the parking lot. The searing heat of the summer sun reflected off the concrete and into my face. A pang of hunger signaled that I had forgotten to eat lunch. I fumbled in my pockets for the car keys and remembered that I had left them in Roy's office. I moved stealthily back into the building only to be met by a secretary who exclaimed, "Pastor, thank goodness I caught you; you have a phone call. I think there's an emergency at the hospital."

I paused, looked down at the floor, and smiled to myself.

The ranch and the cattle and the coyotes were a thousand miles away.

I was back home again.

Back to reality.

SHOCKED!

"Guess what, Bruce?!" The fourteen-year-old junior-high student exclaimed.

"What?" I asked with a lilt in my voice, hoping to match the excitement and enthusiasm she radiated.

"My name's Vicki, and my friends and I have been telling all our friends at school today about the youth revival services at our church tonight . . . and the discussion groups . . . and the fellowship time after the service . . . and the refreshments."

"And guess what, Bruce?" she continued, hardly pausing for a second breath.

There was no time for me to respond to her second "guess what?" I really don't think she expected one, for her one-way conversation continued unabated.

"And we're telling everyone that we have the *best team* in the whole world leading us in our revival . . . and . . ."

As a first-year seminary student I was tempted for a moment to leap into the conversation and caution her about her words, "best team in the whole world." After all, I was a member of the team. And I had been cautioned again and again by my teachers and mentors that humility is a virtue for young preachers and that "pride goeth before destruction." I didn't want "destruction," whatever that meant, so at times I worked hard at being humble—so hard that I occasionally felt *proud* of the results. But on this special occasion, I didn't want to put a damper on this young girl's enthusiasm and (forgive me, Lord) I sorta liked the ring of "best team. . . ."

"Oodles and oodles of our friends are coming to the services tonight," Vicki continued with sustained enthusiasm, "and the church is gonna be packed out with kids from our school . . . and . . ."

"That's great," I interrupted. This kind of news made the long, 500-mile trip from Fort Worth to McAllen more than worth while—even if I did have to cut some classes to make it. Also I had missed a special exam in a course on Christian Ethics. But I reasoned that everybody including the professor should realize that being in a youth revival in McAllen, Texas was far more important than taking another exam in a class on ethics.

YOUTH REVIVAL, AHEAD!

Long before daybreak, four of us had stored our meager luggage in the trunk of Foy Valentine's 1937 Dodge, piled in and headed south. Foy's car was known as The Fireball of Van Zandt County, and it was appropriately nick-named. Van Zandt County was Foy's home, and "Fireball" was a not-so-subtle reminder that the old Dodge's motor constantly overheated.

But who cared! We were off to the valley of Texas—to McAllen and a youth revival. The thought never once entered our minds that we wouldn't make the trek in time for the evening service.

"Fireball" purred along faithfully on the two-lane highway. We did, however, have to stop at every third filling station to cool her down with water, and we kept our eyes open for creeks and streams where we could fill the extra bucket that we carried on the back floorboard—just in case.

We laughed and talked and sang our way through Waco, Austin, and San Antonio. We got to know each other better as we swapped stories about our backgrounds and shared dreams for the future. In all of this a bonding took place and we became a team without realizing what was happening.

Ardelle Hallock (now Clemons) had already graduated from Oklahoma University and from Southwestern Theological Seminary. To the envy of the rest of us she was now gainfully employed, working with students at Rice University and Baylor Medical School in Houston. The idea of receiving a regular check each month—regardless the size—was beyond our wildest imaginations. Ardelle's assignment for the weekend was to lead discussion groups and plan fellowships following each worship service.

Asa Couch, a graduate of Hardin-Simons University, was the designated song leader for the revival. His role was to organize and direct the youth choir, lead the congregational singing, and sing a solo when needed.

Foy and I were to share the preaching responsibilities, alternating service by service. I was delighted with this arrangement for almost everything I knew or had heard or had read could be summed up in a couple of ten-minute sermons. I needed all the help I could get.

The vast open spaces loomed before us after we left San Antonio. I stared in amazement at the miles and miles of ranches occasionally dotted with grazing herds of cattle and oil wells that pumped day and night. There was certainly nothing like this back in Siler City, North Carolina!

"Fireball," watered frequently along the route, hummed through a series of small towns with fascinating historical names—Three Rivers, George West, Alice, and Falfurrias. Finally she coughed into McAllen, the last town in Texas before crossing the Rio Grande into Mexico. There it was—the Valley—land of oranges, grapefruits, and some of the best vegetables in the world.

And . . . a whole town . . . (we thought) . . . waiting for us to lead them in a youth revival. Well, at least *one* teenager thought so.

AN UNEXPECTED GUEST

"Guess what, Bruce?" Vicki exclaimed for the third time.

"What?" I replied, returning to reality and forgetting for the moment "Fireball" and the miracle of a 500-mile day's journey through open spaces.

"I've got a special friend who has never been to a Baptist church. And she's coming tonight. And you know what, Bruce?"

How long can this go on? I thought.

"Her name is Juanita and she plays the accordion. I asked her if she will play it in the service tonight—just before you preach. She said she would."

"That sounds wonderful, Vicki," hoping the "guess what?" game was over. "Just tell her to check with me before the service so we can coordinate the music and the message."

Ten minutes before the evening service a tiny brunette carrying an accordion nearly her size was introduced proudly to me by her friend.

"I'm glad you will be playing in the services tonight," I said when I met her.

"I'm scared," Juanita replied. "This is the first time I've ever, ever been in a Baptist church."

"Don't worry. We're all your friends," I reassured her. "We're glad you're here. By the way, what song do you plan to play?"

"I thought I'd play 'Ave Maria,'" she replied with a smile. "That's my favorite."

I gulped. Personally, I like "Ave Maria." But at a Baptist revival? I knew that Asa would have the congregation and choir singing old gospel songs like "On Jordan's Stormy Banks I Stand" and "Since Jesus Came Into My Heart." I knew also that the choir would sing rousing choruses like "Christ For Me" and maybe "Do Lord; O Do Remember Me." For the life of me I couldn't see how we could fit "Ave Maria" into this mixture.

And time was running out.

"Do you play any other songs?" I asked hopefully.

"Oh, I play lots of them," Juanita answered with a smile. "I've been playing this accordion since I was nine years old."

That was my answer. So I thought.

"'Ave Maria' is beautiful, Juanita, but why don't you choose another number—just for tonight?"

"That's fine with me," she replied. "What do you want me to play?"

"Oh, you pick it out," I replied naively. And if that wasn't bad enough, I added, "I trust you completely."

THAT'S WHAT I GOT FOR TRUSTING HER

Seven-thirty. Packed house. Asa pumped us up with "On Jordan's Stormy Banks," "We're Marching to Zion," and added as a bonus "Jesus Saves." Asa, a tall student, had long arms and his hands flapped in rhythm with the music as he led. It was quite an experience and quite a spectacle!

Eight o'clock. Almost time for me to preach. And time for our special guest, the "first-timer-at-a-Baptist-revival," and her accordion number.

Her "Guess What?" friend gave her a glowing introduction. I bowed my head, pondering my sermon and trying to pray as the little girl slipped her arms through the straps of the instrument and hoisted them over her shoulders. She then placed her fingers on the keyboard, smiled, stretched the bellows, and hit the first chord.

I was startled. So was the congregation. Never had so much sound come at one time from any musical instrument. The fanfare was overwhelming. I forgot all about my sermon, looked up and leaned forward in my seat, wondering what familiar hymn or gospel song would follow those resounding opening notes. I could no longer bow my head and pray. I had to see this for myself. There she stood . . . to the right of the pulpit . . . just in front of me . . . before a capacity audience . . . weighing all of sixty-five pounds but handling that accordion like a master!

As she angled her body slightly to one side I detected a smile on her face. She had found a home in this Baptist church. There was no more fear. With greater effort than ever she played and pumped (or whatever you do to an accordion)!

I listened . . . and wondered . . . and became confused . . .

And groaned.

I had heard these notes before. Somewhere. But not in a Baptist church. Definitely not. And they weren't to be found in *any* Baptist hymnal!

And then it came to me. I groaned again.

Juanita was giving a rousing rendition of "La Cucuracha!"

Spanish for "The Cockroach!"

She ended with a flourish, looked at me with a warm, soft glow on her face and sat down. She had given the number her best.

I looked at her with my mouth half-open in amazement, managed a hint of a weak smile in return, and prayed for energy to stand. . . .

And for something—anything—to say.

And guess what?

I'm the only person in all the world who has ever preached a sermon following "The Cockroach!"

Maybe that's why I enjoy stepping on those rascals today!

12

Divine Appointments

"Please hold my calls," I said to my secretary. "I've got two sermons to prepare and I'm running out of time."

"Looks like things are on their usual schedule around here," she quipped. "But I'll do my best," she added with a smile.

Ten minutes later she tapped lightly on my door, stepped inside my study, and said in a soft voice, "I know I promised not to interrupt, but there's a man out here who wants to see you. He's from out of town and says he'll only take a few minutes. He seems very nice."

"Who is he?" I asked, realizing before the words were out that it really didn't matter. In all my years pastoring a church I had never found a good balance between an open-door policy for people and a protected time of study and sermon preparation for myself.

Without waiting for her to answer, I hurriedly rearranged the clutter on my desk, shoved a few loose items into the already-crammed drawer, and stood to greet my visitor. Instead, he hastened through the door and greeted me.

"Hi, Pastor," he said as he extended his hand. "I'm Chuck Melton from Tampa, Florida. I've been looking forward to meeting you for a long time."

I had no idea who the man was other than what he had just told me, but I was impressed by his firm handshake and warm smile. He was dressed in casual but neat clothes and his well-trimmed, tanned body looked as if it had just stepped off a beach. I quickly guessed that he was about fifty years of age.

"Sit down, Chuck," I insisted as I pointed to a chair. "It's nice to meet you."

"I bring you special greetings from my pastor, Tom Branson," he said, flashing a broad smile. "Tom's spoken often of you. Why just two months ago he mentioned you in one of his sermons. Very good sermon, by the way. He told me that whatever else I did on this trip, I had to meet you. He said you were classmates in the seminary and struggled through Greek and Hebrew courses together."

"Yes sir—Tom said Bruce McIver was about the best; and I'll tell you something," he continued with a grin and a mock confidential tone, "I think he was right." Then he chuckled out loud, released my hand, and patted me on the shoulder.

"Do sit down, Chuck," I invited again, basking in the pride of that moment and wishing that some of my deacons could have heard this stranger's words of affirmation from his pastor, Tom.

Tom? Branson? For the life of me I couldn't pull up a face to go with the name but I wasn't about to let Chuck know. *Oh well*, I mused silently, *I'll just leave it alone and later in the conversation I'll probably remember. After all, it's been a long time since I sat in Hebrew and Greek classes at the seminary.*

WINNING WAYS

"By the way," Chuck added, "before I forget it I must pass on a message from Tom. He said he wants to extend you an invitation to preach for several days in our church in Tampa. He said he'd arrange for a house on the beach for your family when you come. He wanted me to mention this to you today, but he'll be in touch with you soon to check on your availability and talk with you about some possible dates."

Availability? Heavens, I thought, *I'll cancel most anything I have on my schedule for a week like that! Lawanna and the girls will love the beach. It will be a great family vacation and with my preaching responsibilities there, most of the expenses will be covered.* I still couldn't get a face on Tom, but I was liking him better the longer Chuck and I talked.

"Now," I said warmly to my new friend as I leaned over in my chair, "what can I do for you?"

His tone changed and he answered in hesitant, measured words punctuated by pauses. "Tom suggested," he began, "that I look you up . . . since I'll be moving . . relocating . . . to Dallas."

"Move? Relocate?" I asked.

"It's a long story, Pastor, but I'll try to be brief. I hadn't intended to get into this—but . . . since you're a special friend of Tom's . . ."

My mind churned again. *Tom who?*

"It began about a year ago," he continued. "My boy . . . only boy . . . nineteen years old . . . was killed in Vietnam."

"I'm so sorry, so very sorry," I said with genuine concern.

"The sad thing is," he choked, "it was a senseless death. Strafed by our own planes as he and his platoon tried to take a hill. I think they called it 'friendly fire.' You may have read about it in the papers. The whole terrible incident got a lot of coverage back here in the States." He brushed a tear from his eye with one hand and paused to collect his emotions. There were tears in my eyes too. Words were not necessary.

"But that's behind us," Chuck said as he cleared his throat and straightened up in his chair. "We've got to get on with our lives. My daughter and I and my mother will be moving to Dallas. We'll sell our house in Tampa . . . change will be good for us . . . need to get away and start over. . . ."

"Your daughter and your mother?" I probed, trying to be as sensitive as possible.

"Yes, my wife died three months ago. Cancer . . . battled it for three years . . . before. . . ." His voice trailed off. There were more tears, and more silence.

He took out a handkerchief, wiped his eyes, blew his nose and added, "But life goes on. All of this has been a shock but we're ready to put down new roots and start over. It's important for us to locate in a good neighborhood and to find the best public school possible for my daughter. And of course we'll be looking for a new church home, but I'm not really worried about that," he added with an all-knowing smile. "After the things that Tom has said about you, I think we've already found our church—and our pastor."

"Look, friend," I responded. "You've had more on your shoulders and in your heart than any person should have to carry. I'll do everything possible to stand by you through this transition."

"Thanks," he replied as he stood, straightened his shoulders, and moved toward the door. "Your seeing me today helps more than you can know. I'm staying for a few days at the Holiday Inn on Central Expressway. I flew in early to scout out housing and schools. My mother and my daughter are driving now from Florida with some of their personal possessions. They'll be here in a couple of days. Later, when our house back there has sold, we'll make the final move. Just pray for me; that's the main thing."

I did, and then watched him walk out of the building. "Life's not fair," I said slowly to my secretary. "I haven't met anyone carrying more grief and heartache than that man. We've got to do everything we can to help him."

ANOTHER VISIT FROM CHUCK

The next day my secretary rang me and announced, "Mr. Melton from Florida is here to see you for a moment."

"By all means, send him in."

A smiling Chuck walked through the door and into my study. "Hi, Pastor," he greeted me warmly, "I was in this area of the city and thought I'd drop in and say hello to you."

"I'm delighted, Chuck. I've had you on my mind and in my prayers since yesterday. I want to help any way I can. Have a seat."

"No, Pastor, I won't take up your time. Just visiting with you yesterday was all the help I need. I slept much better last night knowing that I had found a new friend in a strange city. I just wanted to stop by for a minute and say thanks to you. Your old buddy, Tom, thanks you also."

Tom? Maybe he lived in my dorm? Or, maybe we drank coffee together between classes?

"Thanks for coming by, Chuck. Are you sure there's nothing I can do for you?"

He paused at the door, pondered for a moment, and said, "Well, I could use the name of a good attorney. I have some legal transfers that must be made. I'll also need a banker. Any suggestions?"

"I think I can help on both counts," I answered gladly. "Robert Fanning is an attorney who comes to my mind immediately. He's done some work for me personally and I'm sure he would be glad to talk with you. And Hugh Williams, the chairman of deacons, is affiliated with a large bank here in Dallas. He's actually in personnel and administration but he can guide you to the right persons to take care of your needs. I can give you several other names if. . . ."

"Those two names will be sufficient," he said as he took a piece of paper from his pocket. "Let me write them down—Fanning and Williams. This will help a lot. Thanks." And he was gone.

I had a good feeling. Helping people is at the heart of ministry—even if it interrupts sermon preparation.

On the third day the secretary rang again. "Chuck Melton just dropped by. Do you have time to see him?"

"Of course I do. Send my friend in."

"Chuck," I welcomed him, "it's so good to see you again. How are things today?"

"They're OK, I guess—but they could be better."

"What's wrong?" I asked in concern.

"I don't want to bother you," he began, "but a couple of things have happened.

MORE TRAGEDY STRIKES

"Last night after dinner at the hotel, I went down to the Schoolbook Depository where President Kennedy was shot. Three young thugs accosted me and robbed me at gunpoint while I walked around the area. They took my wallet, my money, and all my identification. They even took the watch off my wrist."

"That's terrible, Chuck," I exclaimed. "I'm so sorry it happened to you, and I'm embarrassed that it happened in our city. What are your plans? How can I help?"

"I've talked to the police and they're doing all they can. I'm paid up through tomorrow at the hotel and I've asked the highway patrol to try to find my mother and daughter who are now driving this way."

"Do you have any money at all?" I asked.

"A dollar and sixty-eight cents," he answered as he emptied his pockets."

"That won't go far in this city," I said as I looked at the single dollar bill and the few coins he placed on the desk. "But we do have an emergency fund here in the office. I can get enough out of that to pay for your meals for a couple of days. I'll also check to see if I can get the hotel to extend your credit until your mother arrives."

"No, Pastor," he protested, "you've already done too much. I'll make out . . . somehow."

"That's what friends are for, Chuck. Besides," I added with a grin, "I've got to help you because I don't want Tom to become upset with me. He might cancel his invitation for me to preach in Florida. I wouldn't like that; neither would my wife and children who are already excited about a week at the beach."

We both chuckled and I excused myself and walked down the hall toward the financial secretary's office. We made it a practice not to keep a lot of money on hand, but fortunately we found an adequate amount in the benevolent fund to take care of Chuck's food and incidental expenses for two or three days. He protested mildly but I put the money in his hand and insisted that he take it. He thanked me and moved toward the door.

"By the way," I asked innocently, "how did you get from the Holiday Inn on North Central Expressway to our church today?"

"I rode the city bus," he answered.

"Well, you're not riding the bus back. I'm going to take you in my car. Now don't argue with me; just follow me out to the parking lot and we'll be off."

"No, Pastor, you see . . . er . . . I really don't want to impose on your time and I have to go all the way to downtown Dallas to take care of some business."

"Don't argue, Chuck. I've got to go in that direction to make some visits at the hospital. Now, here's my car. Be my guest and get in."

Chuck didn't have a lot to say during the fifteen-minute drive to the heart of the city. I figured that he was worn out from the events of the night before and from the emotional drain of wondering when his mother and daughter might arrive. So we drove most of the way in silence. I stopped the car and let him out on Elm Street as he had requested. I gave him my home telephone number and told him to call me anytime he needed me. We shook hands, waved good-bye, and I was on my way to the hospital. And he was off to . . . somewhere.

CONNED BY A PRO

When I arrived back at the office two hours later there was a note on my desk: "Hugh Williams wants you to call him." I immediately dialed his number at the bank.

"Pastor," he asked, "do you know a Chuck Melton?"

"Sure do, Hugh," I answered proudly. "He's one of the finest men I've met in a long time. Why do you ask?"

"He was in our bank a couple of hours ago," Hugh replied. "He told me that you and he had spent several hours together this week and that his pastor knew you, and that Bob Fanning was his attorney. He said something about losing his credentials and then asked me to approve and initial a sizable check that he wanted to cash. Since this was out of my area of responsibility at the bank, I asked him to give me a few minutes to check on it.

When I returned, he had done a vanishing act. The secretaries said he acted strange . . . and nervous. Frankly, Pastor, the whole thing seemed phony."

I thanked Hugh for his call, stared at the dangling cord of the telephone receiver, and slowly hung it up with a sigh. As I surveyed my study and gazed at the chair Chuck had sat in—three days in a row!—I muttered a word that I had learned as a boy back in the hills of North Carolina.

It seemed the appropriate thing to do.

I never figured out how Chuck (if that was his real name) made it back from Downtown Dallas to wherever he must have parked his car near the church; I never knew if he had a mother and a daughter, or if his son was killed in Vietnam, or if his wife died; I never received an invitation to preach in Florida and my family never had that that special vacation on the beach.

I never found out who "Tom" is, or if he even exists.

I was "conned" by a "pro."

TWICE DEAD

Then there was the day when another stranger dropped by the office to ask for help. Larry Shotwell, one of our ministers, sat down to visit with him.

"How can we help?" Larry asked.

"My mother . . . my mother . . . died . . . Odessa . . ."

"Your mother died in Odessa? Odessa, Texas?"

"Yes, she died two days ago. They're holding up the funeral 'til I get there. But I'm out of money. I don't need much; just enough for a bus ticket."

"We'll do what we can," Larry responded kindly. "Could you tell me your name?"

"Name's Lee. Johnnie Lee."

"Thank you, Johnnie. Let me check on something for a moment," Larry said as he stood and moved across to another desk in the reception area. He discretely checked a large notebook where the names of those requesting help were listed. He scanned the book for a moment, closed it, and walked back across the room.

"Johnnie, I'm so sorry about your mother," Larry offered. "I've just checked and you were in here six months ago. Your mother had also died then. You've lost her twice in the same year!"

Without another word, poor Johnnie was up—and out . . . and gone.

He never came back. Apparently his mother got better.

THE STRANGER

What a wonderful surprise, I thought as I looked out my bedroom window early on Sunday morning. *Snow*. Snow in Dallas the Sunday before Christmas. It looked as if the entire city was covered with a soft powdery blanket, untouched by human footprints and unmarred by automobile tire tracks. For me it was a magnificent picture of nature at its best—a reminder of boyhood days in the hills of North Carolina. I lingered by the window, allowing the child in me to absorb the miracle of the moment, and then moved slowly downstairs to brew a cup of coffee and to look over my sermon notes for the last time.

An hour later I drove alone toward the church for the first morning worship service. The family would follow later and attend the second service. As I steered the car carefully, listening to the crunching of the snow with every turn of the wheel, I knew from experience that the number of people in church this day would be greatly reduced because of the weather conditions. There would be gaps in leadership, adjustments in schedules, and lighter offering plates. But the little boy inside me was so excited, I couldn't let these thoughts get in the way. It was Christmas. And it was snowing!

As I slowly turned into the church parking lot, I was in for a happy surprise. People moved toward the church buildings from all directions. The older folks walked carefully and gingerly, hanging on to one another while they searched for hidden sidewalks. But they grinned with every slippery step. I grinned back. The little children frolicked in the sparkling snow, giggling away any thought of caution. I stepped out of the car and waved in all directions, "Merry Christmas!" The entire parking lot came alive with laughter and excitement, "And a 'Merry Christmas' to you, Pastor!"

I smiled as I stepped into the warmth of the beautiful building, feeling deep down inside that it was going to be a good day. The sun was now shining, peeping through the low-hanging gray clouds. The landscape was beginning to sparkle as the soft, powdery snow silently melted and then froze quickly into glittering ice crystals. And surprisingly, the people were gathering. What more could a pastor in Dallas ask for on a December Sunday morning!

The celebrative, almost childlike, spirit displayed on the parking lot continued as people moved inside the sanctuary for the beginning of the worship service. Some who had not sung a note in months picked up the hymnal and sang Christmas carols with gusto. Little children looked up and smiled at their parents and parents reached down and hugged little children. There was a warmth in the service that seemed to touch every person. Happily, this generous spirit spilled over into the offering plates and they overflowed with special mission gifts to help less fortunate people. It was Christmas! Christmas for everyone, and it was written on the faces of families and friends who had gathered within the walls of our church to worship.

When I stood to preach I urged the people to remember the central theme of Christmas; more specifically, the central Person. I talked about Christ's love for all people and I underscored the humble circumstances of the Advent, His coming to us—an inn with no available room, a cattle stall, a simple manger, a young girl named "Mary" and a carpenter named "Joseph," and a handful of lowly shepherds.

Then, I shared a paragraph that I had recently read in The *Saturday Review:*

> "Last night John Elzy, watchman at the Grand Eagle Department Store, while making his rounds of the bargain basement, found the body of a man lying under a counter. He was thin to

> the point of emaciation, apparently in his middle thirties, and was shabbily dressed. His pockets were empty and there were no marks of identification upon his person. Store officials believe that he was trampled in the Christmas rush and crawled under the counter for shelter. But they are unable to account for what appear to be nail wounds in hands. The police are investigating."

I concluded my sermon with a prayer, and then we sang the closing hymn:

> O come, all ye faithful, joyful and triumphant,
> O come ye, O come ye to Bethlehem!
> Come and behold him, born the King of angels!
> O come, let us adore him, O come, let us adore him,
> O come, let us adore him, Christ the Lord.

The hymn was easy to sing for everyone was feeling "joyful and triumphant." After visiting briefly with members and guests, I slipped out the side door and moved quickly toward my office. Time was important. I had only fifteen minutes to catch my breath, freshen up, drink a glass of water, and then head back for the second worship service. As I turned the corner and started walking down the hall, I noticed a cluster of people gathered in front of our church library. Two Dallas police officers stood in the midst of them. My heart raced and my pace quickened as I approached the group.

THE DISTURBING VISITOR

"Is anything wrong?" I asked anxiously. "What's happening?"

One of those standing in the group responded by pointing through the large glass library window and saying, "There, Pastor. Look there."

I looked through the window into the children's reading section of the library. Seated at a table designed for little boys and girls . . . in a chair designed for little boys and girls . . . was a stranger. He appeared to be about six feet tall and about thirty years of age. He was extremely thin and his long black hair fell in matted clumps to his shoulders. His clothing was ill-fitting and tattered. The dirty brown sweater that he wore was at least two sizes too small and was held together with one remaining button. His sockless feet were covered with a pair of old-fashioned canvas tennis shoes that had no laces. Oblivious to the commotion on the other side of the glass partition, he slowly turned the pages of a children's book, looking intently at every picture.

As I silently stood in the hall and studied the stranger, I heard someone in the small group of onlookers ask, "What are we going to do, Pastor? What on earth are we going to do?"

I heard the questions but I could not respond. Silence. Words would not come.

Finally I managed to ask, "Does anybody know him? His name? Where he lives?"

"No."

"Has anyone spoken to him? Are these the only clothes he has? Doesn't he have a coat?"

"We don't know, Pastor. We've never seen him around here so we thought we ought to call the police. . . ."

One of the policemen, obviously uncomfortable with the situation, moved over next to me and whispered, "We got the call to come out here, but there's nothing we can do; he's not bothering anyone. I guess we'd better be moving on. The streets are bad, and they'll be needing us out there."

I mumbled some kind of thanks to the policemen as they walked away and tried to think of something to say to the person who kept asking, "What are we going to do with him?" Before I could frame an answer, I heard singing from the sanctuary:

> Joy to the world! the Lord is come;
> Let earth receive her King;
> Let every heart prepare Him room,
> And heav'n and nature sing
> And heav'n and nature sing. . .

I knew instantly that the second service had already begun. I was late and I was caught in a dilemma between a congregation meeting for worship and a nameless man looking at pictures in a children's book. I also wrestled with all kinds of emotions as I stared through that glass window—frustration, empathy, bewilderment, discomfort, embarrassment, and anger. I was angry that the police were called because a stranger in tattered clothes found his way into our buildings. I was angry because I kept hearing, "What are we going to do?" I was angry because I just didn't understand the question; or maybe I was angry because I *did* understand it.

While I tarried, pondering my own frustration, the young man closed the book. He then rose slowly from his seat, placed the book carefully back on the shelf and made his way out of the library. He passed in front of the little group of onlookers without a word being spoken . . . by anyone. We watched as he walked down the hall in the opposite direction from the sanctuary and the sounds of "Joy to the World." He paused at the exit door, braced himself against the cold wind, and stepped outside. He then climbed on his old rusty bicycle that he had left leaning against the shrubbery and peddled away in the snow.

He was gone.

The crisis was over and the halls were cleared. There were no more policemen.

I looked at my watch again and moved slowly toward the sanctuary. The worship service was nearly half finished. But I still had time to read the Scriptures, lead in prayer, and deliver the sermon. And I had time to tell again the story published in The *Saturday Review* about "a shabbily dressed young man . . . a stranger . . . thin . . . emaciated . . . trampled in the Christmas rush. . . ."

But this time the young man in the story had a face—for I had a strange feeling that I had just been watching him through the window of the library.

13

Exit Laughing

What you gonna do when the river overflows?
I'm gonna sit on the porch and watch her go.
What you gonna do when the hogs all drown?
I'm gonna wish I lived on higher ground.
What you gonna do when the cow floats away?
I'm gonna throw in after her a bale of hay.
What you gonna do with the water in the room?
I'm gonna sweep it out with a sedge—a broom.
What you gonna do when the cabin leaves?
I'm gonna climb the roof and straddle the eaves.
What you gonna do when your hold gives way?
I'm gonna say, "Howdy, Lord! It's Judgment Day!"

The author of the lines above is unknown, but I'm sure I've bumped into him many times along the way. There's a special sense in which he and I are brothers in asking, "What you gonna do?"

"What you gonna do" if you fail high-school English? . . . if you're not accepted into the university . . . if she says "no" . . .

if she says "yes" . . . if you don't get the job . . . if you don't get the raise . . . if you're forced to take early retirement . . . if the Social Security check doesn't arrive on time . . . if the children don't call . . . if there's a "blip" on the EKG . . . if health fails . . . if you end up living alone? What you gonna do?

People's lives can reflect better answers to this question than any combination of just words.

DOING THE GOSPEL

John and Doris Hurt had been long-time members of our church. John, a former writer for the Associated Press, was the editor of The *Baptist Standard*, a weekly news magazine for Texas Baptists with a circulation of nearly 400,000. No pastor ever had better friends and encouragers than I did in John and Doris Hurt. On many Sunday evenings after a long day of preaching and pastoral responsibilities, I found solace in their den eating Doris' homemade ice cream and listening to John say, "Now, Pastor, you worry too much. Just settle down; everything's gonna be OK." I knew deep down inside that everything *would* be OK, but in my fatigue I needed to hear someone say it. I also needed someone who would accept me right where I was . . . just as I was . . . not as "pastor" but as a friend whose ragged edges occasionally needed to be sanded and smoothed (and soothed). John and Doris did that often.

Then one day while I was recovering from a second heart surgery in a hospital in Milwaukee, I was told that John had died. My energies had been drained by the lengthy operation and all I could do in the intensive care unit was whisper—half-prayer, half-whimper—"What am I going to do? What am I going to do without my friend?"

A few weeks later, back home in Dallas, Doris visited me.

She said, "People ask me, 'What are you going to *do?*'"

Then she smiled and added, "I tell them I'm going to *do* Proverbs 3:5-6 and Philippians 4:4-7."

After Doris left I reached for my Bible to review the verses and to check my memory. I read slowly and quietly:

> Trust in the Lord with all your heart
> and lean not on your own understanding;
> in all your ways acknowledge him,
> and he will make your paths straight.
>
> Proverbs 3:5-6 NIV

> Rejoice in the Lord always. I will say it
> again: Rejoice!
> Let your gentleness be evident to all. The Lord
> is near.
> Do not be anxious about anything, but in everything,
> by prayer and petition, with thanksgiving,
> Present your requests to God. And the peace
> of God which transcends all understanding,
> will guard your hearts and minds in Christ Jesus.
>
> Philippians 4:4-7 NIV

Today, nearly seven years after our visit, I have retired as pastor of Wilshire Baptist Church. Doris has sold her house and now lives with her son and his family in Washington, D.C. far away from her friends and church here in Dallas. She has suffered a broken hip and has experienced a general deterioration in health, but not in attitude.

But if you were to ask her today, "Doris, what are you going to do?" she would undoubtedly answer with a hint of a smile, "I'm *doing it!* I've been *doing it* all along. I'm *doing* Proverbs 3:5-6 and I'm *doing* Philippians 4:4-7."

And to that I say, "Amen!"

"THE SEMINARY SHUTTLE"

"It's a miracle, Bruce; it's nothing short of a miracle," Warren Hultgren exclaimed to me as he visited our home in Dallas thirty-eight years ago.

"What's a miracle?" I asked.

"The pastor search committee of First Baptist Church, Tulsa, has interviewed me, investigated me, researched me, and they still want me to come as their new pastor."

"That's great, Warren," I chuckled. "But are you sure they know *everything* about you?"

"They have really done their homework," he replied. "In fact, I told them in our last meeting that there was one thing they had not found out about me. Then I lifted my pants leg—and showed them a mole behind my right ankle!"

"What was their reaction?"

"They loved it! And they still want me to be their pastor. Bruce, it's a miracle."

We laughed together.

That's one of the things I've always liked about Warren. He could laugh at himself, and he refused to take himself too seriously. He had a brilliant mind, a winsome personality, and an unusual gift for public speaking and preaching. There was no question in my mind: "miracle" or not, First Baptist, Tulsa, had made a good choice.

As Warren drove away, I remembered warmly the beginnings of our friendship. It was in the mid-forties just after World War II, and we were struggling young students in the seminary at Fort Worth. Like most everyone else we were poor, living a day at a time, hoping for some speaking invitation, or preaching opportunity to come our way. The challenge of preaching was real, but so was the thought of the ten or fifteen dollars that we might receive for our efforts. Ten or fifteen dollars went a long way back in those days.

When money ran out completely, as it often did, we could get a loan of a few dollars through the financial office at the seminary. A dear old man, resembling a character out of a Norman Rockwell painting, was the financial officer in charge of loans. Our visits to him became so regular that when he saw us coming he would raise his pen in a trembling hand and ask in a quivering voice, "How much today, young men?" We always managed to pay him back . . . somehow . . . just in time.

WANDA AND "MR. MCGREGGOR"

Warren's wife, Wanda, a charming, delightful person, worked at the Public Housing Administration offices in the heart of Fort

Worth. Jean, my first wife and Kathie's mother, worked in personnel at the telephone company. One cold day they were riding home on a bus called "The Seminary Shuttle." It was late in the afternoon and the bus was crowded beyond capacity with people standing in the aisle. Most of the riders were "regulars" and related in some way with the seminary, either as students, wives of students, or faculty members. Dozens of conversations buzzed throughout the rickety old bus above the growl of the engine.

"Where's Warren?" Jean asked Wanda.

"Oh, he's preaching a youth revival in Tomball near Houston. He'll be gone three days."

"How are you getting along without him, especially on these cold nights?"

"I'm managing to stay warm," Wanda said with a smile. "I'm sleeping with Mr. McGreggor."

Silence. Awful silence. Conversations stopped in mid-air, fifty heads turned, mouths fell open in disbelief, and a hundred critical, beaded eyes focused on Wanda.

In the stunned silence of that moment Wanda and Jean . . . slowly and painfully . . . realized . . .

They were the only people on that bus who knew that "Mr. McGreggor" was the Hultgrens' one-year-old, jet-black Scottish Terrier.

They gasped, reached up and rang the bell, and exited quickly at the next stop—three blocks short of their destination—and giggled all the way home.

It's been nearly fifty years since that episode on the bus. Meanwhile, Warren and I have accumulated a combined total of sixty-five years of pastoral ministry in Tulsa—and Dallas.

Yep, friend—it really *is* a miracle!

WHAT *DID* "OLD JOHN" SAY?

Several years ago I slipped into the chapel of a funeral home on the outskirts of Dallas. The mother of one of our members had died and I wanted to pay my respects by attending the memorial service. I was late so I sat on the back row.

Someone sang a couple of traditional hymns and the minister stood to speak. With poise and dignity he began his message. He quoted from memory several passages of Scripture and threw in a couple of moving poems. His timing was perfect and I listened and watched in fascination. There was no question about it; this pastor was good—real good.

He's really on a roll, I thought. *I'd give anything to be able to speak like that at a funeral—or anywhere else!*

By now, he had moved with ease through the comforting passages in the Psalms and had quoted from memory a portion of the often-used words of Jesus to His disciples: "Do not let your hearts be troubled. Trust in God; trust also in me" (John 14:1 NIV).

From my perfect observation point on the back row, I marveled at what I was hearing. This was a funeral worth attending!

The minister moved on to Revelation, the last book in the Bible, written by John while he was in prison on the island of Patmos. "I can see old John now," the minister resounded in a clear voice, "I can see old John now, on the isle of Patmos, looking out from that dungeon cell . . . into yon distant horizon . . . and saying . . ."

He paused, and I sat on the edge of my seat, waiting with great anticipation to hear what it was John said.

Nothing.

WAITING . . . FOR OLD JOHN'S ANSWER

The minister cleared his voice, shuffled slightly, and moved on—only now he wasn't on the isle of Patmos. He was somewhere back in the Gospels, recounting another of the teachings of Jesus. This continued for a couple of minutes. Then this eloquent speaker took us right back to the isle of Patmos, with John.

"I can see old John now, on the isle of Patmos, looking out from that dungeon cell, into you distant horizon . . . and saying. . . ."

Another pause, another shuffle, another clearing of the throat. We were now back in Psalms and he was quoting the twenty-third chapter. For another couple of minutes he talked about sheep, shepherds, and green pastures.

Then he gripped the pulpit suddenly, cleared his voice for the third time, and said, "I can see old John now, on the isle of Patmos, looking out from that dungeon cell, into yon distant horizon . . . and saying . . ."

He paused and looked blankly at the mourners.

By now, I wanted to help him. Badly. *Say anything*, I thought. *Make something up! Say God loves you, or peace unto you . . . or have faith . . . anything! Just say something!*

Not a word. He just stood there while the audience waited . . . and waited.

Finally, he breathed and whimpered through a frozen smile, "Folks, I guess you've figured out by now that I . . . can't remember *what* John said!"

The audience sat stunned for a moment. Then one or two family members chuckled softly. They were joined by others and people chuckled out loud. Finally, the sounds of laughter resounded throughout the chapel.

I watched the minister and agonized for him . . . until I saw his frozen smile melt and heard him join the others—the family too—in laughter.

The mother was buried.

Life went on.

But we still don't know what it was that "old John" said back there on the isle of Patmos.

QUICK! SHARPEN A PENCIL!

During the years I served as pastor of Wilshire, I conducted hundreds of funeral services. My goal in each was to be brief, helpful, and if possible hopeful. On some occasions when I wasn't certain I was on safe ground, I would read from the individual's personal Bible. I often found that underlined scriptures and marginal notes in the person's own handwriting were helpful in both preparing and presenting my memorial service message. Of course, I always had the permission of family members—after someone had discreetly checked to make sure that no big bills had been stashed away in the middle of Leviticus or Ecclesiastes!

One day I received word that Dorothy Black, a member of Wilshire, was in the hospital and facing serious surgery. Dorothy was one of my favorite people—charming and gracious.

As I left for the hospital to visit her, I remembered with gratitude her words of encouragement, her positive attitude, her sense of humor: *Lord,* I thought, *give us more people like her!*

I parked the car, entered the hospital, and headed straight for her room. Characteristically, she greeted me with a smile.

"You didn't need to come, Pastor," she chided mildly.

"But I wanted to visit with you and the family before surgery," I replied. Then I looked around and noticed that she was alone—which surprised me. "By the way, where *is* the family?"

"Well, my daughters were with me until a few minutes ago . . . but I sent them to my home."

"Sent them to your home?"

"Yes," she continued with an impish smile, "I told them to get out of here, get over to my house, find my Bible, and start marking it up like crazy because if I die, Bruce won't know what to say about me!"

Needless to say, I cracked up over that one.

That was twelve years ago. Dorothy came through the surgery beautifully . . . and she's still smiling.

LAST LAUGHS

If, as Shakespeare wrote, "all the world's a stage," then thank God for one-liners—for without them where would any of us be in those moments when words fail us and something—anything—must be said in order for the "show to go on?" I love it when I hear a good one-liner. Here are some I love best:

"We cannot love anybody with whom we never laugh."
—Agnes Repplier

"Laugh at yourself first, before anyone else can."
—Elsa Maxwell

"With a fearful strain that is on me day and night, if I did not laugh, I should die."
—Abraham Lincoln

"If you're not allowed to laugh in heaven, I don't want to go there."
—Martin Luther

"You don't stop laughing because you grow old; you grow old because you stop laughing."
—Michael Prichard

"Humor is the hook on which we hang our memories."
—Carl Singer

"Laughter is the hand of God on the shoulder of a troubled world."
—Grady Nutt

"A cheerful heart is good medicine."
—Proverbs 17:22 NIV

"Laughter is like a diaper change. It's not a permanent solution—just something that makes life tolerable."
—Anonymous

"I made the joyous discovery that ten minutes of genuine belly laughter had an anesthetic effect and would give me at least two hours of pain-free sleep."
—Norman Cousins, in *Anatomy of an Illness* (New York, NY: Bantam Books)

"I cried until I laughed."
—Anonymous

"Where there is no laughter, and where there are no tears, not much is happening."
—Anonymous

I have long maintained that if Jesus wept, He also laughed. I sometimes like to recall the words of Rufus Jones, a preacher of another generation. When a pious old lady approached him after one of his sermons—laced liberally with humor—she scowled and asked, "Now really, Revered Jones, do you think Jesus laughed?"

"I don't know lady," the Reverend replied. "But He sure fixed me up so I could!"

Enjoy life. Live it to the fullest. Keep laughing—and don't accept any invitations to ride in hearses—that is, *unless you're riding up front!*

About the Author

BRUCE MCIVER is a graduate of Mars Hill College, Baylor University, and Southwestern Baptist Theological Seminary. A native of North Carolina, he grew up listening to stories. Storytelling was a way of life and a recognized form of entertainment.

During his early years of ministry he taught and worked with students at Southwest Texas State University, San Marcos, and at Texas Tech in Lubbock. For thirty years he pastored Wilshire Baptist Church, a dynamic church located in the heart of Dallas. Now retired, he remains active as a member at Wilshire and is in demand as a leader of conferences and seminars. He spends his time speaking, preaching, and writing—telling some of those stories he grew to love.

Although he has spent most of his life and ministry in a busy metropolitan area, his boyhood roots are recalled from time to time in the pages of his first two books—*Grinsights* and *Stories I Couldn't Tell While I Was a Pastor*.

The author and his wife, Lawanna, live in Dallas and are the parents of three daughters. They have three grandchildren.

A NOTE TO THE READER